From the hippest, smartest sex site on the web, Nerve.com, comes the only sex manual you'll ever need.

Which body part is the wallflower of the sexual school disco? What is the real meaning of 'thinking outside the box'? Not sure how to choose the right condom for your man, the most effective lube for your lady, or the best way to spend a quiet evening alone?

This encyclopaedic guide by Nerve.com's Em and Lo is a sassy, hilarious and fully illustrated overview of original sin. Packed with step-by-step guidance and practical, well-researched advice, *The Big Bang* covers all the bases — from safer sex and birth control to female ejaculation and bondage for beginners. Whether you're new to the game or consider yourself a pro, whether you're a swinging single or married with children and whether you're straight, gay, or somewhere in between — you'll never knock boots the same way again.

'*The Big Bang* is this generation's smarter, funnier and raunchier version of *The Joy of Sex*' — *Time Magazine*

'If you are looking for a premier spot to lounge your libido, there's no swankier address than Nerve.com' — *Vanity Fair*

'*Playboy*'s body with the *New Yorker*'s brain' — *Entertainment Weekly*

THE

illustrations by lorelei sharkey
photography by matt gunther

BIG BANG

NERVE'S GUIDE TO THE NEW SEXUAL UNIVERSE

Em & Lo

(emma taylor and lorelei sharkey)

Hodder & Stoughton

Copyright © 2004 by Nerve.com, Inc

First published in Great Britain in 2004 by Hodder and Stoughton
A division of Hodder Headline

The right of Emma Taylor & Lorelei Sharkey to be identified as
the Authors of the Work has been asserted by them in accordance with
the Copyright, Designs and Patents Act 1988.

10 9 8 7 6 5 4 3 2 1

A CIP catalogue record for this title is available from the British Library

ISBN 0 340 83050 6

Typeset in 9.5/14.5pt Trade Gothic by Barneby Ltd, London
Text design by Nicky Barneby
Printed and bound in Spain by Book Print, S.L.

Hodder and Stoughton
A division of Hodder Headline
338 Euston Road
London NW1 3BH

CONTENTS

part 3: SEX FOR WINNERS!
Safer Sex and Sexual Fitness

INTRODUCTION

Great sexual eras are like happy periods of life: they are only fully appreciated in retrospect. The trick is to appreciate the moment as it occurs (incidentally, this is the trick to everything). So let's start now: we are in the midst of a great sexual era. It rocks. It's scrumptious. We could barely find time to write this book.

I don't mean to discount the depravity of our forefathers — the Greeks kept busy; the indigenous Trobriander Polynesians were a frisky lot; the 19th-century Parisians got a lot of mileage out of their absinthe; and those '20s flapper dresses looked, well, functional. The '60s and '70s were pretty randy — it's hard not to envy the two-for-one deal of free love as political protest. And I don't mean to suggest that the shadow of AIDS and other sexual diseases has passed — we still have to dress for inclement weather. But all that said, it's better now. People know more, they smell sweeter, batteries last longer and there's less gender-role rubbish, which means there are twice as many people putting their hands on other people's knees. Oral sex isn't scandalous anymore, it's just good clean fun, or good dirty fun if you like it better that way. More and more people are doing it up the butt and why not? But there are still enough taboos in effect to keep us blushing now and then. A little guilt — without all that 'eternity in hell' overkill — is good; it keeps things exotic (see the chapters on fisting and kink if you want to put a little colour in your cheeks).

Back in the early days of Nerve I used to say that we didn't want to fix sex, we wanted to appreciate it. Americans have gotten a bit carried away with the fix-it mentality; after all, we spend a lot of time fixing things that don't need fixing (breasts and butter, to give you two obvious examples). Although this book intends to leave you a better lover than it found you, its fundamental philosophy is less 'fix it' than 'tinker with it till it feels good'. When you boil down the collective wisdom in the pages that follow (from an oceanful to a poolful), the essence of the advice is to communicate, say please and thank you like your mum taught you, relish the whole experience and for goodness sake, have a sense of humour.

It's good to be good at sex, but there is such a thing as being too good, or too attentive to being good. Sex is a social, recreational sport — like, say, Crazy Golf or board games. The real point of it, procreation aside, is to bond with your fellow players. If you become obsessed with execution, you can miss the point and make other people uncomfortable. (There is nothing worse than the Crazy Golf player with the caddy and wind-speed gauge.) And like the game Othello, sex takes a minute to learn but a lifetime to master. That's why you bought this book. So we'll do our best to turn you into a pro while maintaining a little perspective.

Some of you may have bought this book because you thought it was about the origin of the universe. Well, physics is relevant here — not only do the basic principles hold up in the sack (each body exerts an equal and opposite force; a butt plug and a dildo dropped from the ceiling tend to hit your lover's stomach at the same time), but also sex, as my father likes to remind me, has a lot to do with the origin of things. Just as there was a big bang that kick started this whole universe, there was a little bang that made you and me that may just have awoken the neighbours.

The point is that sex is bigger than us — it's a powerful force in our lives that reminds us that we are animals, in both senses of the word: we are passionate and like it or not, we are carnal, butt-smelling mammals running about in the muck. We want sex because we are part of a species that wants to live. Think of the momentum of massive rivers, the weight of the ocean in its bed, glaciers sliding, tectonic plates grinding — this is the kind of primordial force, articulating itself over millions of years, that is throbbing in your pants (and it doesn't give a damn about embarrassing you in public). It is wildly affirming and at the same time humbling.

Far from being a culminant moment of human grace and style, sex is slobbering, repetitive, instinctual business that connects us more to the humping of prairie dogs and rhinos than the cinematic dance of Tom Cruise and Nicole Kidman. In the absence of directors, lighting crews and make-up artists, we scrunch up our faces, hyperventilate and show each other our cavities. Sex is an exercise in communal humility and that's why it's such a powerful bonding experience. We look ridiculous and we do it because we can't resist carrying out our genetic instructions.

This is all good. As individuals getting to know one another and as a species, we need more humility. If you embrace the absurdity of it and really, truly enjoy it, you will be the best possible lover. If you then also employ the tips in this book — forget about it. Your lover will follow you around like a lapdog for the rest of his or her life. Use your power for good.

— Rufus Griscom, CEO and publisher, Nerve.com

part 1

SEX FOR BEGINNERS

Just the Basics

AH ... AH ... ACHOOOO!!!!

The Anti-Climactic Orgasm Chapter

What's it like, an orgasm?

Exquisite relief from torture.

Why torture?

Because it's real torture not to have the orgasm.

So why do you torture yourself, why don't you just have it?

Because it feels so good just to almost have it.

Better than to have it?

In a way, yeah.

Really?

In a way, no.

— Dialogue from the 1986 film Seven Minutes in Heaven

Who would have thought an obscure teen flick from the '80s could capture the essence of the ultimate sexual sneeze with such precision and grace? Intense arousal *is* torture: you sweat and swell; your heart beats faster, adrenaline rushes through your system, your blood flow increases, your breathing accelerates, your entire body gets stiff, your jewels start to glow like rubies ... until the sexual tension is just too much to bear and your body screams 'Enough already!' Only then are you granted relief through an orgasm: a few blissful seconds of rhythmic muscle contractions that release all that pent-up sexual energy back into the universe, like a whistling teapot from Xanadu. Aw yeah.

For men, an orgasm begins with semen being forced into the urethra — it's called 'ejaculatory inevitability' (that's the point of no return to you). The testicles draw up close to the body and the bladder entrance closes tightly to inhibit urination. Meanwhile, contractions in the urethra, prostate, perineum and penis, spaced about 0.8 seconds apart, propel the man juice up and out. The entire event consists of three to four major contractions and then a few minor ones and then . . . Zzzzz. It'll be time for round two only after a good rest.

Women, bless 'em, don't need sleep to recharge their batteries. When ladies get aroused, blood rushes to the genitals and general pelvic area, causing the nerve bundles to expand and the clitoral network, vagina and anus to swell. The vaginal opening gets tighter, the inner third of the vagina expands, the clit stands at attention, the inner lips thicken and deepen in colour, the areolas pucker, the nips sit up, the breasts swell and some women (and, less commonly, men) experience 'sex flush', a redness or rash that appears on the upper chest or neck caused by the increased blood flow. Then, when she just can't take no more, the uterine wall pulsates and the vagina, clitoris and anus all contract, again in 0.8-second intervals, forcing the blood back to the general population. Some chicks even ejaculate, too (see page 99). A woman can have anywhere from three to 15 earth-shattering contractions and then a bunch of little tremors, all of which spread throughout the entire pelvic area for a grand total of up to 28 seconds of pure heaven. (According to Masters and Johnson, the longest recorded orgasm achieved by a woman was 43 seconds long. Lucky bitch.) See the anatomy appendix (page 271) for a more medical description of male and female arousal and orgasm.

As it turns out, women can come harder, longer and more often in one sesh than men (generally speaking, of course). Their chances of attaining the Big O get even better before or during their periods or when pregnant, as increased blood flow adds pressure to the pelvic area and may heighten sensitivity. Women can also reach orgasm from a greater array of stimulation: it's usually clitoral or G-spot provocation, but sometimes nipple attention, a good squeeze of the pelvic muscles (see page 257), or even a particularly steamy fantasy is all it takes. And no, none of these Os is inferior, as Freud would have us believe: orgasms, no matter how they're achieved, are all good — some are just more intense than others. Shall we go on? According to most sexologists, all women are physically capable of being multi-orgasmic — that is, they can have one or more orgasms after the first, with little to no ebbing in their level of arousal. Masters and Johnson also report the female phenomenon of 'continual orgasms' or *status orgasmus*, a series of orgasms that follow each other like a conga line in double time. Then there's the 'extended massive orgasm', a mythical monster that can rear its roaring head for as 'little' as ten minutes or as long as an hour. Sceptics don't believe this beast exists, arguing that women are not actually having an orgasm for that long, but rather are extending the moment before orgasm. 'You say potato, I say potatOOOOOOOOOH!'

But before we start an epidemic of puss envy, know this: very generally speaking, it's more difficult and takes more time and effort for women to reach orgasm. Some women never come (we doubt the same could be said for men) — not because they're necessarily incapable, but because they haven't figured out how to (yet). And some penis enthusiasts argue that multiple orgasms are not exclusive to the female sphere. Come again? Well, it starts to make sense when you consider that a guy's orgasm and his ejaculation are not the same thing, even though they usually happen simultaneously. Ejaculation, which is strictly the release of semen, can occur without orgasm and sometimes an orgasm, which refers to the muscle contractions and feel-good mental surge, can happen without ejaculation (it's rare). Most men aren't able to have multiple orgasms because they immediately go into a refractory period after ejaculation, during which Mr Man quickly goes limp. Yet some men seem to have multiple orgasms by withholding ejaculation; others claim to be able to have more orgasms, without ejaculation, after the initial orgasm with ejaculation, before the refractory period fully settles in. (For some men, putting their boy to sleep can take anywhere from a few minutes to a few hours.) Tantric teachings contain various methods on how to achieve multiple orgasms for men (sorry, that's a whole 'nother book).

Even if we're just talking plain old meat-'n'-potato orgasms, they can vary greatly from person to person and from orgasm to orgasm per person, whether male or female. The orgasm is a kind of barometer: the number of contractions, intensity and length depend on diet, fatigue, time elapsed since last orgasm, mood, stress, age, state of one's relationship, method of stimulation, self-esteem, anxiety, how good the porn is . . . An orgasm is nice work if you can get it and you can get it if you try (usually). Read the rest of this book for some new ideas on how to apply yourself. But don't get discouraged if you don't get every job. In this field, it's all about the application process.

ME TIME

Nerve's Masturbation Manifesto

15 Reasons Why *Everyone* Should Masturbate

1. Getting a grip on yourself helps teach you the pattern of your own sexual response: what you like, what you don't like and what you hate more than anything else in the whole wide world.
2. Friggin' your riggin' helps you gain control over when and how soon you come: once you can recognise the point right before the point of no return, you can put on the brakes and avoid premature crashes.
3. Polishing your china helps you sleep — right before a nap, or as part of your bedtime ritual.
4. Playing with yourself is a great procrastination device/study break/boredom reliever. Way better than smoking or television.
5. DIY sex puts a smile on your face by releasing endorphins. So self-administer a mercy fuck after (or better yet, during) a bad day at work.
6. Jacking off can help kick start a tired and listless sex drive.
7. Southern comfort puts you first for a change (assuming you're not usually a selfish bastard). Do something nice for yourself: walk your hand home.
8. Beating off evens the playing field when you want it more than your partner does. With the wave of a hand, presto: no more frustration!
9. Doing the handstroke is a self-fulfilling prophecy; the more you do it (and

the earlier you start doing it), the more likely you are to do it into your old age. That image might gross you out now, but wait till you're 70.

10. Doing the hand jive is cheap and you're easy, unlike most of your dates.

11. Not jerking off at all, according to sexologists, is more likely to lead to psychological problems than jerking off incessantly. This is an about-face from the widespread Victorian belief that shaking the bacon would drive you nuts. So stop the insanity!

12. Hand-to-gland combat gives you fresh breath. As long as you brush your teeth when you're done.

13. Testing the plumbing before a date helps keep your head in the game.

14. Widespread wanking creates a more sensual world, adds to the supply of international karma and thus brings us closer to world peace.

15. Masturbation is the shortest distance between you and an orgasm. Need we say more?

Once Upon a Hand

The Bible never explicitly deems masturbation a no-no. It's the Christian inter-pretation of the Old Testament that's to blame. Here's how the story in Genesis goes: Onan's married brother died childless. According to religious law, Onan had a responsibility to impregnate his brother's widow so that his brother could achieve immortality. Onan wasn't down with siring anyone else's kids, so in the middle of getting busy with his sis-in-law he 'spilled his seed on the ground'. Pretty sneaky. So God took him out. Here's how the Church took it: anytime a dude's seed doesn't end its journey in a vagina, that's a sin. Hence the mis-nomer 'onanism' for masturbation, rather than for coitus interruptus. Funny how the Church makes such a to-do over jerking off, yet doesn't enforce the tradition of men putting buns in the ovens of their dead brothers' wives.

For centuries after, everyone just pretended that sex wasn't meant to be fun. Then, in the 18th century, a Swiss physician named Tissot compounded the problem by trying to introduce 'science' to the matter — he claimed that not only was sex not fun, but its resulting shifts in blood flow could actually lead to nerve damage and insanity. If sex was risky, then masturbation must have been a death wish. Across the pond, American physician Benjamin Rush bought

Tissot's line of BS and dashed off a series of inflammatory articles on the subject that scared the hands out of everyone's pants. Throughout the 19th century, men wore spiked metal tubes over their johnsons and boys' hands were tied to the bedposts at night. And women? Well, they just didn't masturbate, of course. (Though a few American doctors did claim that romancing the rose could cause — or at least exacerbate — everything from cancer to 'haggard features'.) And here's where it gets really good: staunch anti-masturbationists like Will Keith Kellogg believed that a bland diet would promote sexual restraint — and thus Kellogg's Cornflakes were born. We shit you not.

It wasn't until the '50s that supersexologist Alfred Kinsey came to save the day. He stuck his tongue out at Freud for calling masturbation immature and proved that most mature Americans enjoyed the occasional nubbin rubbin', without consequence — and that for the majority of mature American women, it was the only way they could get their rocks off. Over the next few decades, masturbation mavens Betty Dodson (*Sex for One*), Lonnie Barbach (*For Yourself*) and Shere Hite (*The Hite Report*) joined in the 'hey diddle diddle' chorus. And in 1972, the American Medical Association finally declared masturbation a 'normal' sexual activity. But don't get too excited: in 1994 US Surgeon General Joycelyn Elders was canned for giving self-love the, er, thumbs-up.

Lady Fingers

Chicks don't always come during intercourse, but they almost always do during masturbation. At least, if they're prepared to put in a bit of practice, they do. That's why psychologist Lonnie Barbach dubbed women who've never come 'pre-orgasmic', rather than 'anorgasmic' — there's always hope. The first orgasm is usually the hardest to achieve. It's also often mild and fleeting, but it gets better. Oh, it gets way better. And once they're orgasmic on their own, women have a much better shot at getting there when they've got company.

Plus, any kind of orgasm will probably help relieve menstrual cramps and PMS and fight yeast infections by increasing blood flow to the pelvic area. Those are good enough reasons to learn how to flick the bean and flick it well.

The following guide to jilling off should help, whether you've never come, you'd like to be multi-orgasmic, or you're just in need of a masturbation makeover. Remember, variety is the spice of sex life: the more roads there are to your happy place, the more easily you and your partner can get there.

Prepping

Get a mirror and check yourself out. It may sound crunchy, but the more familiar you are with what you've got, the better you can work it. Men have waged wars for that view; your partners find it sexy and so should you. (No more rhymes now, we mean it! Anybody want a peanut?)

Set aside time. Spend a rainy Saturday afternoon at home. Call in sick, sleep late, take the phone off the hook. If you've never come before, give yourself an hour every few days to practise, but with no expectations of orgasm to avoid disappointment.

Put the moves on yourself. Light some candles, take a bath, drink a glass of wine, play that totally cheesy album you'd never admit turns you on, read the dirty parts of Anne Rice novels, watch gay porn. It's all about getting to (and staying in) the right mental place.

Warm up. If you insist on foreplay from your partners, then why not from yourself? Rub baby oil on your boobies and thighs, play with your nips, cup your vulva with a hand and rub gently. Make yourself feel like it's the very first time.

The Basic Rules of Thumb (and Four Fingers)

Take your own sweet time. Keep going until you feel like stopping, whether you've come once, 20 times, or not at all. Stop and start. Take snack breaks.

Listen to your body. If you do, we swear we'll never utter that cliché again. Ask yourself, 'Do you like that? Does that make you wet?' (Porno voice optional.) Pay attention to the answers. Because who lies back and thinks of England when it's her own time she's spending?

But don't keep your head in the game too much. Don't chase the orgasm. Just enjoy the attention. Try and forget that orgasms even exist (yeah, right). If you keep getting close and then missing, back off for a bit and then build up again, more slowly this time.

Techniques for Chicks

Digital stimulation (aka paddling the pink canoe): Use your palm. Use your knuckles. Use one hand to pull the mons tight and expose your clitoral head. Draw a circle around your clit with your middle finger. Make a double-handed fist and lie on it. Keep one hand on the genitals while the other goes wandering. See 'Handwork for Her' for a whole slew of more specific ideas (page 39).

Do the hump: Ride inanimate objects on your bed — pillows, piles of clothes, stuffed animals (for all you sickies). Or walk around the house and grind whatever feels good — the bathroom sink, the washing machine on spin cycle, the sofa arm, the desk corner.

Going in: Try a little penetration action, either throughout the sesh, or right as you climax, in your vagina or maybe even your butt. You may not need this to reach an orgasm, but then again, maybe you do. Either way, it'll probably feel good.

Be a thigh master: Squeeze your thigh muscles, or rub your thighs together. Cross your legs at the ankles, cross them at the knee — hell, cross 'em in both places to really tighten things up — all the while contracting and relaxing your pelvic muscles (see page 257). Some lucky ladies can get off from this alone. Imagine the possibilities: the bus! the train! the board meeting! Even if you don't perfect the hands-free manoeuvre, a little lemon-squeezing will always enhance your me time.

Break out the toy box: The pros say you shouldn't use a toy until you've succeeded with your own hand. We say, whatever floats your little man in the boat. Maybe a vibrator is all you need to transform you from a 'pre-orgasmic' woman into a multi-orgasmic one. But, if you've never come without battery-powered assistance, at least give the *au naturel* instructions here and in the 'Handwork for Her' section on page 39 a shot (because god forbid the batteries crap out in the homestretch). See 'Sex Toys' for your toy shopping guide (page 126).

Experiment With …

Muscle tension: Most sexperts recommend doing whatever it takes to make all your muscles soft and squishy. (Try diddling after a yoga class or full-body massage.) Then again, some people find that tensing up gives them focus.

Position: Stand up, kneel on the floor, sit in a chair, crouch against the wall, lie on your front, stand on your head.

States of undress: Over clothes, under clothes, in the buff, with just your shoes on. Do it in trousers with a crotch seam you can grind against (jeans work best). Or tug on your undies so they rub in all the right places.

Quickies: You don't always have to be a sensualist. Sometimes it's just about scratching an itch: put down *The Times*, rub one out, then return to the crossword, all in less than four minutes!

Location: Do it in semi-public (a locked bathroom stall at a bar, the back row of an empty cinema) or in public (kneel on the floor at a party with your heel at your crotch, or cross your legs, squeeze your thighs and contract your pelvic muscles on an overseas flight).

Aquatics: Lie under the bathtub tap, use your detachable shower head, straddle the jets in the Olympic-sized pool, invest in a waterproof vibrator. Just make sure the water's not scalding hot and don't aim a strong stream of water directly into your vagina — it can cause a fatal air embolism. (That's when an air bubble gets into your bloodstream — if the bubble reaches your heart or lungs, it can kill you.)

Perishables: After washing it and slapping on a condom to avoid infection, try a cucumber, a courgette or a carrot. Don't use anything that might snap in two.

Others: Take a workshop (check with your nearest female-friendly sex shop). Or if the whole circle jerk thing doesn't do it for you, rent or buy an instructional video (e.g., *Betty Dodson's Celebrating Orgasm*) and follow along at home.

Boys' Night In

We realise we're preaching to the choir here, but there are four more good reasons to perform organ solos regularly: first, ejaculation flushes out the prostate gland, which may help to prevent blockage and subsequent infections. Second, many docs believe that erections are like sit-ups for your dick — that is, the more you use it, the less likely you are to lose it. Third, it's a great strategy to help prevent premature ejaculation: you can work on your stamina during dry spells so you're not a two-pump chump when your tall glass of water finally arrives. Finally, regular flushings keep sperm fresh and therefore stronger, so when they do meet a vagina, the little guys are better prepared to meet the egg challenge: while two to three days' abstinence prior to ovulation is advised for couples trying to conceive, no ejaculation for, say, seven days can impair sperm motility. There's only one — OK, two — caveats to all this: while you can never run out of sperm, hypermasturbation (i.e., three or more times in a day) can lower your sperm count on that day because the tadpoles never have a chance to rejuvenate (to say nothing of all that chafing). Also, chronic masturbation can lead to 'retarded ejaculation', the childishly hilarious term for an inability to reach orgasm. The moral of the story? Pull your pud often, but with caution.

Dick Techniques

Tom Thumb and His Four Brothers: There's a whole slew of simple, effective, one-handed techniques, all of which we're sure you've already mastered. But let's review for the newcomers (new *comers*, get it?): grip your rod like a microphone (or a can of Budweiser if you prefer), with four fingers over the top and your thumb underneath, keeping as much of your hand in contact with your stewart as possible. Rub up and down. Repeat. For wider range of motion (but less contact), use four or fewer fingers along the ridge and your thumb underneath, *sans* palm. Either of these grips can be inverted by twisting your wrist (before you've taken hold) so your thumb faces down, then you go in for the kill. Or try keeping your thumb out of it altogether and just use your fingers and palm to rub the top, while the underside rubs against your stomach. And if you've got good coordination and a stellar imagination, use your non-dominant hand in order to simulate the feeling that someone else is actually giving you a handjob and you're not a desperate loser.

Look, Ma, Two Hands: While using any of the above single-handed grips, 'polish' the head of your knob with the palm of your other hand or use your fingers to circle the tip — sort of like patting your head and rubbing your stomach at the same time, except you don't look as stupid and it actually feels good. Or grab your penis like you would a cricket bat, fist over fist. (Don't feel inadequate when your peter doesn't poke out of the top fist: that only happens to dudes whose first name is that of their childhood pet and last name is the street they used to live on, like Chester Longwood.) Then, either move your grip up and down or hold your hands still and thrust your hooded cobra in and out; if you want to get tricky, gently twist your wrists as you go. Or cup your hands around your rig as if you've captured a firefly and continue the up/down or thrusting motions. Make 'OK' signs with both hands and use them around your shaft like a ring toss. And if your groin's a sucker for the non-dominant hand trick above, try reaching that hand across your abdomen to approach your balls and thighs from the other side while you employ a single-handed technique with your dominant hand.

Face in the Mud: Lie on your stomach to create more of a sensation of actual schtupping; put down a towel or wear a condom to make clean-up a breeze. (Condoms during solo sex will also help condition your penis to enjoy them during tango sex.) You can use an object — like the mattress, pillows, wadded-up sheets, dirty laundry, etc. Or use some of the above grips with the thrusting motion. Moving your arms and hands won't be an option since, duh, you're lying on them.

Spanking the Pony, Literally: Slapping — it's not just for porn stars anymore. Whether back and forth between two hands or against your stomach, a pillow, maybe even a thawed chicken breast, this whole slapping thing can actually feel good.

Ascetic Masturbation: The following techniques are all about restraint, about making the most of teasing, about resisting the urge to take the shortest route between two points. In other words, these are all techniques you'll never try. But what the hell, here goes . . . Grab firmly with one hand but don't move, just take your thumb and circle the head. Go slow and steady; you won't win any races but the tension you'll build up will pay off in the end (we think . . . we hope). Here's another: bring yourself to the brink of ejaculation and then right as you start to climax, let go and relax all your muscles. No, we're not crazy. The orgasm may be a little flat but you won't ejaculate, you'll stay erect and you'll immediately be ready for another round or five. (You may have accidentally stumbled upon this with a partner when you suddenly stopped moving and thought about your grandma to keep from coming too soon, but still felt a flutter.) Then of course there are the hands-free methods requiring a lot of mind and body control and maybe a little sorcery that only Sting can pull off. But he wouldn't take our calls.

See 'Handjobs for Him' for more specific ideas (page 34).

Dick Tips

Accessorise . . . With a well-worn soft cotton sock, an extra-large condom with lube on the inside, a ski glove with satin lining, a pearl or beaded necklace, running water, a velvet blanket . . . shop-bought toys like masturbation sleeves, cock rings, your girlfriend's vibrator (see 'Sex Toys' page 117) . . . genital moulds of triple-X stars, blow-up dolls and Real Dolls for the adventurous and/or slightly touched in the head . . . and, of course, the old standby: porn.

Play with the boys. Tug on your balls, rub them, fluff their fur, massage the nooks between them and your thighs. Press on the skin between the balls and the anus, known as the perineum (aka the taint; i.e., 't ain't the ass and 't ain't the balls). This will indirectly stimulate your prostate (the male G-spot). Or go straight to the source by sneaking a finger about five to seven cm in the back door (see 'Doing the Butt' on page 79).

Want a more impressive money shot? Abstain from any 'happy finishes' for several days to build up semen steam. Drink lots of water. Once you begin a sesh, make it last for as long as possible, to increase sexual tension and arousal. But remember, an orgasm is an orgasm is an orgasm. Having a come stream that can leap tall buildings in a single bound is no more a prerequisite for great masturbation (or great partner sex, for that matter) than having a six-pack is. Some men may never have explosive expulsions simply because their urethral opening is not small enough to create the pressure necessary for long-distance spurting. And even those with the smallest of holes will experience a decrease in velocity with age. Them's the facts of life.

If you've got foreskin, flaunt it. Pull it up over the head and use it as a masturbation sleeve. Pull it back and focus on the head (you'll probably need lube in order to stand this hypersensitive stimulation for very long). Or just focus on the foreskin itself, rather than the shaft beneath.

Dick Duhs

Don't stick your dick anywhere it could get stuck, except your ear. We're talking bottles, small car parts, letter boxes. Because once it gets stuck, it swells; and once it swells, it hurts; and once it hurts, it starts to panic; and once it starts to panic, it's A&E City for you and Mr Choking Victim. Same goes for hoovers, even if you can safely fit him in the attachment. Because once the On switch is flicked, no matter how much of a dreamer you are, it will never give you a safe blowjob that actually feels good.

Don't try to make your gherkin bigger. Don't use penis pumps, weights, herbal remedies, etc. They just don't work (see 'Self-Help for Your Peter', page 245).

Don't subject your erect hot rod to extreme heat. Before applying any hot compresses to the area in question, test them against your wrist; you should be able to hold your nuked pudding pack (see sidebar) in your hands for at least 30 seconds without any discomfort.

Don't look your money shot in the eye. Ejaculate can sting if it gets in your peepers (something to keep in mind when you're marking your territory on a partner).

Don't do your best impression of the *Silence of the Lambs* **psycho with a boner.** Overstretching an erect penis can actually fracture it and chronic attempts in middle-aged men may lead to Peyronie's disease (aka curved dick).

techniques from teenagers

Philip Roth's protagonists (remember Portnoy's baseball mitt?) have nothing on the following techniques, which are often employed by virgins to replicate the feeling of a real human orifice . . . and usually fail miserably. But the high production value of these homemade 'vaginas' is half the fun. So if you have the time, patience and home economics skills, then get in touch with your pimply inner child. Just don't get carried away — many a teenaged masturbator with an overactive imagination has ended up in the A&E with a fractured penis in need of surgery:

- *Coat the inside of a sandwich-sized plastic bag with lube, stick your johnson in it, then kneel down by your bed and stick the whole package between the mattress and the box spring. Needless to say: thrust.*
- *Fill a large plastic baggie full of something soft and mushy — pudding, oatmeal, cooked pasta — get all the air out of the bag, seal it, warm it up in a microwave (we said warm up, not heat up), lather one side with lube and wrap it around your flesh sausage.*
- *Carve out a penis nook in any number of fruits: honeydew melons, grapefruits, watermelons, large potatoes. Banana peels make good DIY sheaths, or just cut off one end of a large unpeeled banana, scoop or squeeze out the fruit and insert dick (you may need to reinforce the skin with some duct tape, just not too tight).*
- *Get a piece of thick foam (i.e., deeper than the length of your erection) and a swath of soft material. Carve out your desired crevice shape in the middle of the foam, tuck the middle of the fabric in the hole so the rest of the material covers the rest of the foam, place on bed, get on top and go to town.*

take my breath away: what's up with autoerotic asphyxiation?

Autoerotic asphyxiation (AeA), also called breath control — or BC — involves stopping the flow of oxygen to your brain to heighten masturbatory pleasure. Which is kind of like jumping off the roof to beat the lift to the lobby. Not to be confused with the psychological rush many people (especially women) enjoy when a lover carefully yet firmly grips them by the neck during the throes of passion, AeA is a physical rush enjoyed mostly by men — kind of like drinking Red Bull. It's usually arrived at via strangulation, hanging or suffocation while masturbating. The reason it feels so good is that your body — hello — needs oxygen and freaks the fuck out when it doesn't get it. We see you in the back row there, sir, raising your hand to tell us that there are 'safe' ways to enjoy AeA. We're just not buying that piece of land in Florida today, thank you. There's simply no way to do it without putting yourself at serious risk of cardiac arrest, or worse. Even if you don't accidentally hang yourself by falling off the chair or fainting, you are at risk for seizures, stroke, damage to the larynx or windpipe and spinal cord injury. And if you do it often enough, you can incur some serious cumulative brain damage. Even if you do it with company, you're still at risk, because there's no way of knowing when any of these things is about to happen, there's not enough time to give a 'safety signal' and CPR is effective less than ten per cent of the time. Talk about a stiffy. If you're convinced that this is the only way you can get off, then you should seek help from a pro — that shit's out of our league.

All-Play: How to Spice Up Your Tired Old Masturbation Routine

A foolish consistency is the hobgoblin of little orgasms. Oh, but at least they're orgasms! We know how difficult it is to give them up on the long and frustrating journey towards sexual versatility, including masturbatory versatility. But you must be disciplined and full of resolve! Deprive yourself of your usual method. (Hide your pillow. Unplug your trusty old vibe. Sit on your hand.) Invest in some quality new toys. Get a detachable shower head with various massage settings. Buy some squash. Set aside entire days to experiment. See how long you can go. See how fast you can do it, in a pinch. You may have conditioned your body to come only one way; you need time and patience to train your body to like something new. It's like hating the taste of olives, but loving the concept of them — you have to force yourself to eat them at dinner parties and gourmet supermarkets, enduring countless varieties and brands that make your stomach turn, until you finally start to love them. Think of various positions, gadgets and methods of masturbation as different kinds of olives you must try — eat them slowly and don't spit them out, even if they don't taste that good at first. Eventually, you won't be able to get enough of those smooth, plump little gems that burst with flavour around their hard, firm nuts!

Below are a few of our favourites. Give them a taste. But remember, at the end of the orgasm, it's your prerogative to be a boring masturbator. So don't let us pressure you into a kinky wank.

- **Experiment with your breathing.** Slow, fast, deep, shallow. You might even try holding it for a few seconds at crucial junctures.
- **Show off.** If you've got a special someone in your life, do it in the passenger seat while they're driving — and don't let them pull over. Or do it while they're tied up on the phone with their parents. Or while they're tied to the bedposts.
- **Watch yourself do it in the mirror.** Put Carly Simon's 'You're So Vain' on the stereo. Everyone should try this at least once.
- **Do it with a butt plug in.** It's hands-free anal stimulation and a great method of ass conditioning for bigger and better things — and you might just like it. Or, if Pavlov's theories hold any water, you might just grow to like it.
- **Make some noise!** So maybe you can't talk dirty in front of your partner (yet), but what about when it's just you and your genitals? Don't feel silly: if no one hears you, it's like a tree falling in an empty forest.
- **Move, you lazy bastards.** It's called being sexually active for a reason. Thrust your hips, contract your pelvic muscles, arch your neck and back — it'll help trick your bod into believing it's 'the real thing'.
- **Go for sensory overload.** Try feathers, silk sheets, warm oil, ice cubes, a soft brush.
- **Lube it.** If you're a gal, use your own, or better yet, a store-bought water-based brand that has more staying power — especially if your coochie often gets numb or oversensitive (see page 263). If you're a guy, use it, full stop. This isn't about need, it's about want. And who wouldn't want the silkiest, smoothest handjob a man could give himself? Sure, lube isn't appropriate for every self-love sitch (e.g., you're seeing a new special friend for dinner straight after work and can't exactly wash your balls in the company's

lavatory sink). But when your booty call card has run out of minutes, there's nothing better.

- **Get your mind into the gutter (or into someone else's pants).** Fantasy plays an important role in breaking out of your routine and sustaining a mood. Tell yourself a dirty story and give yourself a starring role. Choose your own sleazy adventure (and your sleazy co-adventurer): it's not cheating. Try out that impossible position. Have a threeway. Have a fourway. Host an orgy. Fuck your bank clerk. Indulge your rape fantasy. If you get writer's block, use erotic novels, magazines, comics, or videos as a catalyst. Or log onto a sex chat room (assuming your libido can survive smiley faces, 14-year-old horn-dogs and LOLs up the wazoo).

I See You! I See You!: Mutual Masturbation

Masturbation is not just a consolation prize for the lonely hearts. It's not cheating on your partner and it's not cheating your partner out of an orgasm. It doesn't mean you're not getting it enough from your partner, nor does it mean you're oversexed. And it's not a dirty secret that you have to sneak in when your partner's working late. Think of it this way: you eat together, shop together, choose wallpaper patterns together — why not diddle together? It's called mutual masturbation and it rocks: you do you, your partner does themselves and you both get to watch and play. It's simultaneous voyeurism and exhibitionism. Do it as foreplay, or make a night of it. Get a head start while your partner's otherwise occupied and then let them join in. Get a sex toy you can share. While your hands do the walking, try talking dirty to each other. Or indulge in a snogging sesh — only above-the-shoulders touching is allowed, while all below-the-belt fondling must be self-administered. Do it in bed, sit facing each other, sit facing a mirror together, do it while watching a film. Consider it basic training for phone sex. And be sure to take mental notes: it's the best way to see what really works for your partner.

Masturbation Myths

We are so over all these misconceptions and urban legends about shaking hands with the unemployed. But we want you to be, too. So here goes, once more, with feeling.

Do I masturbate too much?

No. We're pretty sure of that. As long as you're paying the rent, calling your parents regularly and not hurting anybody, then it's OK to be addicted to self-love. If you've got dick or vadge burn or calloused hands, it probably just means you need more lube.

Do I masturbate the wrong way?

No, not unless it hurts. (When you didn't mean for it to hurt, you dirty bird.)

Will it make me depressed?

Not if you're a generally content person. However, there is this: although many of the most obvious physical sensations relating to sex (arousal and orgasm) are caused by nerve impulses, other more subtle sensations occur when chemicals are released into the bloodstream, inducing the post-sex mellow-out (one reason why some paraplegics can still enjoy sex). These chemicals (like the hormone oxytocin) are also responsible for the urge to cuddle and for that time you accidentally blurted out 'I love you' during a one-night stand. When solo, this denouement may feel a bit sad and lonely. Or maybe you're just bummed to hit earth and realise you're not actually fucking that hottie from the produce aisle. So walk it off. You can always do it again in ten minutes — and this time, make it a threeway by adding the hottie from the checkout register too.

I'm a guy and I still get wet dreams. Does that mean I don't masturbate enough?

Nope (though if you have to ask, maybe you're not paying your schlong enough attention). Sure, some dudes stop soiling their sheets once they learn how to rub one out in their waking hours, but many keep on nocturnally emitting all the way into adulthood. Others only have wet dreams when they're sexually active. And some never ever get a wet one. New evidence shows that wet dreams are not as closely tied to 'sperm build-up' as 'scientists' once purported. Plus, chicks have wet dreams (i.e., nocturnal orgasms), too, so you can take your sperm build-up theory and shove it.

Can I teach myself autofellatio?

Rhesus monkeys can autofellate. We'd guess a few members of Cirque du Soleil can, too. You, my friend, cannot.

Am I the only one who's never been in a circle jerk?

Yup.

3

THE NICETIES

Foreplay Is Everything

Let's get one thing straight: the amount of time we dedicate to describing foreplay here is in no way indicative of how much time you should spend doing it. (For those of you on the short bus: the time you spend on it should be much, much longer.) Foreplay is not first and second base; it's not one minute of kissing, two minutes of dry-humping and one nipple tweak before you get to 'the good stuff'. There's no 'correct' order to different kinds of touching and there's no beginning, middle, or end — foreplay is the ongoing dedication to heightening your partner's sensual pleasure. (Yes, we'd like some wine with that cheese.) Which means that all of the stuff mentioned below should be sprinkled liberally throughout the entirety of your sesh. And sometimes, this stuff is your sesh. Foreplay doesn't always have to be a means to a penetrative end.

Let's get another thing straight: don't shoot your wad all at once, so to speak. This is a GO SLOW zone. We've got one word for you: tease, tease, tease! It's always sexier to have your partner beg for more rather than ask for less. Did we say go slow? (Ignore this advice if you and your fiancé are having a quickie in the only bathroom at your family reunion and the bean salad is suddenly not agreeing with Grandpa Joe.)

Thirdly: when people talk about stamina in the bedroom, they're usually not talking about penetrative pumping time. Most women wouldn't call an unrelenting 40-minute cervix ramming pure ecstasy. But give 'em 40 minutes of slow, deliberate, dramatic teasing, building up to a little bit of cervix ramming — now *that*'s what we're talking about. In fact, Kinsey found that a whopping 92 per cent of women who received 20 minutes or more of foreplay felt the earth move.

But enough with all the touchy-feely philosophising; let's get specific!

Plant the seed. Destroy your partner's concentration at work by making them dream about sex all day: send dirty e-mails and text messages, leave voice mails stating your dishonourable intentions for later that evening. It's foreplay without the work! (Just make sure your boss doesn't screen your e-mail.)

Apply feng shui to your sex life. Interior decorate your physical and mental space to create optimum booty energy. Cue up cool tunes to set and maintain a mood (see sidebar). Kill the overhead lights (or just install a dimmer — they cost about a fiver at the DIY shop). Take a relaxing bath or shower, together or alone — you'll be more comfortable exploring each other's nooks and crannies. And we'd like to believe the old wives' tale that 50 per cent of back rubs end up in some kind of sexual embrace — so bring out the oil. Stop talking about work (or any 'problems') at least an hour before any contact is made. Turn off the TV and just talk to each other, because we'd guess 90 per cent of really good conversation ends up in some kind of sexual embrace.

Play dress-up. Go out of your way to wear something sexy — it piques interest. And we're not just talking about low-cut shirts for women. Be creative, people. Guys, lose the tighty whities and get a pair of boxer briefs.

Leave your coat on, stay a while. Ripping their clothes off immediately is sexy, but not every time. Tease them (and yourself) by touching over the clothes, opening one button at a time, putting your hand inside their shirt or down their pants. If and when the clothes do come off, make sure the socks come off, too. Always.

top ten make-out albums

Eight out of ten Nerve readers recommend the following. Results may vary.

My Bloody Valentine, Loveless
Miles Davis, Kind of Blue
Massive Attack, Mezzanine
Jeff Buckley, Grace
Rolling Stones, Sticky Fingers
Billie Holiday, Singin' the Blues
Al Green, I'm Still in Love with You
Dead Can Dance, A Passage in Time
Tool, Aenima
Cocteau Twins, Treasure

Be unpredictable. The places you think you should attend to first (or really want to) are the ones you should make wait. Focus on parts of your partner that don't usually get touched in polite company: insides of the thighs, hips, arch of the foot, ribs, belly button, pubic bone, taint, back of the knee, underneath the butt, armpits, etc.

Take a lunch break. If you really want to make foreplay last, neck for a while, go out to eat (see a film, go grocery shopping, etc.), then come home and resume play.

Mouth to Mouth

The kiss is the most compact, powerful, diverse, complex, practically perfect sexual act ever invented. We would not be surprised if there were a high correlation between kissing compatibility and relationship endurance. Speaking of which, if you're in a long-term relationship, don't think for a minute that you can forgo making out just 'cause you can get the sex whenever you want. Kiss a lot. More than you do.

We have a theory about why platonic girlfriends like to make out with each other way more than platonic guy friends do: chicks are just better kissers. They're responsive and patient and gentle — not all over the place like they're trying to stake a claim. They also know how important it is to hold your head and play with your hair, thanks to all those Andrew McCarthy flicks they watched when they were teenagers.

A note about tongues and spit: use discretion. Avoid jabbing, poking and hoover suction action. This isn't a sword fight. One tongue at a time is underrated. So is no tongue. There's nothing worse than a sloppy drool ring around your mouth that starts to cool as it dries. Better to be a tease: make them wait for the kiss. Get as close to each other's mouths as you can without actually kissing. Brush your lips together. See who crumbles first.

If you worry about that not-so-fresh feeling in your mouth, brush your tongue as well as your teeth, lay off the butts and coffee, don't leave home without a tin of mints for quick touch-ups and stash a tube of toothpaste by your bed for early-morning make-outs.

Mouth to Everywhere Else

Take your French kiss on a road trip. Lick and suck anything you can get your lips on: fingers, shoulders, the belly button, the neck. Especially the neck — there's nothing like a skilful nuzzle on the nape to fuel your Buffy fantasies. Same goes for the ears. Just be sure to show a little restraint: One wet willy can ruin 30 minutes of diligent foreplay faster than you can say 'Was it something I said?' And while we're big fans of the discreet love bite (known as 'passion purpura' in the medical community), don't be giving any without permission — not everyone gets all secondary school nostalgic about having to don a polo neck in the middle of August.

Boobies

Nips — on both girls and boys — are sensitive creatures, which is what makes them so great! But one wrong move (whatever 'wrong' may mean for you) and they can go on strike at the pleasure plant. Which comedian was it who said that when it comes to nipples, there's a fine line between ecstasy and nausea? Everyone's different, so ask your partner how you can stay on the good side of their line. That might mean lightly grazing over the area with a finger or tongue tip, gently pinching them with an evil grin, sucking on them like a crazy straw, or just leaving them the hell alone. Nipples are not radio dials, so don't try tuning in to China — unless you're absolutely, positively sure they're down with that.

If you've got a pair of boobies in your life that aren't yours, there are some things you should know: not all women love them as much as you probably do. It's hard to when women are constantly bombarded with images of perfectly perky ta-tas selling them everything from underwear to instant rice. It's all fantasy — silicone, airbrushing and duct tape. The reality is, breasts are not usually symmetrical, they often have little hairs sprouting from the areolas and they don't kiss the sky without some help from a push-up bra — yes, it's true! Treat 'the girls' with awe and wonder and they'll come out and play more often. This does not mean attacking them two seconds after the first kiss, like dudes always seem to do in the movies. Squeezing a bosom like you would a stress-relieving ball is so year seven — save that for a full body massage or her monthly breast exam (see page 241). Don't always rip the bra off immediately — those things are expensive and she probably bought that nice lacy number just for you. Do not attempt the one-handed removal unless you are a master. And if you don't have a pair of your own, you are not allowed to call them 'tits'.

If you do have a pair of your own, here are some things you should know: don't hate them, because they're beautiful. Love them and others will too. Use them as an extra pair of hands — they'll be warmly received wherever you put them: on your partner's face like an eye mask; over their genitals like a warm compress; in their mouth like scoops of ice cream; all over their skin like a back tickler. And then of course there's the charmingly dubbed 'titty fuck' — the name alone turns many women off the practice, but guys really dig the visual of their manhood being cuddled by two breasts smushed together. (For more on boobies, see page 240.)

Toe Jobs

Don't forget the feet — why should fetishists have all the fun? Rub and suck the little piggies, especially if she's the kind of chick (or he's the kind of guy) who gets pedicures. But remember, just as some people are protective of their ass-holes (lord knows why), others are shy about their feet — toe-sucking is not in everyone's sexual repertoire. Make sure your partner's cool with you heading all the way down. Here are a few tips to keep you on your toes while you're on theirs:

- If your partner's embarrassed, start off by bathing their little piggies to assuage any fears they may have about stinky feet or toe cheese. Hell, whether they're embarrassed or not, insist on this for your own sake. (Unless you're into that whole self-degrading, grosser than gross, *The Cook, The Thief, His Wife & Her Lover* meat truck scene thing — in which case, you're on your own.)
- A foot rub is a great segue into toe-sucking. Edible massage oil is a nice touch. Just make sure you have warm hands!

- Maintain eye contact. Not only does it up the raunch factor, but their reaction will help you avoid the ticklish spots (very important for not ruining the mood or getting kicked in the face).
- It's just like a blowjob: start slowly, tease, don't just suck, use your tongue to follow the curves (including in between the toes and the line of the arch), take your time, enjoy it, etc.
- No tickling, please.
- Try out positions where you can stimulate your partner's more traditional erogenous zones while continuing to suck the toes for a nice Pavlovian effect.
- Better yet, get in a position where they can stimulate you while you savour those little nubbins — double whammy!
- If you're the kind of guy or girl who gets pedicures, use them to give love, too. Hell, use any body part: thigh, hip bone, butt crack, you name it.

4

CAN I GET A HAND HERE?

Manually Stimulating Your Partner

Let's skip all the lovey-dovey propaganda about how underrated hand-jobs are and get straight to the practical: always wash your hands before introducing them to various bodily orifices. Imagine all the dirty hands that groped the Underground pole before you did; do you really want those strange, stained fingers indirectly touching your honey's holiest of holies every time you do? Keep your nails clean and well trimmed, 'cause Mum was right: they're nesting grounds for germs. Plus, nothing kills a mood faster than a hangnail on sensitive flesh (except for maybe your mum busting in on you). Moisturise regularly to keep your hands soft and callous-free. If you've got cold hands (and your partner's got a sense of humour), do a quick Karate Kid impersonation by rubbing them together fast and furiously. And remember: this is not the time to accessorise — lose the rings.

One way to approach digit diddling is to find out how your partner masturbates (assuming they do so with their hands) and learn to imitate that. There's a cheesy motivational plaque hanging in many a corporate lobby that reads: 'Tell me, I forget; Show me, I remember; Do it with me, I understand'. Obviously they were talking about learning to give great hand. Here's the non-corporate translation: Have your partner coach you verbally; Watch and learn as they masturbate; Put your hand over theirs (like a glove) and then follow their lead as they get themselves off. If your partner doesn't like the spotlight, have a mutual masturbation sesh and keep one eye on their crotch.

But by no means should you limit yourself to your partner's one particular style. There are myriad moves you can try that might not be in your partner's repertoire — because they can't reach, they've never tried, they're a creature of habit, they didn't date Suzie Jenkins in secondary school, or they haven't hired that particular porno.

Handjobs for Him

There's a school of thought that says no one can give a guy a better handjob than he can give himself. After all, he's probably been fine-tuning the old up-down technique since primary school. Well, that's defeatist, not to mention just plain wrong. Our lunchtime poll revealed that about 90 per cent of men *always* appreciate a helping hand. The following tips and tricks should help you win over the remaining ten per cent.

First off, just 'cause it's called jerking off doesn't mean you should literally jerk it like a cigarette machine: a smooth and consistent motion is key. A contest in Texas called Hands on a Hard Body has players compete for a souped-up pick-up truck by keeping at least one hand in contact with the vehicle at all times. When giving a handjob, pretend you're one of those contestants. Sure,

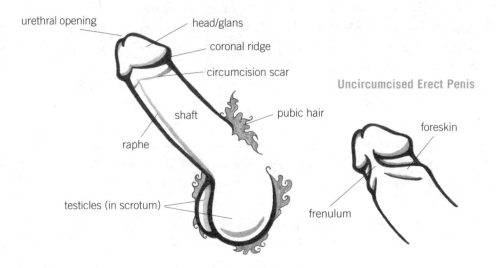

Circumcised Erect Penis

urethral opening

head/glans

coronal ridge

circumcision scar

Uncircumcised Erect Penis

shaft

pubic hair

foreskin

raphe

frenulum

testicles (in scrotum)

you can tease at the beginning, but once you've made significant contact, continued rhythmic contact is appreciated; once you're in the home-stretch, it's more than appreciated — it's essential. Remember the three Fs: focused, fast and firm.

Speaking of firm: the two most common complaints about handjobs are that the grip is too delicate or that it's too rough. Don't hold it like a china teacup but don't hold it like it's going to run away, either. It varies from guy to guy, so for a more

what if your guy wears a polo neck?

Check with your unsnipped fella to see if he wants his foreskin held forward or back during handjobs. We're guessing he'll probably want you to use it as a natural lubricant instead of holding it back. In fact, all the uncircumcised guys we talked to asked incredulously, 'Guys use lube?!'

specific answer you'll just have to ask. One way to ensure a firm grip without pain is to use lubrication. In fact, giving handjobs without lube is like ordering a Big Mac without the Special Sauce — you can do it, but why would you want to? Well, maybe you don't like the mess; maybe you're working with an un-circumcised specimen where the extra foreskin acts as a virtual lubricant; maybe your luvva prefers to have nothing come between you and his penis, not even a thin layer of goo; or maybe you're stranded on a desert island with cotton mouth. In all those cases, you can use 'the grip' method: your hand moves one area of skin up and down over the inner tissue, rather than gliding over the entire surface (the range of motion will depend on the elasticity of your partner's penile tissue). Or, if you're careful, you can move your completely dry hand lightly up and down the shaft. However, any bit of moisture or sweat can make this an uncomfortable experience. When using either of these methods, bear in mind that some men prefer attention focused on the shaft because the glans (or head) of the penis is more sensitive to rug burn. And be patient, for the non-lubed HJ is a fine art: not only does it take more practice to master, it might take him longer to climax.

But if you've got lube, use it. Lubrication gives your hands more freedom of movement, it helps replicate the feeling of intercourse and it's easier to achieve and maintain that oh-so-important steady rhythm. (See page 264 for some good lube brands, as well as DIY recommendations in case you run out.)

The standard position for handjobs is to lie by his side and reach down, mimicking the way he masturbates. But if you're out of practice, you'll get an arm cramp. Plus, sometimes you want a room with a view. Mix it up a bit: he lies down and you sit between his spread legs facing him (either on your knees or with your legs spread over his); he sits on the edge of a bed or chair while you kneel on the floor facing him; you're sitting on the edge of a bed or chair and he's standing facing you; he's sitting up and you're behind him, kneeling or sitting with your legs spread, reaching over or around to his front.

Style Notes

The following ten ways to give him a helping hand work best when you're comfortable and well oiled. Don't hesitate to shift your weight or add more lube as you go along — just try to keep one hand on the job at all times. And remember that careful attention to the head, especially the frenulum (see illustration), is always appreciated — that area's got the highest concentration of nerves on the penis.

- **Look, Ma, One Hand:** This standard move is like 'the grip' (mentioned above) except your hand is much looser as it glides over the shaft and head. Wrap one hand gently around the base of the shaft, with your thumb and index finger closest to the head; slowly move up towards the head, closing your grip as it slides over the head until just the tip remains barely in your grasp. Without ever stopping the fluid motion, gently put it in reverse and slide your hand back down the shaft the way it came. Gracefully repeat and gradually pick up speed. You can throw in a slight twist in one direction on the upstroke and a slight twist in the opposite direction on the downstroke. With your free hand, make a handy-dandy dick holder by putting your fingers and outstretched thumb palm-down on the groin area (with his penis standing in the corner made by your thumb and index finger, see illustration) or by encircling the base with your thumb and index finger — this will help keep his penis from flopping around too much as you work it with your other hand. You can also gently stroke, cup, or hold the twins, because really, they need their fun too. Or lightly massage his perineum and anus, if he's into that.
- **Glazed Twist:** Wrap one hand around the base of the shaft with your thumb and index finger closest to the base (an inverted grip); slowly move upwards. When you get to the top, run your palm and fingers over the head, keeping

as much of your hand in contact with the head as possible. As your hand rounds the head, the move should seamlessly turn into the downstroke of the 'Look, Ma, One Hand'; that is, your hand comes down on the other side of the penis, pinky edge first. If your left hand is busy with the twins, slide your right hand back into the starting position (keeping your fingertips on his penis at all times) and begin again with the same hand. But we suggest using two hands: as the right hand moves down towards the base, use the back of that hand as an approach ramp for the inverted grip of your left hand. As the right hand exits on the downstroke, the left enters on the upstroke and the two hands keep switching places fluidly after each revolution (see illustration).

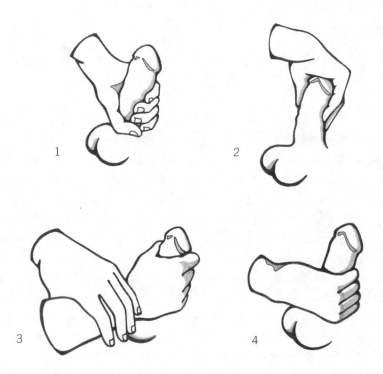

- **The Alex Chee Inverted Plum Roll (ACIPR):** A gay friend of a gay friend of Nerve's named Alex Chee claims to give the best handjob in New York City — it's a variation on the Glazed Twist and yes, it is fabulous. Before trying it at home, Alex recommends practising his patented move by rolling a plum around in a cupped palm. When you think you're ready for the real thing, begin the Glazed Twist on your partner, but when you get to the head, pretend it's the plum rolling around gently in your palm (except your hand is upside down and gravity is not an issue). Since the head is most sensitive, especially on uncircumcised men, you may not be able to do this for very long before he spanks your hand away. An involuntary neck twitch or shudder is a good indication that you should return south to the base, thus completing one long revolution of the ACIPR (see illustration).

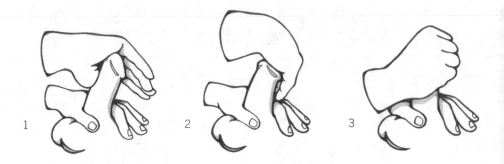

1   2   3

- **Linkin' Logs:** Weave your fingers together on one side and interlock your thumbs on the other side to create a virtual vagina/anus for his penis. Move up and down, keeping a firm grip. Use a gentle mortar-and-pestle twisting motion or give a light pulsing squeeze along the way.

- **The Tug Boat:** If he's not quite standing at full attention, use a gentle upward squeeze with one hand for the full length of his shaft. When you reach the head with that hand, begin the same motion in the same direction at the base with your opposite hand and so on. It's like climbing down a rope. To receive points for artistic merit, begin the upward stroke *under* the balls with your hand in a V shape; as you gently work your way over his berries toward the twig, close your grip.

- **Like a Prayer:** Press your flat hands together like a prayer and let his penis slip through the small opening at the heels of your palms. As you slowly move up and down, keep your fingertips pressed together. After a few strokes, create an opening between two of your fingers to let his pecker peek through for a bit of air; the insides of those two fingers on each hand should run down along his member and then back up as you return to the upright and locked prayer position (see illustration).

- **Indian Arm Burn (IAB)**: Create a cylinder by placing one hand in the shape of a C on top of the other hand in the shape of a C. Insert penis. As you slowly move up and down, gently twist your hands in opposite directions, so your wrists move away from each other. When you can twist no farther, change twisting directions so your wrists move back towards each other. Contrary to this technique's name, you should *not* be wringing out his dick like a wet blanket.
- **The A-OK**: Same as the IAB, except instead of using all five fingers of each hand, just use the index finger and thumb if you're looking for a more deli- cate touch (or if your hands are just 'too big' for the IAB . . . wink wink, nudge nudge).
- **Thumb Press**: Pretend you're having a very gentle thumb war with your own two thumbs up the raphe (or underside ridge) of his shaft — kind of like a back or neck rub, moving your thumbs in tiny circles. Use your fingers on the other side to keep his penis straight and steady (see illustration).

The Grand Finale

To rub or not to rub . . . when he climaxes, that is the question. Some guys like you to maintain the same steady pace all the way through the orgasm; some guys like you to keep going but gradually slow down as he comes; some like you to 'milk' the come out; others like you to pulse with each spurt; some want you to stop moving but keep a gentle hold on the dick; some want you to let go after the first few spurts; and there's one guy out there who likes you to let go completely right before he comes (his name is Steve — be gentle with him).

Handwork for Her

It's all about the clitoral head, that nubbin of fun peeking out from beneath its hood. But then again, it's about everything but that. Without attention paid to her surrounding territories (see illustration), the magic little button ain't so magic. And then your audience of one might start booing and throwing rotten tomatoes (which is only good if you're into that food-play fetish called sploshing).

Take the scenic route on your way to the clit. Thighs, buttocks, belly and pubic hair are all good starting points. Hell, start all the way down at her toes. The longer the journey and the more the build-up, the better, since the glans of the clitoris is often too sensitive for direct stimulation right off the bat; the more aroused a woman is, the more heavy aircraft her landing dock can take.

Lube — it's not always necessary, but it can't ever hurt, as long as you're using a product that's glycerine-free and water-based, like ID Personal Lubricant, Bodywise Maximus or Liquid Silk (see page 267 for more suggestions). No DIY lubes down there, please (except for saliva or her own love juice) — using any oils or products containing sugar (especially internally) can promote yeast infections.

Women are far less predictable than men when it comes to pace and pressure. Just because she's enjoying something immensely doesn't mean she'll

Vulva

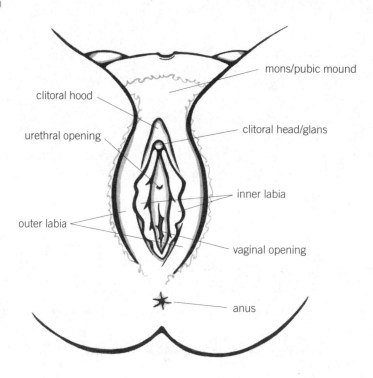

clitoral hood

urethral opening

outer labia

mons/pubic mound

clitoral head/glans

inner labia

vaginal opening

anus

enjoy it more if you do the same thing harder and faster. And just because she's enjoying something immensely today doesn't mean she'll enjoy the same exact thing tomorrow. So when in doubt, ask. Even if you have no doubt, you should still probably ask, you cocky little fucker, you.

the myth of the magic button

The clitoris is a complex organ that extends throughout the genitals. The little man in the boat is just the glans, or head, of the clitoris. However, when we say 'clit' we are referring to the glans — the part of the clitoris you're most familiar with. See page 271 for more on anatomy.

Vary your position. To simulate the angle of her fingers when she masturbates, lie by her side and reach over; sit behind her and reach around while she's sitting; or have her lie on top of you (you're both on your backs) and reach around. To give her something she can't give herself, have her lie on her stomach or lean over something (e.g., the back of a sofa) so you can diddle her from behind. (In this position you can give her G-spot a personal thumbs-up, see page 101.)

There's no money-back guarantee on the bag of tricks below — mix and match and watch for the best results. Just follow two rules when letting your fingers do the wanking: one, if she seems to really really be enjoying something, don't change a thing; and two, the beginning of intercourse or oral sex shouldn't mean the end of the handwork — like beige, it goes with everything.

General Work

It's not always about penetration. Can we get an 'Amen!' from the lesbians? Try to think outside 'the box' with the following tips:

- 'Warm up' the vulva as a masseuse might: lay your hand over the entire area and let it rest there for a few seconds, then move it around in a gentle circular or rocking motion. Or use a long, pulling stroke from her perineum to her pubic bone, repeatedly brushing your hand and wrist over the entire area. You can also use the pads of your fingers to massage the mons pubis and run your fingers through her pubic hair, assuming she hasn't gone slaphead. If she's particularly sensitive down there, run your fingers in the direction the hair grows. If she's particularly thick-skinned, start patting the area with your finger pads and ask her if she'd like it a little harder; if she says yes, then work your way up to a good repetitive 'front bottom' spanking. All of these moves come in handy should her clit get overstimulated and require a break.

- Use one hand to pull up the skin of the mons pubis while the other gets busy: it might help coax out a particularly shy clit and she might like the tightening effect.
- Chicks have a perineum, too! Press on it in a gentle, circular motion once she's warmed up a bit.
- Try wearing a latex glove; she might like the sensation.
- Offer her your arm as a humping post, with the wrist bone pressed against her clit, the fleshy part of your palm (under your thumb) up against her labia and your fingers cupping the back of her upper thigh. She may squeeze you with a vicelike grip, or rock back and forth on your hand like Rainman.

Outer Work

She's got labes — know how to use them.

- Gently pinch the outer and inner lips between the thumb and index finger of each hand, working your way up and down each set of lips simultaneously.
- Put your index finger on one of her inner lips and your middle finger on the other, then scissor-kick your fingers in alternating directions, so her lips are rubbing against each other.
- Separate the labia with your first and third fingers while you stroke between her lips with your middle finger.

Inner Work

We're loath to use the terms 'fingering' and 'finger-fucking' in this section — and not just because they make our skin crawl the way words like 'moist' and 'panties' do. No, they also give the wrong impression. Actually fucking her with your fingers is only part of it (which is why we use the term 'handwork'). But chances are she's going to want it at some point. Before diving in, make sure that your nails are smooth and clean and remember that most of the nerve endings are in the outer third of the vagina — no need to head straight for the cervix (unless she's into that). Pay attention to what's going on in there, too:

your fingers are a much more reliable witness to the inner workings of the vagina than a dildo or penis (which is usually a little distracted at the time).

- OK, OK, we'll say it: *finger-fuck* her, as if your finger(s) were a penis or a dildo, moving in and out. But remember the first lesson of screwing: it's not all about the jackhammer. (For more on more fingers, see 'Fisting', page 109.)
- The G-spot, the spongy tissue felt through the ceiling of her vagina, is best reached using the old 'come here' finger crook (try doing *that* with your penis). The middle finger works best for its length and dexterity, while your first and third fingers provide balance and external stimulation. Experiment with different pressures and motions — the spot should expand as she gets more aroused. But provoking the G may not necessarily be arousing to her: some women love it (some even ejaculate from it), some women can't feel it and others find it downright painful. (For more on the G and female ejaculation, see page 99.)
- Imagine there's a clock inside and play with each hour, paying attention to what time makes her tick. With all the emphasis placed on the G-spot, you'll never discover whether or not she likes a little indirect anal stimulation from a finger pushing down on the bottom of the vaginal canal, towards the bum.

Clitoral Work

We're talking about the little man's head here, not the rest of his boat. He's a sensitive ponytail guy, so he needs a lot of open communication. Some women may not like direct contact and would rather you use the hood as a buffer (most of the below strokes can also be done over the hood). Others need you to push hard on it like a broken door bell. And some even have a favourite 'side' — it's only polite to find hers, if she has one.

- Circle around and over the clit with your index finger.
- Roll it gently between your thumb and index finger.
- Tap on it quickly, alternating between your index and middle fingers, like a typist on speed hitting 'jkjkjkjk' over and over.
- If you've got a tough little cookie on your hands, try flicking the bean — literally. But be careful (and don't blame us if she slaps you).

- Place one to four fingers (or a thumb) over the clit area, press firmly and then 'vibrate' your hand gently but rapidly, either up and down, in a circular motion, or from side to side, never losing contact. It's no Hitachi Magic Wand (page 126), but you've got a nice smile — and you're safe to use in water, too!
- During any of the 'Inner Work' moves above, keep your thumb out to provide clit stimulation.

The Grand Finale

To rub or not to rub . . . when she climaxes, that is the question. Some chicks like you to maintain the same steady pace all the way through the orgasm; others like you to keep going beyond the orgasm for a second or third round; some chicks like you to keep going but gradually slow down; some like you to push with each orgasmic contraction; some want you to stop moving but keep your hand placed there firmly; and there's one chick out there who likes you to let go completely when she comes (her name is Stephanie — be gentle with her).

5

HEADING SOUTH

The Art of Oral Sex

Oral sex is all about keeping your head in the game. You've got to have focus, dedication, an Oxford Blue in scuba diving — but most of all, you've got to have fun. Remember, this is a privilege, not a chore. Make your partner feel like there's no place you'd rather be. Play. Tease. Explore. Plant a tree. Get your face in on the act. Make a mess. Build up a crescendo. *Worship.*

We're firm believers in a quid pro quo policy when it comes to oral sex: you've got to give it to get it. Which is why you should initiate and not wait to be asked to head downtown. That said, an occasional request for oral sex after a bad day at work or your pet's funeral is reasonable (however, pushing your lover's head downwards and using their ears as a steering wheel is not). You'll get a higher rate of response to these requests if you keep a clean house: wash all your nooks and crannies every day, if not right before the blessed event. You could even run your fingers through your pubes to remove any strays and — dare we say it? Yes, we do! — dingleberries. Don't forget to brush your teeth, too: not only will it give you fresh breath your partner will appreciate, it will help keep your oral lovin' fresh when you start appreciating their genitals in return.

Boys and girls, the basics are mapped out for you below. Learn them, live them, love them! But don't be on cruise control: be tuned in to your partner's verbal and physical cues. While you should probably have a basic plan, it's the detours, wrong turns and spontaneous visits to Graceland that make the journey worth writing home about.

Exploring the South Pole: The Art of Fellatio

The blowjob is a frequent victim of analysis paralysis. While there are certainly many ways to give a great BJ, there are very few ways to give a bad one (unless, of course, you literally blow on it). The key here is confidence. It's like the *Little Engine That Could*: if you *think* you can give great head, then you probably can. First of all, don't even worry about how you look down there — with your mouth on his dick, you're the most beautiful person in the world (even if *you* think you look like a spastic jackhammer). Second, get into the head space that's most comfortable for you — whether that's taking control ('I am an all-powerful sex god') or relinquishing it ('I am your love slave'). Once you've got those bases covered, you can focus on the nitty gritty, as follows . . .

Getting Going

Start slowly. Don't act like you've been starving on a desert island for weeks and a big juicy sausage suddenly washes ashore. (You don't remember that scene from *Robinson Crusoe*?) Lick the glans (head), lick the frenulum (the supersensitive strip of skin beneath the glans on the underside), lick the testes (balls), lick the inner thighs (inner thighs). If his genitals are a blank canvas, then your tongue is a soft paintbrush and your strokes are swirly like van Gogh's. Take your time. Breathe. Be a tease. For example, when he's hard, open wide and descend on him like a hover-craft, letting as little of his penis as possible come in contact with the insides of your mouth. Or shower his shaft with kisses. Before things get too spirited, take a quick trip back north for some more deep kissing, face-to-face.

He doesn't have to be rock hard for you to take him into your mouth; in fact, he doesn't have to be hard at all. Open mouth, insert flaccid penis, close mouth and feel him grow like a magic sea monkey! Lightly tap your tongue against the shaft

hold the mayo?

Ejaculate is non-fattening, with only about five to seven calories per serving (the average serving size being one to two teaspoons). Sperm originate in the testicles along with male hormones, but the latter are absorbed directly into his bloodstream — so swallowing won't make you more manly. HIV and other sexually transmitted diseases, however, can be transmitted by swallowing his bodily fluids and from oral to genital contact.

or swallow gently to help the little man along. But don't start moving your mouth up and down (aka 'The Basic Bob', see below) until he's at least semi-erect.

Slippery When Wet

We have one word for you: saliva. And lots of it. Don't be afraid to get wet and messy — it's more fun for everyone that way, not to mention easier. Keep a glass of water and/or a tin of mints handy to help with cotton mouth. In fact, mints (or watered-down toothpaste or mouthwash, or even champagne) will give him a tingly sensation, while keeping things slick, aromatic and tasty for you. If you like or need more lube than you can get from your salivary glands, or if you find the taste of penis a little bland, there are some synthetic water-based lubricants (like ID's Juicy Lubes line) that come in different flavours (e.g., banana, passion fruit, strawberry-kiwi). Other fun (though sticky) condiments include honey, jelly, whipped cream, liqueurs and mayonnaise (OK, hold the mayo). Go easy on menthol items, as they can burn, especially in the peepee hole. And no intercourse or anal sex after food play without a thorough washing first. To keep things cool, clean and simple, just use a little crushed ice every now and then. A hot tea chaser works well, too — alone or in tandem with the ice.

The Basic Bob

This is what makes a blowjob a blowjob. He's on his back, you're between his legs and your mouth's taking him in and out. We don't mean the 'Walk Like an Egyptian' move so popular in pornos, but a more fluid, undulating, artistic up-and-down. Some people stretch their lips tightly over their teeth, like Grandma without her dentures — just to be safe. But lips loose and soft in the shape of an O around the shaft should provide enough buffer between his chorizo and your choppers. Besides, lips (full or thin) just feel good. Either way, no need to become a high-powered hoover. Your sucking function should be set to Off or Low — simply moving your mouth up and down will create adequate suction. Besides, sucking too hard can make it difficult to get into a smooth groove, while increasing the chances of your teeth getting in the way. And don't forget to continue to make the most of your tongue — the top, the tip, the sides, the underside. It should be in constant motion, providing a non-stop source of lube and stimulation. *Very* important.

A note on approach: it may be more comfortable for you (and suspenseful for him) to edge his hot dog in slowly, going a little farther with each downstroke of your mouth. However, to make a winning first impression, envelop the shaft as far as you can with the first significant bob.

Handy Work

There's no need to deep throat all the time — if at all — if you use one or both of your hands (or even just a finger and thumb) as an extension of your mouth. Your mouth is between five and eight cm from your teeth to the back of your throat, while his erect penis is usually 12 to 18 cm in length: it's not cheating to give yourself a helping hand. In fact, we'd say that *all* good blowjobs should incorporate hands — at least eventually. A gradual escalation is key. Start with just your mouth, add a thumb and forefinger, then more fingers, then maybe your other hand. Here's how:

● Make a ring with your finger and thumb or a mini-megaphone with your hand(s), hold it up to your lips (which are pursed in the O formation) and keep your hand against (or at least within an inch of) your kisser as you perform the Basic Bob. Once you've mastered that, take it to the next level: when you get to the top of the shaft using the megaphone/Bob combo, slide your index finger over the head to one side and then go back down (so his ding-dong is now between your index and middle fingers) with your mouth immediately following. For even more advanced play, try twisting one or two hands and/or your head (in the same or opposite directions) as you go up and down — we're not talking Indian burns here, just a gentle shifting from left to right on the way down and then back again on the way up.

- You can also use your hands to pull the penile skin taut and increase the head's sensitivity: wrap your thumb and index finger around the shaft a couple of centimetres above the base and pull down. It's a 'handy' move if you've got lockjaw (or the two of you are in the red-lit bathroom of an inner-city dive bar while ten drunks wait outside to pee) since it will probably make him climax more quickly. Whether or not you take up the skin slack, a hand or two at the base is never a bad idea — no need to get spanked in the face with a rebounding penis that accidentally slipped out of your mouth. Then again, such accidents have been known to open the door to a whole new world of penis-slapping fun.

flavour savers

The following ingredients may affect the way both men and women taste and smell down there, for better or worse.

The Good: *melon, kiwi, pineapples (and juice), celery, strawberries, cinnamon and a vegetarian diet will help keep your love juices tasty. The jury's still out on a powdered drink for men called Semenex, guaranteed to 'give you the best tasting cum [sic] possible — or your money back'. Not yet available in the UK, but you might want to reserve your tin (or your judgement).*

The Bad: *broccoli, salty foods, alkaline-based foods such as meats and fish, dairy products and some medication and vitamins can make you taste a little stale.*

The Ugly: *asparagus, coffee, booze, cigarettes and some drugs (e.g., cocaine) can make you taste bitter and bad.*

Gag Me with a Spoon

On second thought, don't. Gagging is never a pleasant experience. But when you've got a kielbasa banging on your throat's back door, it's a natural reflex. Happily, it's one that you can learn to control. Take him in as far as you feel comfortable and then sit quietly for a moment, giving your mouth time to grow accustomed to the sensation. Practising on a courgette (or a kielbasa, or a guy you don't like as much) can also help condition your mouth. Relax your

too much of a good thing

When it comes to giving head, endurance on the part of the receiver is not a virtue. Fellating is fun but it's hard work; after 20 minutes, it's just hard work. Give your fellator a break by giving in when the spirit moves you (i.e., when you're about to come, don't start thinking of footie stats or your grandmother). Also, if you climax in record time, your partner feels like a star.

throat muscles and use the Jedi Mind Trick to overpower your urge to gag. (It's kind of ironic that homophobic frat boys would probably make the best deep throaters, due to their extensive experience with beer bongs and shotgunning.) As you begin to bob (slowly), inhale at the top and exhale (through your nose, if possible) on the way down. Pick up the pace gradually and don't forget to keep breathing. If your partner has a tendency to thrust, hold on to his dick with both hands while resting your forearms on his hips to weigh him down. Or try cupping his balls with a free hand for the occasional 'Whoa, Nelly' squeeze or tug. If the urge to purge is still overwhelming, then by all means take over with both hands and come up for some air.

Deep Throating Is *So* '70s

All it took was one porno with a catchy name and innocent suckers everywhere became victims of unrealistic expectations and low self-esteem. Anyone who thinks it's necessary to swallow all 18 cm with each bob has obviously never sucked dick. That said, the *occasional* sword-swallowing is an impressive party trick. Learn to DT sparingly over the course of a blowjob and you too can be the porn star your boyfriend has always dreamed of! (Though chances are the novelty will wear off for both of you pretty quickly.)

In order to really get him in there, you've got to widen the natural 90-degree angle of your throat. Using the anti-gag tips above will help. In addition, these two positions will elongate your food trap–cum–love passage for an express trip to your uvula (though neither will allow you optimal tongue action on the sensitive underside of his penis).

- Sit on his chest facing his penis (so your starfish is staring back at him). Or, if you prefer, make it a 69 and sit on his face, assuming this is proportionally possible for the two of you and you aren't easily distracted. Hold the base of his penis to help guide it in. You'll probably notice his Peter pressing on your tongue in this position (rather than on the roof of your mouth, as it usually does when you're facing the other way).

- Lie on your back on a bed and hang your head off the edge. Depending on the height of the bed, the man either stands or kneels by the side of the bed (using pillows to adjust his height) so that his penis is at your mouth level. Use your hands against his thighs to control the depth and speed of his thrusts. Enjoy the ball goggles.

take it on the road

One of the beauties of the BJ is that it can be delivered on the fly, so to speak. Cabs! Changing rooms! Phone booths! Due to time constraints and possible passersby, receivers should be prepared for blue balls and givers should be prepared to swallow (good campers pack out what they packed in).

Positions

While not necessarily conducive to deep-throating, the following positions are better for an all-around best-in-show blowjob.

- Lie on your sides. Your head is propped on a pillow facing his knob — that way, he has more room to thrust and you won't have to work as hard.
- Kneel or sit in front of him while he stands. Guys love that whole 'praying before the altar' thing.
- Practise irrumation, or 'face fucking' as it's charmingly known: lie on your back with your head on a pillow while he hovers over you, supporting most of his weight with his arms and gently moving in and out of your mouth. Meanwhile, you can take care of his testes, perineum and anus (see below) — or you can take care of yourself.

Bonus Points

Is your blowjob looking tired and lifeless? Use the following tips and tricks to give yourself a fellatio makeover:

- Make lots of eye contact. Stop short of creepy staring contests.
- If you've got long hair, tie it back so he can see what you're doing — or have him hold it back in a sexy clenched fist if you want to be all hardcore.
- If you've got long hair, let it down so it caresses his throbbing man parts (a million romance novels can't be wrong).

- Take out his penis and rub, flick or spank it against your neck or cheek (a million pornos can't be wrong).
- So he doesn't feel left out, stick a finger or two in his mouth to give him something to suck on (assuming they haven't already been massaging his prostate).
- Rub his tummy. Don't ask why, just try it.
- Pay attention to the twins.
- Gently massage or push on the perineum (aka the taint).
- Insert a lubed finger — sans long fingernail — up his bum a bit to massage his prostate, aka the male G-spot, aka the sure-fire way to make him your slobbering love puppy. (See page 79 for more anal tips.)
- Pinch or tweak his nipples, but only if you know he likes it — 'cause some guys sure as hell don't.
- As you come up the shaft, pause at the top and twist your head back and forth a few times like those bobbing dashboard dogs, with your tongue focusing on the frenulum. It's like the Alex Chee Inverted Plum Roll (see page 37), except you use your mouth instead of your palm.
- Straddle, squeeze, or hump his leg(s) to let him know that this isn't just a job for you, it's an adventure.
- Take your clothes off and keep his on, or vice versa.
- For women only: in the middle of intercourse, hop off and head south for a taste of the exotic.
- For professional use only: gently — and we mean *gently* — slide your front teeth against his shaft during the old up/down. Did we mention GENTLY?

Get Your Foot on the Accelerator

After you've romanced his stone for a while, gradually speed up until you've reached a rhythm that's comfortable for both of you. At this point, it's OK to treat him like that desert island sausage. And it's no longer OK to tease. Increase the vacuum of your mouth just a bit. When all verbal and physical signs from him suggest that the cliff's edge is fast approaching, don't slow down and don't make any drastic changes in motion. One of the biggest complaints from men is that their partners don't go hard or fast enough at the end. Well, maybe they should just ask for it harder and faster at the end, shouldn't they?

Insecure cocksuckers tend to be afraid they'll cause an injury, make a mess, or look like an ass (bless their hearts). Don't be afraid: he'll tell you if it really hurts, he doesn't care if it's sloppy and he thinks you look fabulous. If you're still unsure, you'll just have to suck it up and ask for direction . . . and then suck it up. Keep going, you're doing great and soon you'll get to . . .

The Big O

Rumours of standard blowjob-induced orgasms are vastly exaggerated. Sometimes the guy on the receiving end feels as much pressure to come as you might feel to make him come, in which case no one's having fun. Don't feel compelled to get him off.

If you do get him off, the grand finale is completely up to you. Whether you spit, swallow, or finish him off with your hand, it's still a blowjob. If you opt for a re-enactment of Old Faithful, be sure to have him warn you just before he's gonna blow. In fact, even if you plan on getting a protein shot, it's nice to know when it's about to be served.

If he forgets to tap you on the shoulder, there are other warning signs: his penis swells; his balls draw close to his body; his hips really thrust (if they weren't already before); his body tenses up; his glans blushes; his breathing gets heavier; he shouts at the top of his lungs, 'Good Christ, I'm coming!'

Many gay guys don't swallow because they like the visual — which is always a good excuse. If you, too, 'like the visual', quickly switch to a full-on, two-handed handjob, or hold his penis against your cheek as you pump it with your cupped hand, or get on one side of his body so you can play his ridge like a flute (focusing on the frenulum), or let him finish himself off. If you want to get really dirty (both figuratively and literally), take a sperm shower. He'll probably appreciate the visual — and the honour.

fellating your unsnipped fella

No need to undress him right away. Slip your tongue inside his foreskin and circle around the glans, remembering that uncircumcised guys are usually more sensitive there. Gradually edge the hood down with your tongue or fingertips. While blowing him, you can hold the foreskin (loosely or taut) down at the base, or pump it up and down the shaft, or just let it do its own thing. Be sure to hold the foreskin back out of the way when he comes, for an unobstructed shot and a cleaner finish.

If you don't want to interrupt the flow of a good blowjob, or if he's a stealth bomber, hold the ejaculate and his penis in your mouth through his last spurt, then gently slide your mouth off and spit in a nearby receptacle: your hand, a lined wastebasket, your glass of water, the bathroom sink, his mouth. On the other hand, you could always swallow. It can convey real intimacy — plus, you don't have to hold it in your mouth while you search for the trash can and it makes clean-up a cinch! Some people actually like the taste and throw in a sincere 'Mmm, mmm, good' to prove it. If you're not one of them, you can protect most taste buds by putting him way back in your mouth and starting to swallow as soon as he erupts.

Put on the Brakes

Once he comes, stop everything — in our experience, it hurts if you don't — unless you know he's the kind of guy who likes a bit of post-O dick stroking. But do hold it in your mouth, motionless, for a few seconds or more — he'll have flashbacks of Mrs Danforth stroking his head in reception class.

Thinking Outside the Box: The Art of Cunnilingus

If the world is your oyster, how should you eat it? That depends. Your favourite vagina might like a good mashing and a little teeth action on Mondays and a light touch on Thursdays. It might prefer direct tongue-clit contact every day of the year, or it might insist that the tongue sneak around the clit, never ever actually touching down. Be sensitive to your partner, but not in that *Steel Magnolias* way. Figure out what she likes and doesn't like by gently pushing her boundaries and pulling back if she pulls back. You've got to be patient: women don't like to be rushed. In fact, many of them *can't* be rushed — they require steady and prolonged stimulation in order to get off. So act like you've got all day.

Assuming the Position

No need to get all fancy with the positions — if she's lying on her back and you're between her legs, you can't lose. To increase your skin-to-skin ratio, to gain more control and to pull her closer, hug her thighs or bum with your arms (either under or over her legs, depending on whether her knees are bent).

Placing a pillow or two under her ass allows you better angles for exploration. It also signals that you want her to be comfortable and that you intend to stay down there for as long as it takes. She might want a pillow under her head — girls like to watch, too, you know.

Here are some more variations on the position theme:

- Have her pull her knees up to her chest to really open things up.
- To give your neck a break, move onto your knees by her side and approach from above (see illustration).

- Your partner adjusts the pressure to her labia and clit by squatting on all fours over your head (the old 'sit on my face' move).
- Kneel between her legs while she sits on the edge of a bed or chair.
- She stands with her legs spread wide while you approach from underneath. (She'll probably need something nearby to hold on to for support.)
- Both lie on your sides with your head resting on her inner thigh and her legs over your shoulders so her calves rest against your back (see illustration).

- She's on all fours and you come from behind, like a dog sniffing another dog's butt.

Taking the Scenic Route

You may be an eager beaver, but don't dive right in. (Unless, of course, the two of you are still in the red-lit bathroom of an inner-city dive bar and 20 drunks are now waiting outside to pee.) Be a merciless tease. Beat around the bush. You don't even have to remove her knickers right away; just work around or over them. You want her on the edge of her seat, not fast asleep, so mix it up. Nibble a little on the hips and then follow the curve of the pelvis with your tongue. Get close enough with your tongue to touch your partner's pubic hair, but not the actual flesh. A few minutes of this along with puffs of air from your mouth onto the vulva should warm her up nicely. Note to diners: we said *puffs* of air — never actually blow air into the vagina, as this can cause a fatal air embolism. Bummer.

Getting Down to Business

We're not at the clit yet, but you can whip out your tongue now. Remember, you should still be in tease mode. Point your tongue and swirl it between her thighs and outer lips, gradually moving in towards her inner lips. Once there, run your tongue up and down in the grooves between the lips, starting gently and gradually increasing the pressure. Flatten your tongue and deliver a big slow lick from her perineum to her pubic bone. Suck on the lips, first one side, then the other. Kiss her like you're kissing her mouth. Nibble gently (we said *gently*). Get the whole area wet with saliva and keep it that way.

Approaching the Clitoral Head

The clitoral glans comes in all shapes and sizes: some are smaller than others, some protrude from the hood like erect nipples, some never show their face (those can be a real bitch to find). If her clit is a shy one, place a hand on her mons and push up a bit to help coax it out of hiding. Once you've got the glans in your sights, touch down gently with only the very tip of your tongue. You may not even want to move it, just hold it there for a moment. Slowly start to move her clit side to side, maintaining constant contact and a light touch. Then, take it in your mouth and gently wind your tongue around it in a circular motion. You might be able to feel the head getting engorged in your mouth. A little suction can be nice, but don't be trying to give her a love bite down there. Run your tongue up and down the sides and tickle underneath it.

As you immerse yourself in your work, don't forget to check in with the boss. Let her guide your head. Get feedback from her. If she's totally unresponsive after three or four minutes, perhaps you need to change the angle, position or pressure of your tongue. Does she have a favourite 'side'? If she bends one leg and keeps the other straight, you'll have better access to it.

Avoid too much porno wagging (jabbing at her with your tongue stuck out and your face miles away so the camera gets a good view). That can feel so cold and distant sometimes. Get your face all the way in there. Give her clit an Eskimo kiss with your nose — and not just with the tip; pressure from the bridge can rock her world. Or how about a nice chin rub? (If you're a guy, be aware that your designer stubble might prickle. Then again, that might be a good thing.) Pretend you're giving her an adamant, non-verbal 'uh-uh' by rapidly shaking your head back and forth (with your tongue in, or out and stiff). Or hold your head still with her bean between your top and bottom front teeth while you flick it with your tongue.

'p' is for pleasure?

Cunning linguists love to debate the pros and cons of 'alphabetising'. If you missed the memo, this is writing the alphabet with your tongue, either on the clit itself, or over the whole vaginal area (occasionally grazing the clit when you cross your t's or dot your i's). Proponents claim the unexpected twists and turns are very effective, while naysayers argue that it's too mass market. Conduct your own field research and report back.

Swimming at Your Own Risk

- The following manoeuvres are for advanced divers only. (OK, so they're not *that* crazy.)
- Put your index and middle fingers along either side of her clit and gently spread and squeeze as you lick.
- Don't be afraid to make a little noise. The occasional 'Mmmmm' not only

feels good physically, it lets her know you're having a good time, too. Humming is also nice if you can do it without cracking up. Or without cracking her up.

- Hot tea and crushed ice are party tricks she'll fall for, too. Just keep anything with sugar away from her coochie to avoid infection and keep ice on the outside to avoid damaging delicate internal linings.
- Make eye contact occasionally, but don't engage her in a stare-down — give her space to go to her happy place.
- Put your idle hands to work: rub the mons or the belly, tug on the lips or the pubes, gently massage the perineum, play with her boobies, graze everything you can reach with your teasing fingertips.
- Use your tongue as a surrogate sausage. No, you don't need a dangler like Gene Simmons, since most of her important nerve endings are in the outer third of the vagina.
- Lovingly stick a well-lubed, manicured finger up her ass, or just topically tickle it. (Do not insert fingers that have visited the poop chute into her vagina.)
- Think of vibrators and dildos as good shipmates — you work up on deck while they work down below.
- See the entire section on 'Handwork for Her' (page 39), then mix and match with this chapter.

Slow and Steady Wins the Race

If she starts acting like you're doing it right, it's not necessarily a cue to increase the speed or pressure. In fact, when you find something that works, stick with it. Many women literally get off on repetitive action, steady tempo and unwavering pressure; suddenly stopping or changing motion when she's close to the end could be the sexual equivalent of a 'return to start' card in a board game. It can take women anywhere from three to 30 minutes to reach their peak arousal state. Not that you're complaining, though — you were born to do this.

But being destined for greatness doesn't mean you won't get tired. Close your mouth and let your jaw rest every so often — rub and stretch your lips until you feel ready to open wide again. If you're a guy, alternate stimulation between your tongue and penis, but don't always think of tipping the velvet as foreplay to getting your dick in her. Speaking of which, if you are having intercourse, take regular cunnilingus breaks to extend your play.

The Final Stretch

Even if you follow all the above advice (you little teacher's pet), your partner may not climax. Don't sweat it: ya done good and we're pretty sure she'll have had a damn good time. Then again, sometimes good head is the *only* way a woman can come. Assuming the earth does move for her and you realise it as it's happening, you'll probably want to stop fiddling with her clit — it can get even more sensitive at the moment of orgasm and heavy friction can be painful. Like a guy's balls, sometimes the head of the clitoris will draw up into the hood before a woman comes. Whatever happens, do not let go! Continue putting pressure on the chickpea or hold it gently in your mouth until the spasms subside. And if she's squeezing your head in a death grip à la WWF, don't panic — just keep doing whatever you were doing and pray for the best.

JUST DOING IT

The Ins and Outs of Intercourse

The animal kingdom, pornos and the probably mediocre sex ed you had at secondary school are all terrible places to learn about intercourse. A few lessons from them and you'd think sex is intercourse and intercourse is just good hard jackhammering. Where's the romance? Where's the variety? Where's the nuance? Where's the clitoris?

For guys, the formula for intercourse ecstasy is usually fairly simple: insert dick; thrust; thrust some more; come. Unfortunately, only the rare, lucky woman who likes cervical stimulation will get off from this equation. And hetero guys: you're probably not dating one of them.

Fewer than 30 per cent of women can orgasm from intercourse alone — and we'd guess half of those 30 per cent are faking (shame on them). It's not surprising, considering the vast distance between the clitoral head and the vaginal opening (shame on Mother Nature). A dick or dildo with the very best of intentions could drill all day long without ever making clit contact, which is what most women need in order to climax. But change the angle, add a finger (anyone's), or join forces with a vibe and you could beat those odds together. And let's not forget about the G-spot (see page 100), another key to orgasm for some women, which actually is inside a woman's vaginal canal. But again, merely inserting something and pumping away ain't gonna cut the mustard. The G enjoys *shallow* penetration at a very specific angle.

Before we jump into bed with tips on the nitty gritty of technique, let's pause for a brief lesson in intercourse etiquette: don't prize it above all other sex acts to the extent that it's the only thing you're ever after. But don't forget to approach intercourse with respect, either; after all, you're tapping into the reproductive circle of life. And don't ever assume you're entitled to — or obligated to engage in — intercourse, no matter how naughty or naked you've already got. If you're not sure, ask (that means you, too, ladies), because when you're in bed together, there's no such thing as a stupid question — except for maybe 'What was your name again?'

Now, let's get it on.

Knocking on Heaven's Door

For those of you taking the plunge, or rather, doing the plunging: just because you've been invited in doesn't mean you should rush across the threshold every time. Hang out on the porch for a while, ring her doorbell a couple of times. Use your dick or dildo like a finger or tongue, teasing the labes and the clit. Use your hand to control the motions and maintain your stiffy. (No sneaking around to the back door, though — the germs that hang out there aren't welcome in front.)

When it's time to come in and play, you or she can spread her lips with a few stroking fingers, or guide the dick or dildo with a hand. You can enter in one fell swoop (just make sure that everything's well lubed, see page 263) or take your teasing time. Go inch by inch, or even centimetre by centimetre. Go in a bit, then back out again, then in a bit more and back out again and so on.

And both of you: look into each other's eyes, will ya? It adds a nice personal touch.

The Doing It To-Do; List

- **Do it in slow motion.** Super-fast thrusting is more likely to make her numb and him too sensitive. You both want to go for rhythmic, graceful motions worthy of Juilliard.

seeing red: getting busy when aunt flow's in town

Don't assume that if she's surfing the crimson wave it means no sex — chicks have sex during their period all the time. For many women, it's their horniest time of the month. And orgasms can relieve menstrual cramps. We've even known people who — gasp! — go down on women who are menstruating. Unless you're restricted by a religious tradition, or you've got brand-new white Ralph Lauren sheets, there's really no reason not to. Well, except for the fact that the presence of blood can slightly increase the odds of transmitting certain sexually transmitted diseases and infections (and especially her odds of contracting pelvic inflammatory disease, as the blood can help carry the offending organism farther up the reproductive tract, see page 194) — but if that's a concern (and isn't it always?) you should be using barrier protection anyway. Even if you don't usually employ oral sex dams for cunnilingus, it's a good idea to grab one at this time of the month — any infections she might have will be more highly concentrated in her menstrual blood than they usually are in her vaginal secretions. You should also be aware of the commonsensical misconception that a woman can't get pregnant while she has her period; while the chances are reduced, there is still enough risk to warrant using birth control.

But maybe your concerns are less pragmatic than aesthetic. Maybe you're worried the post-coital embrace will resemble something out of Texas Chainsaw Massacre. Well, for most women, total fluid per period is only a couple of tablespoons, so just avoid her heavy days and the gore should be minimal. Also, a bath may wash away some of the excess blood, at least externally, so jump her bones when she gets out of the tub — give her a big kiss on the ruby lips and hop back in the tub to clean off afterwards. Or just do it in the shower.

Or perhaps you're suffering from the juvenile delusion that menstruation is dirty, unnatural even. (We've all heard the joke 'How can you trust something that bleeds for seven days and doesn't die?' — that's so funny, we forgot to laugh.) Or perhaps — heaven forbid — your own mum made you feel like it was something to be ashamed of. Grow up, put a dark towel on the bed and enjoy the extra lube and splash of colour! Or just do it with the lights out: wet and squishy is wet and squishy. Period!

- **Do indulge in quickies.** Chicks dig them, too. Empty train carriages, a restaurant's disabled stall on your lunch break, a lift, your car at a lay-by, the back row of an almost-empty cinema, the hall on your way out to dinner, your flat's stairwell on your way home from dinner, on your sofa five minutes before your favourite TV show starts ... on second thought, scratch that: television should never take priority over sex.
- **Do leave more than a hat on.** Total nudity is not always a prerequisite for

great sex. Plus, leftover clothes give the sex a sense of urgency. And that's hot.

- **Do your kegels.** Guys can twitch their dick by contracting their pelvic muscles. Chicks can use their well-toned pelvic muscles to really hug their partner's sausage. (See page 257 for your pelvic muscle work-out.)
- **Do your best Elvis impression.** People assume thrusting can only happen in one plane, back and forth. Pretend you're doing it to Latin music. Tilt your hips in every direction. Swivel from side to side. Rock around the cock.
- **Do swim in the shallow end.** Intercourse is not a race to see who can get to the cervix first. Most of the vagina's nerve endings are in the outer third and that's where the G-spot is, too (see page 100). Imagine that his penis ends just below its head (don't worry, it's only make-believe) and thrust with (or envelop) that bit. It's not like this is any big sacrifice: most of the dick's nerve endings are on the head and the vagina is snuggest at its opening. Everyone's a winner!
- **Do be a team player.** Stimulate her clit with your hand, move her hand there, use a toy, do *something*. Stimulate his balls, perineum and anus with your fingers, use a toy, do *something*.
- **Do keep kissing.** Full stop.

The Doing It To-Don't List

- **Don't have sex in a vacuum.** There's not enough room in there . . . But seriously, folks, fuck as the situation dictates. Maybe you're in the middle of a knock-'em-down, drag-'em-out fight when you start kissing with a vengeance — suddenly lighting some candles and getting out the massage oil would probably kill the mood. Instead, tug on their hair, scratch their back, thrust with fury, call them dirty names, damn it! Or maybe you two just decided to make a baby, in which case slow, face-holding, soul-searching, teary-eyed, missionary sex is probably in order.
- **Don't feel obligated to call it 'making love'.** Especially if it creeps you out as much as it does us. We prefer: fucking, shagging, having sex, having some love, doin' it, bonking, swapping favours, kebabing, fizucking, bobbing, humping, bumping, bumping uglies, schtupping, getting sorted, doing

the hanky-panky, doin' the nasty, getting it on, knocking boots, getting nooky . . .

- **Don't always be a softy.** No, we're not talking about your dick, dudes. (Jeez, you're so *sensitive*.) Most guys underestimate how much women enjoy a little rough play. You don't have to wait for a fight to have back-scratching, hair-pulling sex. And don't freak if your partner asks you to put your hands gently around their neck. It doesn't necessarily mean they're into erotic asphyxiation (see page 18): they probably just like what it does for them psychologically.
- **Don't move.** Try to remain perfectly still, focusing on your partner's breathing and comprehending the magnitude of the union — it's very Zen. (Not ideal for the quickie sessions mentioned above.)
- **Don't think about football (or snooker, darts, or *Coronation Street*).** If you're not present in the moment, you won't realise when your marathoner impersonation is resulting in vadge or dick burn.
- **Don't believe everything you read.** Your partner's preferences, however unexpected, always trump 'official' sex advice — even if you got the advice from this book.

How to Achieve Simultaneous Orgasm During Penetration Every Time

We have no idea.

Assuming the Position

There are 64 different positions outlined in the *Kama Sutra*. We're not even gonna try to compete. You know why? Because intercourse's dirty little secret is that every conceivable configuration is just a creative interpretation of only five basic positions: missionary, woman on top, rear entry, side-by-side and standing. But if naming each of the 100-plus approaches to these five positions makes you feel like Sting, more power to you. In fact, we're going to give clever names to some of our favourite variations — so sue us. (You can also sue us for resorting to the boring male-female model for the most succinct descriptions of the positions below.)

The Three-Pronged Spork (see illustration)

Category: Rear-entry/side-by-side combo

How: Step one: he spoons her and inserts tab A into slot B. Step two: she bends her torso away from him, making a 90-degree angle with her body, while he stays straight on his side. Step three: she swings her top leg back over his hip and places her foot flat on the bed. She places both shoulders flat on the bed so she can turn her head toward him to make meaningful eye contact.

Pros: Regular spoon sex doesn't allow for much movement or depth of penetration — the Spork does!

Cons: What you eventually gain in eye contact, you lose in body contact.

Variations: You want *more*?

When: Early-morning cuddling turns into late-morning sex.

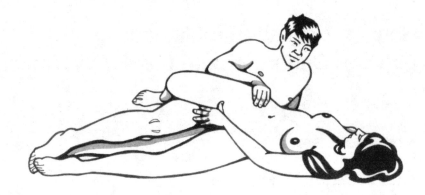

The G-Force

Category: Woman on top

How: He lies on his back; she sits on top of him (on her knees or squatting) and leans back, supporting her weight on her hands. He makes a fist and places it on his lower abdomen so she can grind her clit against it. She can also reach back and play with his twins. He can bend his knees to give her something to lean on.

Pros: Gets at her G; she controls the depth and pace; still feels good if he's only semi-erect; he gets a nice view.

Cons: His chub slips out easily. His chub might not bend that way. His chub might break that way. Also, in this position, a lot of women feel pressured by the responsibility of setting the pace — so make sure she knows she can take her time.

Variations: She rotates 180 degrees (very carefully) so she's facing away from him.

When: She just made partner at the firm.

Excuse Me, Do I Know You?

Category: Rear entry

How: You're both standing; she bends over the back of a sofa, a desk, or the kitchen table (so that her torso is at a 90-degree angle to her legs) and he enters her from behind. He does not forget to reach around with a finger or toy.

Pros: It's easier on your knees than the classic doggie style and just as dirty; it gets at her G; it allows for deep penetration.

Cons: There are none.

Variations: She bends over a big pile of cushions on a bed.

When: It's his birthday.

Is This Seat Taken?

Category: Woman on top

How: He sits on a chair, a couch, or a bed (cross-legged, kneeling, or with legs spread out); she sits (or squats) on top of him, facing him. She can place one foot on the floor for leverage (i.e., off the side of the bed or sofa). She can use two feet if they're on a narrow chair.

Pros: She can lean back for some good G action while staring longingly into his eyes.

Cons: You don't have much range of motion.

Variations: She sits on him, facing away. This is more likely to hit her G, but it's not as friendly.

When: You want to christen your new car.

The Weave

    Category: Side-by-side

    How: You both lie on your sides facing each other with your legs inter-
    twined.

    Pros: He can go for longer; it's handy if you're different heights; it
    makes for shallow penetration (if her cervix needs a break); her
    thighs rub pleasantly against his shaft; you're already in the post-
    sex cuddling position when you're done.

    Cons: It's hard to get any real thrusting in.

    Variations: This is about as complicated as side-by-side sex gets.

    When: You're sharing a very small sleeping bag in a very small tent.

I Can See My House from Here (see illustration)

    Category: Standing

    How: She leans with her back against a wall and he faces her; as-
    suming she's shorter, she props herself up on something low
    with one or two feet — a footstool, a coffee table, a stair, a phone-
    book, an obedient dog. She should tilt her pelvis forward for easier
    access.

    Pros: It makes you feel like you just couldn't
    wait, like that hot sex scene you saw in
    Less Than Zero when you were a kid and
    have been trying to emulate ever since.

    Cons: You both need to be in great shape
    to hold it and you might be concentrat-
    ing so hard on not falling over that you
    never get the standing O you deserve.

    Variations: She wraps her legs around
    his waist and her arms around his
    neck so her weight is evenly distrib-
    uted between him and the wall, aka
    Daddy's Home. Or she sits on a
    counter, a pelvis-high windowsill, or the
    bathroom sink while he stands facing her.

    When: Your partner just returned from a busi-
    ness trip/war/Asda run.

The Princess and the P . . . (see illustration)

   Category: Rear entry

   How: He lies on his back with his legs slightly spread and bent; she lies
       on top of him on her back with her feet flat by the sides of his legs.

   Pros: Good for morning sex when you've both got bad breath.

   Cons: No one gets a view. Very shallow penetration (we're talking 'Is it
       in, honey?' shallow). He feels smothered. Limited range of motion.
       Zero clit stim (you'll both need all hands on deck for balance). Need
       we go on?

   Variations: She lies stiff as a board with her legs straight out; he wraps
       his arms under her armpits and over her shoulders and does mini
       pull-ups. (And if you can get off on that, call the Guinness Book of
       World Records, 'cause you'd be the first.)

   When: You're doing it in the great outdoors, the ground's hard (among
       other things) and he's a gentleman.

The Ass Backward

   Category: Missionary

   How: He's on top but rotates 180 degrees so his head is facing her
       tootsies.

   Pros: She might like the different angle of penetration; she has un-
       impeded access to his tushy; he can suck on her tootsies.

   Cons: He doesn't get much of a view; you're so far away from each
       other; and if he's got the kind of woody that aims straight up against
       his belly, this ain't gonna work.

Variations: One of you turns on your side and then attempts to do a full-body handshake.

When: She wants to do the crossword and he wants to watch his favourite soap.

The Red Cross (see illustration)

Category: Missionary/side-by-side combo

How: She lies on her back with her left leg straight out and her right leg bent at the knee. He lies on his left side facing her, with his body at a 90-degree angle to hers, so that the two sets of genitals meet at the intersection. His left leg is flat on the ground under her left leg; her bent right leg makes an arch over his right leg, which is stretched out straight over her left one.

Pros: He can go long; it's the perfect position for using a vibe on her clit; you're both comfortably reclined.

Cons: No matter how many times you read this description, you're still going to have to get in bed to figure it out. (Or is that a 'pro'?)

Variations: He can really see what's going on if he props himself up on his left elbow and she swings her right leg out so that it slips through the little tunnel under his left armpit until it's comfortable. Make it a genuine Red Cross by doing it when she has her period (see 'Seeing Red' sidebar).

When: You both want to be on the bottom.

Splitting a Bamboo (token *Kama Sutra* position, see illustration)

Category: Missionary into woman on top

How: You're outside under the stars on a blanket. Step one: she leans back on her arms or a collection of pillows. Step two: he sits or squats facing her between her legs. Step three: either she or he uses one arm to manoeuvre her left leg onto his right shoulder. His left hand is on her right leg. Step four: she lets go of her leg (which remains on his shoulder) and leans back on both hands while he pulls her in with both hands on her lower back. This is when he sticks it in, aw yeah. Step five: at some point, she puts her left leg down by his side and moves her right leg up into position. Step six: raise your eyes to the heavens. Check out Orion.

Pros: You will experience everlasting power and transcendence via your connection to the heavens.

Cons: May require a 20-minute warm-up session and a beginners' course in yoga.

Variations: Do it indoors — though you may miss out on the everlasting power and transcendence bit.

When: If you insist on 'makin' sweet love', then this is probably a good way to do it.

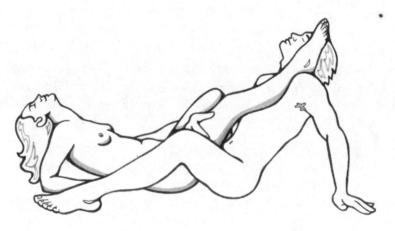

Golden Dildo Award for Best 'New' Position (see illustrations)

The Double Deck-Her (aka Coital Alignment Technique)

Category: Missionary

How: See below. And again. Keep re-reading until you get it.

Pros: Big-time clit stimulation during intercourse. 'Nuff said.

Cons: Assembly instructions required.

Variations: Follow the instructions below, but with her on top.

When: You're in wuv. Or you're dating a sensualist.

Sometime in the early '90s, a sexologist by the name of Edward Eichel claimed he had discovered a brand-new way to do it that guaranteed simultaneous orgasms in the missionary position every time! Obviously he had a rather exaggerated sense of his own accomplishment (otherwise he would have won a Nobel, or at least had a very large building named after him) — but the position has a lot going for it. The basic idea is to provide clitoral stimulation during genital intercourse and you can't knock that. Eichel's 'invention' has actually been around since the *Kama Sutra* — he simply wrote the instruction manual. But it is a toughie to master — the coital alignment technique (CAT) sounds more like calculus than copulation when you try to describe its ins and outs. So for writing the book on it, literally, we'll give him a golden dildo. (But Eddie, if we hear another *peep* from you about CAT being 'divinely inspired' or 'the one true way', we're taking it back, ya hear?)

Here is your mission, should you choose to accept it:

1. He starts in the missionary position and then moves up her body a few inches (i.e., he shifts up towards the head of the bed) so that his pelvis is aligned with hers, directly over it. Just the tip of his dick should be in at this point, so his shaft is pressing up against her mons. Full-on direct penetration is impossible in this position, but that's the point. You're going for constant friction. It won't feel easy or natural until you get a rhythm going (see 4a) but the pay-off is worth it.

2. His legs should be together and straight and hers wrapped around his thighs, so her ankles rest on his calves. She should

stretch her legs so they're as straight as possible — it helps with her pelvic leverage later on.

3. He takes his weight off his elbows and cups her shoulders with his arms under her armpits so that he's resting on her, with his head next to hers on the pillow. (Kind of like a big cuddle, except for the whole penis-in-the-vagina thing.) His upper body should be completely relaxed; both your spines should be as straight as possible. It should feel like the good kind of smothering.

#1–3

4a. What you want is to replace the usual banging and thrusting with a slow, rocking hip action: she starts by tipping her pelvis away from him (i.e., down into the bed) so that his dick comes almost all the way out and she can feel its base pressing against her clit. Then, it's his turn: he pushes down with his pelvis so he moves lower down her body and enters her fully; she tilts up ever so slightly in response to him to let his sausage slide in. And then it's her turn, then his and so on. As he pulls out each time, he should move forward so that his pelvis is eight to ten cm higher up her body, the head of his penis is just inside her vadge wall and the base is against her clit. Remember, that's the whole point: constant pressure on the clit.

#4a

4b. To get the rhythm going, make sure that as one of you is push-ing, the other provides a little resistance — this'll help keep you swinging back and forth in sync. Rather than in/out, think: pressure/counterpressure. (Just like you're sitting facing each other in one of those cute couples swings on a porch, drinking homemade lemonade.) And remember: she should be setting the pace.

5. She can squeeze her pelvic and thigh muscles each time he enters her fully; she'll get more friction and stimulation and he might just forget his own name.

6. Keep going. A lot. Do not — repeat, do not — speed up. This isn't supposed to be acrobatic sex. And remember: ladies first.

In Praise of the Missionary Position

The missionary position gets a bad rap: it's considered boring, un-inspired, old-fashioned, blah. It's embraced by prim housewives, religious types and uptight sexologists as Proper Sex. But positions aren't submissive — people are. If you think missionary sex puts a woman in her place, then you must not think much of women. If you think it's lazy, then you're obviously not working hard enough at it. And if it's not doing it for you, then maybe you just need a little more practice.

The missionary position is kind of like tofu: it's extremely versatile — you just have to add your own flavour. And there's no reason not to: this position gets more skin-to-skin touching, eye contact and kissing per gallon than any other alignment out there. Just remember, ladies, this isn't an excuse to lie back and let him do all the work. Here's how you can super-size your missionary position tonight . . .

- Hold hands to up the lovey-dovey factor.
- She guides his hips with her hands to move him exactly where and how she likes him.
- A pillow or two under her butt can do wonders for deeper penetration, not to mention her comfort.
- She straightens and/or closes her legs for a tighter fit and more labial fric-tion, which might mean more clitoral stimulation (score!).

- The closer her knees get to her ears, the deeper the penetration (but you can start waving good-bye to her clit). She can bend her knees and put her feet on his butt cheeks, or wrap her legs around his waist. If she's really limber, she can throw her legs over his shoulders and make her calves his ear warmers. If she's not limber, no good can come of this.
- He kneels between her legs and lifts her hips up onto him, using his thighs as an on-ramp to his highway of love — it's the closest view of penetration he'll get without using a dildo or watching porn.
- He holds still while she drives: she thrusts back, she squeezes her pelvic muscles, she swivels her hips.

Love Hurts

Pain or burning during or after intercourse could be the result of hitting the cervix, tiny abrasions caused by the friction, not enough lube, an allergy to semen or latex or lube, a lube with nonoxynol-9, an episiotomy scar being irritated, hormone deficiency (e.g., post-menopause or post-natal), a sexually transmitted disease or all of the above. See 'Sex for Winners!' on page 159 for more information. See your doctor for specific concerns.

DOING THE BUTT

A Complete Guide to Anal Fun

Freud really fucked things up. Add ass play to the long list of fun sex acts he turned into big social no-no's. Sure, he said fascination with your own fanny was an important and necessary part of a child's development, but then he diagnosed that same pleasure in adults as immature and dysfunctional. Why should kids have all the fun? Admit it: there's nothing quite like a satisfying poop. After the sneeze, it's probably the closest bodily function to an orgasm.

Freud's not the only party pooper, though; there are myriad reasons why people still have a bug up their ass about anal play, even 100 years later. Homophobia's a biggie: hetero men (and even their girlfriends) worry that using his exit as an entrance will 'turn him gay'. Or at least turn him girly — which stems from a long, uncool tradition of rigidly defined gender roles and sexism. Germaphobes worry that it's too dirty — and not in that good naughty way. Prudes worry that it's too dirty in that good naughty way. Tight asses worry about loose sphincters and incontinence. And some people just don't like the colour brown.

Pshaw, we say. First of all, having anal sex is as likely to turn you gay as renting *Mommie Dearest*. (And believe it or not, many gay men *never* go dirt-roading.) Secondly, for macho rugger-buggers, getting butt-fucked by their girlfriends might be a much-needed mind fuck, a powerful lesson in gender role reversal. There are also simple ways to keep things tidy so you don't end up with a sepia-toned crime scene in your bedroom. As for the prudes, they should

from the 'couldn't have said it better ourselves' file: anal probing

'Nothing can promote long-term awareness and relaxation more effectively than developing the habit of sensitively inserting a finger into your anus for a minute or two every time you shower or bathe. Once your fingertip is inside, use it to feel both of your anal sphincter muscles. Briefly contract these muscles against your finger as you inhale and then release them as your exhale. Complete the routine by briefly massaging inside your anus with a gentle, circular motion.' — Jack Morin, PhD, Anal Pleasure & Health: A Guide for Men and Women

know better than anyone that breaking taboos is half the fun. And with enough relaxation, communication, lubrication and TLC, anal sex can actually strengthen your sphincter muscles. Finally, everyone knows that brown is the new black.

The only excuse you have for not having fun with your ass is not knowing where to start. So let's *rectify* that situation, shall we?

What the Hell Is Going on in There?

If only there had been a *Blue Peter* episode with a talking dildo explaining how a digestive tract becomes an erogenous zone. It probably would have gone something like this:

First let's meet the asshole, the wallflower at your body's school disco. With a higher concentration of nerve endings than any other body part besides the genitals, it's just begging to do the chocolate cha-cha. Beneath its puckered kiss lie two sphincter (ringlike) muscles that form the inch-long, tubelike anal canal. With its elastic folds of tissue, the anus is like those one-size-fits-all miniature gloves: there's no way you think you're getting your hand in there and then you do! When putting on an ass mitten, you'll first encounter the external sphincter, which is controlled by the central nervous system (i.e., you can tell it what to do and it'll listen, most of the time). A couple of centimetres or so deeper lies the internal sphincter, which is under the jurisdiction of the autonomic nervous system (i.e., it pretty much does what it wants, whether you like it or not).

Next comes the windy road of the rectum. It's 10 to 15 cm long and has two curves along its length that give it the shape of a lazy S. The first bend in the road, closest to the exit, is formed by the pubo-rectal sling, which contracts when you have to go, to keep you from shitting your pants. When nothing's on deck and you've learned to relax down there, the sling lengthens, smoothing out the S-curve somewhat, for non-S-shaped dicks and dildos. The second, less pronounced curve comes about seven cm farther down the road. The rectal canal is a no-parking zone (unless you're one of those holders who's always postponing their loo break) — it's designed purely as a passageway. The *colon* is where faeces make their rest stop. It lies just beyond your rectum, about 20–25 cm in from your starfish. When something penis-sized (e.g., a penis) is inserted into the anus, the rectum is usually as far as it gets. (And that's as far as this book goes, too.)

Here's what happens when you take a dump: faeces hang out in your colon until they're good and ready to hit the dirt road. Once the colon sends them on their merry way, your rectal reflex kicks in: the internal sphincter automatically relaxes, while the pubo-rectal sling contracts, sharpening the S-curve. Once *you're* good and ready, you relax your external sphincter (which relaxes the sling) and finally drop the kids off at the pool.

Here's what happens when you get turned on (which may or may not be when you take a dump): the anal tissues get engorged with blood, causing them to blush (hey, it's sexy when your genitals do it). The anal canal may become more moist and a little sweaty and the sphincters twitch and contract — especially if they're being stimulated directly. These contractions feel good and even better when they've got something to hold onto, like a finger or a penis.

Taking Care in There

That's how it's all supposed to work, assuming you don't fuck it up. But you're human and you do fuck things up, so here's how not to. The following tips will whip your butt into shape (literally) so you'll always be ready for some HRA (hot rear action).

> **Eat to poop.** Fibre is one of the best damn things you can do for your sex life. Seriously, if you take no other advice from our book than this, it will all have been worth it. A daily dose will ward off constipation and diarrhoea and keep your works of art big and firm, which means less roadkill on the Cadbury's carriageway and a clean exit (i.e., fewer wipes). Good natural sources of fibre include apple

tools of the trade

The following items should be in the immediate vicinity whenever you're playing the B side:

● **Loo:** *Sometimes shit happens. You might be in the throes of ecstasy when Mr Poopyhead comes a-knockin' (especially if you haven't prepped right). Even if it's a false alarm, it's nice to sit on the pot for a bit, just to be safe.*

● **Dark towels:** *Towels mean clean sheets and easy lube clean-up. Dark towels mean no freak-outs if the lube should turn brown. (Which is uncommon, by the way: it's more about peace of mind than actual necessity.) Or you could just throw the sheets in the laundry pile when you're done.*

● **Condoms:** *Have plenty on hand, in case one breaks or you want to 'freshen up'. Dark-coloured condoms can help downplay the ick factor (though they may camouflage any blood, which is something you should know about). Again, brown and red (especially the latter) are both rare occurrences, assuming you followed all our instructions. Some people use the polyurethane Female Condom (Femidom) in their butts, too, just without the inner ring (see page 210). And because the Female Condom is inserted into the ass (rather than put on the penis), you can more easily switch between orifices.*

● **Latex gloves:** *They offer protection against sexually transmitted diseases (both ways), allow for smoother entry, help prevent anal tissue tears and are the perfect accessory for your doctor/patient fantasy.*

● **Oral sex dams (also called dental dams):** *Important for safe rimming. Glyde Flavoured Dams or Hygienic Dams are made just for this. A cut-up latex glove or a piece of quality cling film (not the cheap and thin generic kind) does the job, too.*

● **Ass wipes:** *Some loo roll companies make moist towelettes with aloe: 'Great for quick and easy cleanup before, during, or after hardcore butt pirating'. Yes, that is on the box.*

● **Wastebasket:** *Preferably lined. You gotta have somewhere to put all those used condoms, gloves, dams and ass wipes.*

● **Enya on the stereo:** *The perfect musical accompaniment, according to nine out of ten anal enthusiasts. (If you're a music fascist, substitute Portishead.)*

skins, potato skins, whole grains, pulses, nuts, prunes, fresh fruits and vegetables. You can also supplement your diet with water-soluble fibres like psyllium husk powder, guar gum and pectin. Man-made poop improvers like Fibrogel work, too. (Note to overachievers: these suggestions are for *oral* ingestion only; don't attempt any DIY suppository action with the above ingredients.)

Eat to play. Food takes about a day to travel through your digestive tract from start to finish, so plan ahead if you know someone's going to be seriously fluffing your duff. Begin eating lightly 24 hours before. Go easy on the dairy, meats and highly processed foods. And if you know something makes you toot, then for heaven's sake, don't eat it.

Don't resist the urge to purge. We know you've got better things to do than shit all day, but if you always hold it, the rectal reflex gets lazy. Which means the internal sphincter has no one telling it when to relax. Which means you have to push and strain and grunt every time you're on the pot. Which means pain, haemorrhoids, small tears and strange looks from the person in the next stall. So when you gotta go, you *gotta* go.

Give a hoot, pollute! While it's certainly bad manners to let one rip in church, on a first date, or at a job interview, chronically keeping your toots to yourself can lead to muscle tension, which makes it hard to relax down there.

losing it

Don't panic if he goes limp while you're knocking on his back door. Totally normal. It's probably just because he's not thinking with his dick for once; instead, he's completely preoccupied with how good his tush feels. Either that, or he's freaking out because he thinks he's gay now.

Anal Anatomy

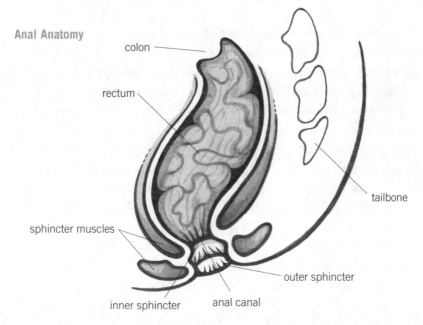

colon

rectum

tailbone

sphincter muscles

outer sphincter

inner sphincter

anal canal

Go caving on your own. It may sound New Agey, but getting to know your anus intimately (yeah, we mean sticking your finger up your own ass) gives you firsthand experience with what's going on in there. It conditions your rear for incoming objects and teaches it how to enjoy itself. With a finger in, see how deep breathing, relaxation and muscle control affect the status quo (i.e., the two sphincters and the pubo-rectal sling). Notice how you feel like you gotta go number two, even though you know you don't. Experiment with what you like and what you don't. Upgrade to a dildo (optional). Remember, nothing's getting permanently *stretched* here: you're simply toning your muscles and teaching them how to relax so they can be infiltrated not only safely, but very, very happily.

Don't stress. When you're anxious or pissed off, your shoulders cramp, your teeth clench and your stomach churns. Why should your doughnut hole get off scot-free? Think of ass play as massage therapy.

House Cleaning

OK, so there's no getting around the fact that messy, smelly dung comes out your abyss every day. But that doesn't mean you can't have a bright and shiny asshole even Mr Muscle would be proud to lick — at least some of the time.

First things first: if you want to poke around down there, make sure there are no roadblocks. The more recently you've taken a dump, the more clean, open and lighter you'll feel. If you have a sloppy dismount, take a rain check on the poking, *obviously*. But if it's a perfect ten, then proceed to the all-important shower. Stick a soapy finger where the sun don't shine. Repeat as necessary. (Just be sure to rinse well with water after, as soap residue can be irritating back there.) Heck, you can stay in the shower and have your sesh under a constant stream of warm water if you're really germaphobic (you'll just have to use a lot more lube — see below). Moistened, unscented baby wipes (now available in handy adult form too!) are good to have on hand for easy touch-ups before, during and after. And let's avoid infection, people: don't forget to thoroughly wash all items that will be doing any digging (hands, penises, tongues, dildos, courgettes, etc.) with antibacterial soap (OK, toothpaste will do for your mouth). And wash those same items *after* the digging, before they go anywhere else (vagina, mouth, another ass). If you're the lucky diggee, be sure to clean house afterwards — lube and ejaculate can carry microscopic faecal bacteria to places where it's unwelcome.

Still got that not-so-fresh feeling? You could always resort to the enema, though it's a controversial practice. Traditional enemas are designed to induce particularly stubborn bowel movements (BMs) — you inject a solution into the anal cavity, hold it for a few minutes, then let the dam break. DIY enemas usually contain chemicals that can irritate the anal lining and upset the delicate bacterial balance (which is why most enema enthusiasts replace the chemical solution with lukewarm water). Some studies have found that enemas (even the water variety) can increase the likelihood of HIV transmission. And if you rely on enemas too much, you'll reach the point where you won't be able to go without their help. So there.

If you insist on hosing your ass down, we recommend a few gentle squirts of warm water with an ear syringe to clean out after a BM. This small amount should be enough to take care of any faecal flakes, while avoiding serious colonic irritation or mid-sex seepage of leftover liquid.

If you've still got that not-so-fresh feeling, consider this: sex is dirty. At least if it's done right, as Woody Allen said. All those showers, anal douches, fibre supplements and good potty habits don't mean *shit* if you have a knee-jerk 'ew' reaction to anal play. Get over it.

Smooth Like Butter

You've got to use lube — no ifs, ands, or butts about it. The anus is not self-lubricating and spit and vaginal juices won't cut it. Besides, you should never go back and forth between the asshole and other orifices for lube pit stops. Try thick, water-based lubricants like ID (in a handy pump dispenser), Spike or

tips for the receiver

- Before you do anything else, you might want to have an orgasm. If you're a bit of a tightass, it'll put all your muscles at ease.
- Anal pubes — and we've all got 'em — can be trimmed if you're worried they're long enough to get in the way.
- Hold the back door open for your guest by 'bearing down', or pushing out a bit (like grunting without making a sound — just try it). It'll give them more room to squeeze in.
- Breathe deeply from the gut, like you do in yoga class. It relaxes your muscles — including the ones around your ass.
- You don't need landing lights: just guide them in with a helping hand.
- At the moment of entry, keep your head in the anal game: don't distract yourself (or your muscles) with any self-diddling until the eagle has landed.
- Once the visitor has settled in, try contracting your anal muscles voluntarily. Syncing up those contractions with the involuntary ones of your orgasm can make it last even longer.

even K-Y — they won't degrade latex, unlike oils. Stay away from lubes with numbing ingredients, since you want all your pain and pleasure sensors fully operational. And don't be stingy — while laying the lube on thick may make your next trip to the bathroom slightly sloppy, it'll make your trip to anal ecstasy speed-bump-free. (See page 263 for more on lube.)

The only exception to the water-based lube rule is if you're travelling up a man's canal and you're not using a latex condom (i.e., you're either using a polyurethane condom or you're riding bareback) — then and only then, do we give you permission to use oil-based lubricants like petroleum jelly or massage oil. (But remember, condoms and gloves should *always* be involved until both partners have been tested together for everything. See the sexually transmitted diseases chapter on page 161.) Here's why: first, oil degrades latex condoms. And secondly, when this much lube is involved, it gets everywhere, including the vagina; because oil can't be washed away easily, it can lead to vaginal infections — hence the male-only stipulation. But even for men, we're not big fans: oil can block your anal glands and cause infection; it often contains perfumes, which can be irritating; and though latex gloves are thicker than condoms, oil can degrade them, too. That said, if you're using non-latex gloves or polyurethane condoms (page 206), or if you're using a sterilised dildo, oil can really help get the tiger in the tank: it's a much hardier lube than the water-

tips for the giver

- *Offer up your bum first: you should be willing to take whatever you want to dish out. Especially you homophobic hetero dudes.*
- *Channel the spirit of Pavlov and condition your partner to associate anal play with intense pleasure: gently rub their black hole (or stick a pinkie in) as they come.*
- *If the receiver has never had anything up their bum, do not — repeat, do not — try anal intercourse with a dick or dildo the first time around. Don't you remember? The tortoise always wins.*
- *Don't be rushing out the door without a proper farewell: a quick and sudden exit can cause the muscles to tense and spasm more than usual. Even if the receiver yells 'Get the fuck out!' always exit in a calm and orderly fashion.*
- *No 'oops'-ing. Rugger-buggers and lad's mags will tell you that the best way into the back door is to act like you were looking for the front and missed. THIS IS LAME. And it hurts like a motherfucker. And it's why so many women are not big fans of anal sex, rugger-buggers and lad's mags.*

based variety; it's a better odour eater; and it makes cosmetic clean-up quicker and easier (i.e., a dry cloth mid- or post-sesh will remove any skid marks in one swipe).

Giving the Finger

Congratulations, you've made it to the fun part! If you and your hot-cross bun luvva have both followed our advice so far, you each now have a shiny new tunnel of love to explore. But don't whip out your dick or dildo just yet. You've got to warm up the ass first: make friends with it, wine and dine it, hold it close. A light pat here, a little perineal rub there, a lot of lube all over.

Then take the tip of a well-trimmed, well-lubed finger and wave hi to the asshole in a gentle, circular motion. It'll wink back. Like a good gynae, narrate as you go along to keep them in the loop. Dilly-dally on or around the hole until you feel it relax, then slowly push in up to your first knuckle (right below your nail) and pause so both parties can appreciate the line that's just been crossed. Once you're past the inner sphincter, aim for the belly button.

At this point in your journey, we'd like to welcome your finger to the lower

the not-so-immaculate conception

It's a common practice among Catholic schoolgirls who follow the letter rather than the spirit of the law to preserve their virginity by engaging only in anal sex. (Or maybe that's just what the dirty old men like to think.) It's certainly a common misconception that you can't get pregnant this way. But of those couples who use anal sex as a method of birth control, about eight per cent end up conceiving. It's called 'splash conception' (the semen slides along the perineum into the vagina) and it happens.

rectum. We hope you enjoy your stay. Come and go as your partner pleases, trying out varying pressures and strokes.

When it comes to the next step, there are two finger camps: the single-finger purists and the poly-digiters. The former worry that two or more fingers might tear an inexperienced sphincter and suggest graduating to a dildo or penis (which have no knobbly joints) after a single finger. The latter argue that additional digits in slow succession are more easily manoeuvred, help condition the sphincter for bigger things to come and are less daunting than dicks and dildos. Let the asshole decide.

For her pleasure: surround her territories by putting one finger in her vagina and another in her tooky. Press along the wall shared by the vagina and the rectum from either side. Just remember not to swap fingers. In fact, reserving one hand for the anus only and the other for the vagina only may help.

For his pleasure: the root of his penis actually extends a few centimetres into his body and can be stimulated from both the perineum and the anal canal. And, about seven or eight cm in lies his holy grail — the illustrious prostate gland, aka the male G-spot. It's Mother Nature's big reward for guys who open themselves up to a little anal action. To hit his magic button, have him lie on his back, stick your index finger palm-up almost all the way in and aim towards the navel, then curve your finger in a 'come here' gesture and rub gently. You might not be able to feel it at first, but as he approaches the big O, it'll get bigger and firmer.

Accessorise, Accessorise, Accessorise

Never underestimate the simple joy of sticking something man-made up your butt. Toys aren't cheating, they aren't just for lesbians and they won't make an A&E urban legend out of you, either (assuming you read the directions). No, toys are your friend. They're excellent partners in foreplay and build-up, or for adding extra stimulation during other kinds of sex — especially the soft and bendy toys made specifically for the caboose. Again, it's not stretching, it's just getting used to the sensation of being filled and learning to relax around an object. Vibrating toys not only stimulate, they also help with the relaxation factor. Take note: silicone-based lubes can damage silicone toys — so check the ingredients of both. And most importantly, any toy taking the back road should have a flared base so it doesn't get lost up there: lubricated pool ball = bad. Nothing that can break up there, either: lightbulb = bad. (If you're reading this section because you've currently got a baby carrot stuck up your ass, just squat and push — it'll eventually find its way out. If you're reading this section because you've currently got a Power Ranger stuck up your ass, get to A&E — you need professional help.) For specific anal accessories, see 'Sex Toys' on page 117.

The Big Guns

OK, now you can whip your dick out. If you're working with a slightly smaller specimen, this is your chance to shine. But whether you're using something small and real or huge and fake (or enormous and living or tiny and inflatable), the following tips all apply. For simplicity's sake, we'll refer to them all as the penis and assume they're all penis-sized (i.e., no 40-cm battering rams that might poke and seriously piss off the colon). We are not, however, referring to an entire hand — if you want to get tricky, see 'Fisting' on page 109.

Lube the penis and relube your partner's anus. Rub your penis against their tootsie tip to announce your presence. It should blow you kisses back (and no, we don't mean farts, we mean contractions). When you see or feel it relax and open, there's your window of opportunity. If you've already got a finger in there, use it as a shoehorn. This is not the time for any no-handed moves; hold the penis to gently — *gently* — guide just the head in. Or sit tight and have the receiving end move towards you to envelop the penis at their own pace.

Pop quiz: Once you've passed the anal canal, in which direction should you go? That's right, kids, aim for the belly button! Soon you'll hit — or should we say delicately *tap* — the first curve of the rectum (Angle A). If your partner's the strong, silent type and doesn't mention this, take matters into your own hands by angling your penis towards their backbone a few centimetres after the inner sphincter before you hit any dead ends (Angle B).

Angle A

Angle B

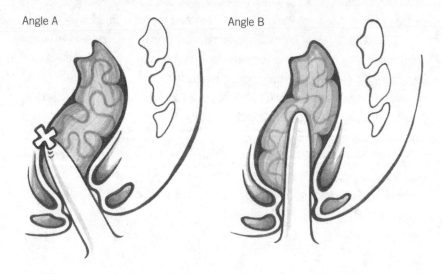

Pole Positions

When it comes to the position of the dirty deed, it's receiver's choice. The stances below each have unique fringe benefits when it comes to control, visuals and depth of penetration, so fuck around and see what works for the two of you. Something to keep in mind: even if the butt-fuckee is on their head, as long as their legs and upper torso form a 90-degree angle, their rectum will straighten out a bit. If your special someone enjoys feeling like a piece of meat, they can slump over the back of a sofa or a table — it'll give them something to hang onto as well. And don't forget to put your idle hands to work, either on your own or your partner's non-anal pleasure points.

Missionary

Penetrator on top, receiver on bottom; allows for medium to deep penetration.

Pros: Eye contact (good for bonding, non-verbal communication and staring contests); comfortable for particularly lazy receivers.

Cons: Receiver can start to feel squished after a while.

Bonus points: Receiver puts a pillow under their butt; pulls their legs to their chest; rests their legs on the giver's shoulders.

Spooning

Both partners on their sides, facing the same direction; allows for shallow penetration.

Pros: Inserter's thrusting capabilities are limited so there are no sudden (i.e., painful) moves; convenient if both partners are particularly lazy; less 'porny' for the prudes.

Cons: No romantic eye contact.

Bonus points: Try the same position facing each other, which technically makes it 'knifing'.

Doggie Style

You know the drill. Allows for deep penetration.

Pros: The spelunker can see where they're headed; the penis is more likely to hit her G-spot (indirectly) or his prostate; best position for smoothing out the S-curve; you're doing it *doggie style*.

Cons: Awkward if you're very different heights; the penetrator may get caught up in the moment (due to the openness of the position) and start thrusting with too much gusto; you're doing it *doggie style*.

Bonus points: You both stand (the receiver bends over as if picking up a bar of soap off the shower floor); the receiver lies on his or her stomach (for less depth of penetration).

The Happy Landing

Receiver on top and the penis owner flat on their back; shallow to deep penetration depending on the receiver's mood.

Pros: Receiver is in total control, *totally*; the one getting sat upon gets to lie back and enjoy the show.

Cons: The sitter may clench their butt muscles to manoeuvre, impairing relaxation.

Bonus points: Try the same position with the sitter facing the sittee's feet.

The Fine Print, Part I: Blood & Pain

If it hurts, stop (duh) — we don't get to sadomasochism for another couple of chapters. And we're not talking about good pain here, like popping a stubborn spot or massaging really sore muscles. We're talking bad pain, like getting your finger caught in a car door, passing a kidney stone, or listening to Celine Dion. If it's sharp and shooting or red and ripping, you're not doing it right. There, we said it: there *is* a wrong way to have sex.

Similarly, there's good drunk and then there's bad drunk. Nerve recognises booze as a legitimate sexual lubricant — who hasn't woken the neighbours with roll-around-on-the-kitchen-floor-with-your-clothes-still-on sex after three dirty martinis? However, you don't want to get so sloppy that you can't distinguish between good pain and bad pain. As for the would-be givers: don't plan on operating your heavy machinery in sensitive anal areas if you've been heavily 'self-medicating'.

There should be no more blood than you'd see after a vigorous teeth cleaning. In fact, if you're doing it right, there probably won't be *any* blood. To be safe, stop at the first sign of red. If the red persists, like for more than a couple of days, go see the doc.

If you feel a little tender down there right after the act, it probably means you didn't use enough lube, you went too fast and furiously, or you didn't read this chapter from beginning to end. Don't worry, you'll recover. Just treat yourself to a warm bath, pamper your ass and kick the anal habit for a few days. If you feel a little or a lot tender down there for some time, long after the act, it may mean an STD. Again, go see the doc.

The Fine Print, Part II: Infections

We'll admit it: poop is a little dirty. Bacteria that make themselves at home in the faeces of perfectly healthy humans can lead to infection or worse if spread, even via microscopic particles, to other areas (mouth, vagina, penis, paper cuts). Which just goes to show: you can't go wrong with barrier protection (dams for rimming, gloves for fisting, condoms for butt pirating). Fingers, toys

from the 'couldn't have said it better ourselves' file: rimming

'To eat or not to eat — ass, that is. My various cocktail party surveys have all indicated the same thing: not many men that I know eat ass. I was a little surprised to learn this, for, from what I hear, most women like it — a lot. The body doesn't have many orifices, after all; you'd think people would want to take advantage of all there are (think of the benefits of having three martinis instead of two). But the curious truth is that while most men are willing to fuck any part of a woman's body — the ass, between the breasts, in the armpit, behind the knee — they still get a little squeamish putting their tongues in the excretory vacuole. It's not that I don't understand — shit gets kind of a bad rap and the uninformed seem to think that rimming has a lot more to do with faeces than it really does (which, by the by, makes me speculate about the hygienic habits of the naysayers). But all trepidation and exaggeration aside, what would one not do to give pleasure? Various Motown hits have enumerated the deserts one might cross, the mountains one might climb for the beloved, so I ask, is licking the anus really so daunting? When in Rome, we are told to do as the Romans. In Southeast Asia, you might well eat fried termites. And in bed with your true love? Don't count it out.'
— Jack Murnighan, Jack's Naughty Bits

and other body parts that come in contact with the anal area should be washed thoroughly with antibacterial soap and water before touching anything else. When it comes to rimming, mouthwash may keep your breath fresh, but there's no research to support the claim that it'll help prevent the spread of bacteria.

Back-door play is also a pretty effective way of spreading STDs like HIV, hepatitis (A, B and possibly C), herpes, gonorrhoea, chlamydia and genital warts. Transmission occurs via infected blood or faecal matter, or skin-to-skin contact — even if there isn't any actual penetration. When there is penetration, microscopic tears will occur in the rectum or anal canal, which is why anal sex is a little like livin' on the edge (it's the highest risk sex act two men can engage in).

Faeces can also carry parasitic infections such as amebiasis and giardiasis and bad bacteria like salmonella, campylobacter and shigella. Rimming is especially conducive to these infections. And, although there have been no medically proven cases of HIV transmission through rimming, a piece of cling film never hurts. Minute amounts of blood in the faeces, as well as abrasions in the anal tissue, put the rimmer at risk. For HIV-positive rimmers, the accidental ingestion of infections like shigella can weaken the immune system. See STDs on page 161 for more info.

The Aftermath

If you feel like you have to go to the loo right after, it's not bad manners to excuse yourself (just make sure you come back). Throw away any condoms immediately. Cuddle.

part 2

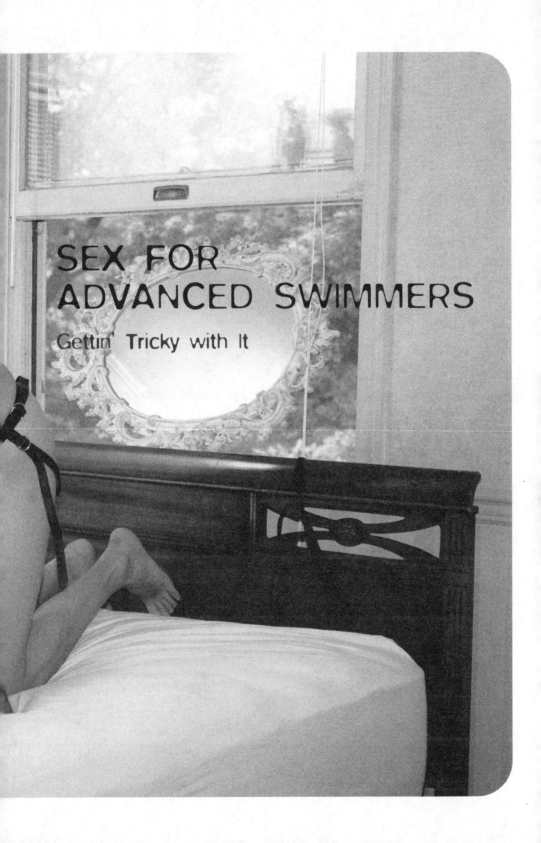

SEX FOR ADVANCED SWIMMERS

Gettin' Tricky with It

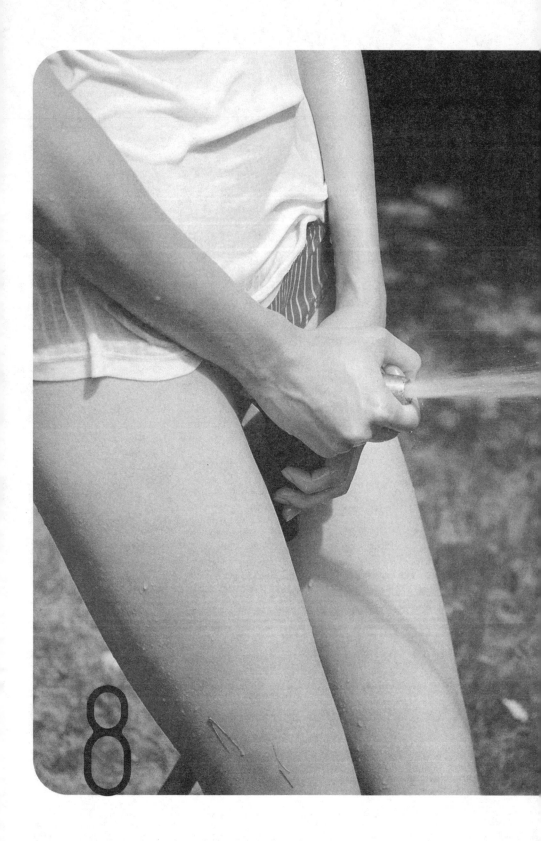

G LUST AND SPECIAL SAUCE

The Mysterious World of the G-Spot and Female Ejaculation

Do all women have a G-spot?

Yes.

Do all women like having their G-spot stimulated?

No.

Can women ejaculate?

Yes.

Is it pee?

No.

Is female ejaculation a result of G-spot stimulation?

Usually.

Can I teach myself (or my partner) to female ejaculate?

Maybe.

Why do cats lick their pussies?

Because they can!

If only it were that simple. Don't get us wrong — these answers are all right on, but each invariably leads to a hundred more questions. (You're so *demanding*.) Before we attempt to answer them all, let's get one thing straight: by 'G-spot', we don't mean a magic button that's guaranteed to transport all women everywhere to orgasmic bliss every time it's pressed; nor do we mean your girl-friend's own personal sweet spot (whether it's in her vagina or her armpit). No, the G-spot is a particularly sensitive area that's stimulated by applying pressure to the roof of the vagina — and provoking it may or may not lead to orgasm and/or female ejaculation. Like almost everything about sex, it depends.

The G-spot has been embraced and shunned by the public more times than David Beckham. And then there are those people who could give a shit about either. The debate (or lack thereof) stems from the dearth of serious medical research on the subject. Oh, yeah and from sexism, too — a lot of people think ejaculating is unladylike. The G-spot and female ejaculation are the misunder-stood goth teens of the sex world.

But not understanding them completely doesn't mean you can't enjoy them. In fact, we kind of like the idea that we still don't know everything about sex. It gives us something to look forward to.

It Ain't Easy Being G

We have the '80s to thank for shoulder pads, Wham! and the term 'G-spot'. Before then, research on the area was pretty flimsy. In the '40s, prominent sex guru Alfred Kinsey found that most ladies who dug having their vadge tickled dug it most on the vadge's top wall. But since Kinsey was all about the clitoral head, he didn't send out any press releases on the matter. The '50s gave us good old German gynae Ernst Gräfenberg, the first modern scientist to identify the erotic potential of the urethral sponge, as felt through the top wall of the vagina (see illustration). But the world was only ready for one orgasmic revolution and Kinsey's clit won out. It wasn't until the early '80s that a pair of sexologists, John Perry and Beverly Whipple, picked up where Gräfenberg left off, replicating his findings and finally giving this hot zone a name in honour of Ernst: the G-spot.

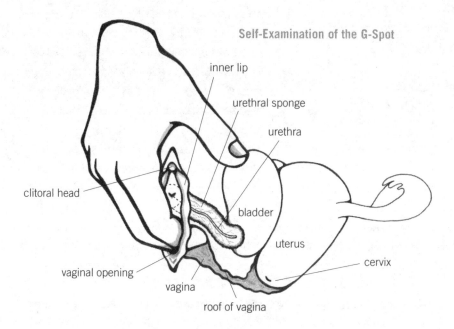

Self-Examination of the G-Spot

inner lip

urethral sponge

urethra

clitoral head

bladder

uterus

cervix

vaginal opening

vagina

roof of vagina

Where Do G-Spots Come From?

If you want to talk about the G-spot, we've got to talk about the urethra. Oooh, fun. The urethra is the slender tube that carries urine (wee wee) from your bladder to your urethral meatus or opening (peepee hole), which, if you're a chick, is usually between your clit and vaginal opening. The urethra runs just above the roof of your vaginal canal, kind of like a ceiling pipe and is surrounded by erectile tissue called the urethral sponge, sort of like insulation. This sponge houses a number of 'paraurethral' (meaning *near* the urethra) and 'periurethral' (meaning *around* the urethra) glands and ducts that secrete and expel fluid (or female ejaculate) respectively. While the G-spot has never been anatomically mapped by medical professionals, it's popularly known as the part of the urethral sponge that may be felt through the ceiling of the vagina, approximately one-third to one-half of the way in — it's usually an oval area or ridge (sometimes called the G-crest) about the size of an elongated five- or ten-pence piece. (However, some consider the G-spot to actually be the *entire* urethral sponge.) When you're aroused, the urethral sponge fills with blood and its glands fill with fluid, causing the area to swell and firm up — which is why many women (or their partners) are only able to locate the G-spot once they're, you know, good and ready.

The urethral sponge (G-spot if you're nasty) is also sometimes — controversially — called the female prostate. Check it out: foetuses, whatever sex they're destined to become, all start out female. It's not until the seventh or eighth week of gestation that the Y chromosome kicks in for the boys. The same embryonic tissue that eventually develops into the prostate gland in boys is what eventually becomes the para- and periurethral glands in girls. New research suggests that the female urethral sponge with these glands and ducts is not just leftover tissue, but is actually its own working organ with similar functionality (see female ejaculation below).

Getting Jiggy with Your G

Warning: following the following tips *will* help you locate your G-spot, but it won't guarantee that you and the G will become BFFs (best friends forever!). For some women, the sensation is too intense, for others it's just plain annoying. Some ladies only enjoy it at certain times of the month, while others get bad flashbacks to urinary tract infections past. None of this means your plumbing's defective, nor does it mean you've got 'issues'.

Stimulating the G involves pressing on the urethra, so it's only natural that you'll feel like you have to take a piss. Thus, just like it's a good idea to stick your own finger up your tush as an introduction to anal play, so is it helpful to do a little self-service at the G-spot station before letting a partner at it. Because just like a finger up your tush gets you over the illusion that you have to poo, so too a finger on the G will get you over the illusion that you have to pee (assuming you've already gone to the loo before doing either).

It takes a bit of coordination to get to your own G, especially if you have short arms. The best positions include: on your back with your knees pulled up and a fluffy pillow under your butt; on your stomach; in a squat; or on your hands and knees. Once you've assumed a good position, insert one or two digits about five cm into your veegee, with the pads of your fingers pressing up against the vagina's front wall. It should feel kind of ridgy and rough, unlike the rest of the vaginal walls, which are smooth. If you're having trouble spotting it, you might want to down a couple of glasses of water, get in the shower or on the pot, stick your fingers inside, aim in the general direction of the G and then actually urinate — if you can feel the pee travelling through the urethra, you've hit the spot.

Still can't find it with your own digits? Use the force, Luke: search for it by registering how the pressure feels inside you and not what your fingertips are feeling. Nothing wrong with enlisting the help of friends, either. Like the Crystal Wand, a 25 cm, clear, treated glass, S-shaped and oddly photogenic dildo of sorts, specially designed to make a beeline for your G-spot (if you don't like it, you can always use it as provocative coffee table art). Or the G-spotter, a handy attachment to the classic 'back massager', the Hitachi Magic Wand. (Page 126 has more suggestions for your toy box.) Your other friends, the ones with actual fingers, can also help with G loving, probably more easily than you can.

Once you get to the G, however you get there, you're gonna need direct, consistent, fairly hearty pressure. Because you're feeling it *through* the vaginal wall, there's no need to tiptoe around the G-spot like you might the clit. Try pushing on it, massaging it, or pulling on it (aka the old 'come hither' move) — and keep on keepin' on. As with all vaginal work, accessorise with lube and latex and trim your nails.

Sorry, guys, but fingers and toys are more likely to hit the spot than a penis. (Ever see a penis say 'come hither'? Didn't think so.) However, some intercourse positions are more G-friendly than others, like woman on top, or rear entry with the woman on her stomach or side. Sorry again, guys, but cervix pounding won't work — you'll miss the G completely. What you're going for is shallow penetration angled towards her navel, using your hand to guide the way. See? We told you size doesn't always matter. But then again, it does matter for those women who don't even notice their G-spot until they're really filled up. Like filled-up-with-a-fist filled up. (Turn to page 109 to find out how the hell to get your hand in there.)

Going with the Flow: Female Ejaculation

While many cynics dismiss female ejaculation as just another New Agey fad that involves mistaking piss for goddess juice, it's actually been documented for centuries. For the ancient Greeks — Aristotle included — female ejaculation was par for the course. Hell, some of them even believed it was necessary for conception. Squirting also pops up in ancient Japanese erotic art, old Chinese sex advice books, the *Kama Sutra* and the writings of second-century physician Galen. It wasn't until around the 18th century, when art and science started focusing on the ways male and female bodies *differed*, that female ejaculation got a bad rap. During the 20th century, even Masters and Johnson, those champions of positive sex thinking, suggested that ejaculation was simply urinary stress incontinence and surgeons actually operated on prolific ejaculators to 'correct the problem'. Still today, people remain confused, embarrassed and/or freaked out by the phenomenon. That's why we're here.

can i drink it?

Natural vaginal lubrication is a transmission fluid, that is, it can contain traces of HIV if the woman is infected. Urine, on the other hand, doesn't. The jury's still out on ejaculate, so best to be safe and consider it to be a transmission fluid.

Female ejaculation is so damn hard to study because it varies from woman to woman. Some women spurt straight across the room, others just leave a big wet spot on the sheet — we're talking anything from a few drops to a series of gushes. (And then there are those super-ejaculators in porn videos who produce it by the pint, but since when can you believe anything you see in porn?)

from the 'couldn't have said it better ourselves' file: injaculation

'Taoists, shamans, Tantric kooks and Sting swear that male orgasm without the expulsion of seminal fluid, vis-à-vis strategic pressure on the perineum — otherwise known as injaculation — can lead to enlightened consciousness, not to mention explosive orgasms. So I decided to give it a shot and started flogging the bishop in my own time-honoured (if not particularly mystical) tradition. A couple of minutes in and fast approaching the point of no return, I located what Taoists refer to as the "million-dollar point", aka the perineum. I pressed hard there and felt a strong, constant pulse. Just before orgasm, the pulse became arrhythmic and graduated to a panicked pounding. Then, immediately prior to the moment where I'd typically soil the bed linen, I saw for a brief second what all those ponytailed 40-somethings had been proselytising about. The build-up to orgasm was momentarily more intense than usual, but the feeling soon vanished as quickly as it had arrived. I continued to press hard for a minute or two, concentrating on the subsidence of pressure in my rig. I withdrew my fingers from my undercarriage and propped myself up on my shoulders, disturbed and underwhelmed by the whole ordeal. Then, as noted by the injaculation's proponents, I realised I could "go again" straight away and did, several times, until I got bored and a little bit depressed. The real shocker came after I went to the bathroom to find that my pee had more head on it than a pint of Guinness. In other words, I'd just come in my bladder. And that's fucked up.'
— Grant Stoddard, Nerve's 'I Did It for Science' Guinea Pig

Some women ejaculate right before a G-spot orgasm, some do it independently of orgasm, others do it in sync with their G climax and still others can do it from external clitoral stimulation alone (though some degree of G-spot stim is usually the 'open sesame' for the floodgates). Some women don't ejaculate at all ... or do they? One theory speculates that *all* women produce ejaculate, but for various reasons don't know it: maybe they confuse it with vaginal lubrication and/or urine; maybe they resist the urge to let go and unknowingly flush it out later when they pee; or maybe they produce so little that it trickles out inconsequentially.

What the Hell Is It?

One thing everyone agrees on (at least everyone who believes it exists) is that female ejaculate is expelled through the urethra during orgasm or arousal as a result of pelvic muscle contractions (i.e., orgasm) and/or the glands overfilling. It's definitely not pee though, at least not as we know it. There may be *traces* of pee in the fluid (it's coming out of the pee hole, after all). Or you may pee slightly when you come, if you haven't emptied your bladder recently. But the fluid we're talking about here — thin, watery, transparent or milky, slightly sweet-tasting and not very pungent — ain't no piss.

Some researchers say it's prostatic-like fluids from the paraurethral glands, others say it's just a chemically altered form of urine from the bladder. Some say it's a combo of both. Hell, it could be orange juice for all anybody knows. The next time you have the privilege of being in the presence of female ejaculate, sniff it yourself and decide.

The most convincing argument we've heard yet comes from a study cited in Rebecca Chalker's must-read for anyone with a clitoris in their life: *The Clitoral Truth*. A student of human sexuality who also happened to be a seasoned ejaculator took a bladder relaxant drug (that turns urine bright blue) before several masturbatory sessions. When she ejaculated, the expelled fluid was either clear or only slightly tinged with blue; when she subsequently peed, the expelled urine was bright blue every time . . . Eureka!

Let Your Love Flow: Tips for Would-Be Geysers

While we recommend you don't go chasing waterfalls (the last thing women need is another ridiculous sexpectation put upon them), the following tips may nurture your inner ejaculator:

- **Go it alone first.** There's less pressure and you can take as long as you want without boring anyone.
- **Let it go.** You're going to feel like you've got to pee, but don't worry about pissing the bed — if you've gone to the loo beforehand, there shouldn't be a problem. But even if there is some piss, is it really a problem? Golden showers are sexy.
- **Bear down.** Take 'letting go' a step further by actually pushing out when you feel the urge to pee, like you're in a pee-off and you're about to take the lead.
- **Do a 'dry' run with urine.** Stimulate the G when you know you've got to P. When the urge is overwhelming, just let it flow. Practising with urine first will teach you how to let go and get messy. When you're ready for your ejaculate to go solo, do the exact same thing — just empty your bladder first.
- **Don't block the exit.** A large toy, a penis, or a hand might cut off the urethral

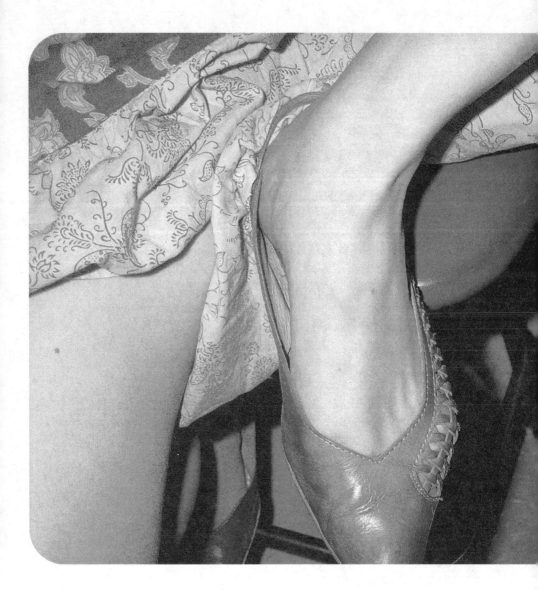

opening. Keep up the stimulation, just get them out of the way as best you can.

- **Get hot and bothered.** Being super sexed-up, overcome with lust and engulfed in the flames of desire means a number of things: (1) your G-spot is easier to find and can take more pressure, which means more experimental poking; (2) your pelvic muscles are more relaxed, which makes it easier to let go; (3) you're more likely to have an orgasm, causing pelvic contractions, which help expel the fluid; (4) you're super sexed-up, over-come with lust and engulfed in the flames of desire!

- **Have an orgasm first.** Ejaculating might be easier after your groin has already been warmed up and relaxed by an explosive O.
- **Make clean-up a cinch.** Put down towels or a waterproof pad (you'll find them in the incontinence aisle at the chemist's) or a fitted vinyl or PVC sheet (available at most sex shops) so you're not stressed about wetting the bed. Or do it in the bathtub; if you actually run a bath, the warm water will also help you relax.
- **Drink water.** When you're thirsty, your body gets retentive with all its fluids, including female ejaculate.

9

GOING DEEP

Fisting for Pacifists

Ah, the simple pleasures: long walks on the beach at sunset, the Sunday papers in bed, someone's entire hand up your inner rectum all the way to your sigmoid colon . . .

Fisting (aka handballing or fist-fucking) may not be the first thing you think of when you think of makin' sweet love, but it can be an extremely fulfilling — not to mention filling — experience. The trust, communication and time required for both vaginal and anal fisting usually translate to intimacy with a capital 'I'. And for female fisters, it's the only time they can really be *inside* their partners.

Most people fall into one of two fisting camps: those who haven't tried it and think 'eeeew' and those who *have* tried it and think 'cooool'. The best way to bridge the gap between the two is to dispel some of the myths surrounding the act — like the rumours about cathedral-sized vaginas, the inevitability of in-continence and punching your way in with a rock-'n'-roll fist (more on those below). Good information is important for safe fisting. Size does matter here and not all partners will be able to do it. (The six-foot-four, 16-stone rugby player and his five-foot-one, seven-stone ballerina girlfriend probably don't have vaginal fisting in their future.) But with practice and patience, many couples can make love-mining a rewarding part of their sexual relationship. Fisting — it's not just for freaks anymore!

Safety Tips

- There's good pain and bad pain. Fisting might feel funky and slightly uncomfortable at first, but it shouldn't make you say 'ouch' out loud. At the first sign of bad pain, stop.
- Stay off the sauce: drugs and booze numb your pain reflexes, impair your judgement and make you stupid. Both parties need to be in control of all their mental and physical faculties when going deep.
- Keep the lights on. You need to see what you're doing. (But not the fluorescent overheads: you don't need to see *that* much.)
- For those in the remedial class: remove all rings and bracelets.
- Trim your cuticles and file your nails down. Way down. If you can scratch an itch, they're too long.
- Call us crazy, but we suggest stopping at any sign of blood, even if it doesn't hurt (though veterans say that a small amount of bleeding during and immediately after anal fisting is expected). If pain and bleeding persist for more than a day, see a doc.
- Some experts believe you should wait several days before having intercourse after vaginal fisting, or anal sex after anal fisting, in order to allow the healing of any internal abrasions that may have occurred.
- For the fistee, this is an emotionally and physically vulnerable experience; for the fister, it's a power rush. It can be incredibly intense for everyone, so if you're not in a trusting relationship where you're comfortable with this kind of exchange of power, you might want to reconsider bending over. (The power dynamic also explains the prevalence of fisting in BDSM circles, see page 135.)

Tools

- **Rubber gloves:** They help prevent infection and the spread of disease caused by abrasions, either on hands or internal cavity linings. Gloves also facilitate a smoother entry and exit. Latex works best, assuming no one's got a latex allergy; if that's a concern, opt for something synthetic. For vaginal fisting, use non-powdered gloves, since talc can be irritating and has been linked to cervical cancer. Elbow-length rubber gloves are a nice touch for more formal fisting occasions, though they may scare the shit out of your partner, literally.

- **A sling (optional):** Many regular anal fisting receivers favour some kind of contraption — be it a harness or a hammock, ceiling slings or stirrups — to help them maintain an easy-access position (*you* try staying still doggie-style for an hour with a fist up your bum). If you don't have a bondage budget, a stack of pillows for support should do.
- **Lube:** Lots of it. Preferably in a pump dispenser for easy, one-handed reapplication. And keep water nearby for 'loosening' dry lube. Use a fragrance-free, *water*-based product, as oil will degrade latex gloves and petroleum-based products can damage the mucosal lining. A thicker lube like Spike has more staying power than familiar brands like K-Y and Astroglide. However, some people find that even the thicker water-based lubes don't cut the mustard when it comes to anal play. In the US, a white gloopy lard-like substance (trade name Crisco), is a favourite among the leather set. In the UK, the cook's alternative is butter or lard. Still others go for J-Lube, a veterinarian's lube. While Crisco and the like *will* degrade latex, its proponents say that gloves are a lot stronger than condoms and can take the abuse. We say: when in doubt, stick with purpose-made lubes.
- **Time:** Lots of it.
- **Communication:** Lots of it.

the myth of the loose woman

Sex Myth No. 327: Women who practise fisting are loose, both morally and physically. On the contrary, when a woman learns how to relax her muscles and her partner approaches her with the right form and enough lube, fisting can actually help tone her vaginal muscles. (See page 259 for more on kegel exercises and vaginal elasticity.)

Vaginal Fisting

The vagina is like the revamped VW Beetle: there's a lot more room in there than you'd think. When a woman is aroused, the inner two-thirds of her vagina expand. Thus, foreplay is absolutely essential (not to mention good manners). Often fisting will evolve from intense handwork (page 39) — the giver wants to feel more of what's going on in there and the receiver just wants *more*. But it's not something that should be attempted with guesswork. Like all good scouts heading deep into the woods, be prepared.

For the Fistee

- Get a copy of *A Hand in the Bush: The Fine Art of Vaginal Fisting* by Deborah Addington and read it with your partner.
- Lie on your back with your knees bent, or prop yourself up on your elbows and knees. The former position is easier to hold for longer; the latter may require a sling or something to lean on. Either way, just make sure you're comfortable because there's no getting up for a quick glass of water mid-fisting.
- Breathe. Deeply. Exhale with each significant move your partner makes, either on the way in or out — it helps relax your muscles.
- You can exert your vaginal muscles — what the midwives call bearing down — to help the hand make a graceful exit.
- Don't expect to climax. The feeling may be too unfamiliar or intense to take you up and over that hill.

For the Fister

- If your partner is lying on her back, your palm should face up, as if you're 'feeding the pony'. If she's on all fours, your palm should face down, like you're going to pet the pony on its head. If she's on her side . . . well, you get the picture.
- Start with one finger straight in — *never ever an actual fist* — and slowly work up to two, then three and four. When she's comfortable with all four fingers, fold your thumb into your hand while keeping your fingers straight, to form a duckbill shape (making it as narrow as possible, like you're trying to remove a tight bracelet). Rotating your hand slightly back and forth may help you ease your way in.
- As you enter the vagina, your hand will most likely form a fist naturally (make sure your thumb is tucked inside the fist). If you don't feel it happening automatically, consciously make a fist just before you're all the way in.
- Once inside, hold still for a long, dramatic pause, to appreciate the holy-shit-the-fist-is-in! moment. She may also need a minute to get used to the sensation.
- Remember that with an entire hand inside her, *nothing* feels subtle. So concentrate on small, fluid movements: clenching and unclenching, twist-

ing, 'knocking' and/or mini-thrusting. Some women like pressure on the cervix sometimes (depending on their cycle). But be gentle — it's more sensitive than a Shirley MacLaine movie back there. Note: your fist should stay inside the entire time.

- Keep adding lube along the way. As they like to say in the sex advice biz, too much is almost enough.
- Continually check in with her, like she's your customer and you're working on commission.
- You should exit as slowly and gently as you entered, making your fist back into a duckbill on your way out. Never ever *ever* pull out suddenly, even if she's really late for work. If your partner spasmed or orgasmed, her vagina may have vacuum-packed your hand inside; insert a finger from your free hand to break the seal.
- Hold her. This can be an extremely intense and emotional experience — we've heard tales of post-fisting tears, shakes and spiritual enlightenment.

Anal Fisting

For prep and safety tips, read the entire anal sex chapter (page 79). No groans from the peanut gallery — this isn't homework; think of it as a choose-your-own-assventure. Seriously, you need to know this stuff. Please don't make us go through it all again here.

Once you've caught up on your reading, you can approach anal fisting like you would vaginal fisting (see the above tips for the fister and fistee), except turn each tip up to 11. Because the anal canal and rectum are non-lubricating and less elastic, more easily torn and less accustomed to incoming traffic than the vagina, you'll need *more* lube, *more* communication, *more* time and *more* patience.

But we don't want to characterise the anus as just a second-rate, high-maintenance vagina, so here are some important tips designed exclusively for that very special moment between a hand and its ass mitten:

- When you've coaxed your bum to accommodate an eight-cm-wide toy, you're probably ready for a fist — or at least as ready as you'll ever be.

- Play the 'Mother, may I take another step' game whenever you want to go deeper inside your partner. If you get a positive response, make your move as they exhale.
- Doggie-style is a winner position, as long as the receiver's got something to support themselves.
- If you've followed our instructions and done all your reading, you should know this already, but it bears repeating: *do not go in with a clenched fist.* Instead, squeeze your straightened fingers together and tuck your thumb against your palm to make a duckbill shape for entry. Let it curl into a fist only once you've made it to the dark side.
- Going in as far as your wrist is as far as our conscience (and our lawyers) will let us go. If colon play sounds like your cup of tea, check out Bert Herman's *Trust, the Hand Book: A Guide to the Sensual and Spiritual Art of Hand-balling* — he's cornered the market on anal fisting advice; and we can't compete.
- Don't expect to get your whole hand in the first time. Don't expect to get your whole hand in the fifteenth time. Great fisters and great fistees alike are made, not born.

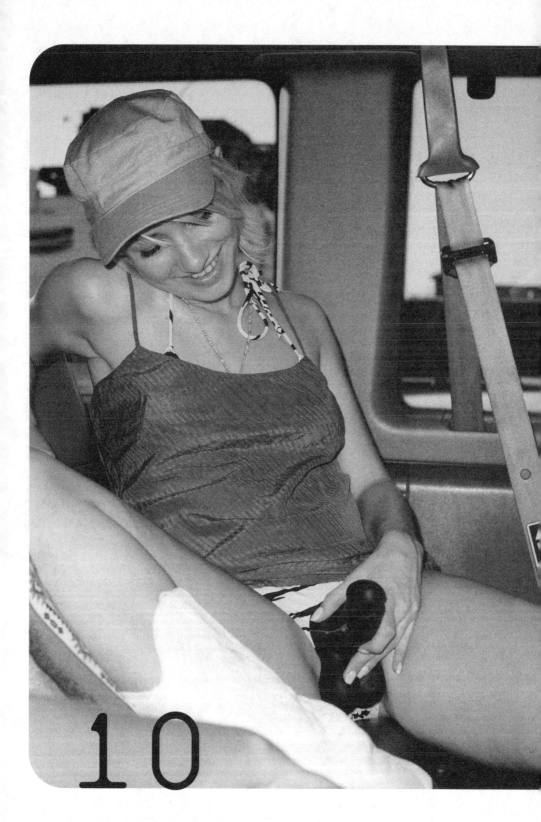

10

SEX TOYS WON'T BREAK YOUR HEART

Plugging in Your Sex Life

The idea of sticking objects up against and inside one's body for sexual pleasure has been around since the dawn of fruit. Images of dildos pop up in Upper Paleolithic art, on ancient Greek vases and in Chinese paintings from the 1800s. For centuries, the use of dildos was prescribed and administered by doctors to women who were thought to suffer from 'hysteria', a mental illness caused by the inability (or unwillingness) to derive pleasure from 'normal' boy/girl in-out sex. Apparently, jerking these ladies off was tough work for the good doctors, who eventually got lazy and invented a mechanical vibrator in the 1880s to pick up the slack. Nobody seemed to think any of this was weird until the 1920s, when the porn industry co-opted these 'medical devices' for their own naughty purposes. It was another 30 years before the American Psychiatric Association woke up and smelled the misogyny, deleting hysteria from their official list of psychoses. A few years later, the Brits followed suit.

Which is not to say that everything's happy-go-lucky in sex toy land these days. In Japan, for example, it's illegal to manufacture objects that resemble an anatomically correct dick — hence the prevalence of really well-made toys adorned with creepy faces and bunnies. And in Texas, dildos can only be sold and bought for 'educational purposes'. Some shops even have you sign a release confirming your honourable intentions.

But you probably don't live in Texas, lucky duck. Which means it's getting easier to score some primo proppage. The Internet, bless its big heart, provides not only the sex ed you wish you'd had in secondary school, but also discreet, shame-free shopping. More education means higher demand, which means better quality products and well-lit, non-sleazy shops to buy them in. In fact, more and more couples make a night out of shopping for sex toys together (which is usually less scary than surprising your partner with a 14-inch [35 cm] dildo in the middle of a nice romantic sesh). Sure, you'll still find people who think of sex toys as a crutch, as unfair competition, or as tools of the devil (especially in Texas). But the smart people realise they're called toys for a reason.

The following is a guide to the kind of gear you can use to climb Mount O.

Dildos

They're usually bigger than a butt plug, smaller than a breadbox and act like a dick. Some are flesh-coloured and about the size of your last boyfriend, others are zebra-striped and have impossible porn proportions. Still others are S-shaped and have only G-spot stimulation (both his and hers, see pages 126 and 130) on the mind. Handheld dildos let you experiment during masturbation with what kind of penetration works best for you (in terms of angle, technique, etc.). They can be used with a partner as an add-on during oral sex and handwork. If your partner happens to be a dude, dildos let him check out what it looks like when his own dick's in — and out and in — there. And dongs make helpful surrogates should he need a break (e.g., if he came already, he doesn't want to come yet, he's recharging for round two). Dildos don't vibrate, but then again, neither do penises.

Harnesses

A harness lets you wear your dildo like a penis. It's what they call a strap-on in the biz. They're usually worn by women who want to be the penetrator (or just want their shiny new cock sucked). As long as your dong has a flared base, it'll fit in most harnesses. The leather, nylon or even rubber straps are pulled snug so the (usually silicone) schlong doesn't wobble and so its base presses pleasantly against her clit. Many harnesses are outfitted with small, strategically placed pockets that hold baby vibrators for extra clit stimulation — either the giver's or the receiver's or both (if both are chicks). Some harnesses or harness attachments allow the giver to get some too by holding a second dildo that goes inside the wearer's puss or ass. Men can get in on the harness action if they want to do their partner with a smaller or larger specimen than their own. Especially good for guys is the two-strap harness that looks like a jock strap and doesn't smash his balls in the process. One-strap harnesses fit like a G-string and are more popular with the ladies. There are even thigh strap-ons: buy two and hump each other's legs simultaneously, you dirty dogs.

Vibrators

Think: dildos that do the cha-cha really really fast. Like noses and 401(k)s, vibrators come in all shapes and sizes, from a buzzing tennis-sized ball on a stick to a cute little dolphin. Those balls and bunnies have given many women their very first orgasm and are often the only way they can come. No shame in that. In fact, if you haven't ever experienced a vibe, make like Mikey and try it. Will I like it? you ask. Does the Pope shit in the woods? Here are some other questions to ask yourself when investing in a vibe:

Do I want clitoral or vaginal stimulation? Or both?

Some vibes are meant purely for external clitoral stimulation (especially those packaged as 'back massagers'), some can be used internally as well and others have extensions that allow for simultaneous penetration and clit stimulation. Those last ones are particularly great for lezzies: one lucky partner gets the vibe inside as well as the clitoral stim, while the other can get on top of her in a face-to-face lovey-dovey embrace for some simultaneous clit stim of her own.

Am I going to use it in my bed or at the office?

If you plan on keeping yours by the bed, a plug-in is probably your best bet: the vibrations are stronger, the toy is sturdier and the buzz won't run out when you need it most. (If the cord cramps your style, get a cordless electric vibe with rechargeable battery.) When you're on the go, you'll need a smaller, battery-powered vibe. Japanese- and German-made models tend to have longer life spans than their American or British counterparts. Just stay

material world

Ancient dildos were fashioned out of whatever nature had to offer: wood, ivory, onyx, gold, you name it. Today, toys are usually made from a wide variety of man-made materials. Some basic commonsense rules for using any of them include the following: clean your toy after each use, according to the instructions. Don't share your toy casually (your nursery teacher will understand). Use lube that's compatible with the material of your toy (silicone lube destroys silicone toys). And store it in a clean, cool, dry place. This means a specially designated box, secret compartment, or sandwich bag (sans sandwich). And the most important thing to remember is this: if a toy is porous (i.e., absorptive) — and they usually are — you should slap on a fresh condom each time you use it, especially if you're inserting it anywhere . . .

- *Silicone: slippery, water-repellent, body-heat conductive, non-porous, unlikely to cause allergies, more expensive but worth it.*
- *Cyberskin: almost creepy in its fleshlike texture and very porous, requiring a high-maintenance cleaning ritual immediately after each use.*
- *Man-made/synthetic rubber: fairly soft and warm, cheap and easy to find, but it's porous, has a short life expectancy, can cause allergic reactions and smells like, well, rubber.*
- *Natural rubber latex: used mostly to make condoms and gloves and the very occasional sex toy, incompatible with oils and can cause allergic reactions.*
- *Hard plastic: cheap, easy to find and easy to clean since it's non-porous, but can have rough seams and isn't very long-lasting.*
- *Vinyl or soft plastic: lightweight and affordable, but porous.*
- *Hard acrylic or Lucite: solid as a rock, non-porous and commonly used for pelvic-muscle strengthening tools.*
- *Treated glass (Pyrex): no kidding.*
- *Soft acrylic: surprise, surprise, it's soft and therefore porous (like on the head of the Hitachi Magic Wand, see chart).*
- *Leather: rare, expensive and hard to clean.*

away from Duracells — their commendable turbo charge can burn out little love motors.

Do I take loooong showers?

Some battery vibes are also waterproof — you can actually submerge them in a tub of warm water, soapy bubbles and rose petals.

How fast and furious do I want it to wiggle?

Some vibes have two settings — On and Off — while others come with a speed control so it feels like you can turn it up to 11. If even the lowest setting is too much, try the vibe through your jeans or over a pillow. Some shake, some rotate, some twist, some buzz, some even lick. But none of them will lie to you.

Am I willing to invest in my pleasure?

Vibe action will set you back anywhere from a fiver to round about 50 quid — but it's worth every penny. If you don't flinch buying a 60 quid pair of painful heels, why would you hesitate to spend that on the key to unlocking your erotic potential? (That's a rhetorical question.)

Do I have thin walls and a nosy neighbour? Do I care?

Some buzz softly like the flapping wings of a hummingbird, while others sound like the strangled whine of a dying cow. If you're using a vibrator with a partner and you (or they) are the kind who's mortified by the slightest little toot during sex, stick with those specially designed for discretion. But if it's just you and the vibe, we say rev it like a Harley engine and ride.

Do I like to watch GMTV makeover segments?

If so, you'll love this: you can give new life to almost any vibrator with an attachment. These accessories can make you feel like you've got a brand-new toy, at half the price. Make your vibe longer and stronger! Turn your passive external vibe into an aggressive penetrator!! Get clit stim where you didn't before!!! Reach your G every time!!!!

Ben Wa Balls

The modern version of BWBs are two unconnected balls you stick up your coochie before going on a walk or skipping rope. Way overrated. If you must insert balls, go with duotone balls — spheres with ball bearings inside them, all connected by a (usually nylon) cord — and then go for a walk. Better yet, get the vibrating kind and stay in bed.

Butt Plugs (Still or Vibrating)

They're basically squat, kooky-shaped dildos with flared bases (so nothing gets lost up there). BPs are designed to go in and stay in, to give your ass something to wrap its arms around. Think small, soft and jellylike — at least to begin with. Once inserted, leave the butt plug be while you carry on making out, having intercourse, washing the dishes. (Or move it around a little if you like.) It won't pop out like a turkey timer, so once you feel ready, slide it out gently to make way for something meatier. Or just roll over and go to sleep if you're done.

Anal Beads

These look a lot like a toddler's toy necklace made in arts & crafts class — small balls (though they do come supersized) intermittently attached along a thin nylon cord. The silicone variety are smoother and can be boiled for easy sterilisation, but they're so expensive to manufacture that they're only custom-made these days. If you've got the plastic kind (cheapskate), smooth any rough seams with a nail file. For some, the best sensation is popping them in one by one; for (most) others, it's pulling them out right before — or during — orgasm. Just don't yank 'em out like you're tearing off a plaster, because anal tissue is delicate and cries easily.

Cock Rings

A cock ring (made of leather, rubber, or metal) traps the blood in your penis and can help you maintain a stronger erection for longer — after all, most people would choose stamina over size any day. It'll also increase your sensitivity down there, which is why some guys find cock rings actually make them come faster. Ironic, dontcha think? Rings can make a penis look and feel bigger (and engorged and veiny and swollen and slightly purple — which usually sounds better to the party not wearing it). Vibrating ones that provide clitoral stimulation (or even better, vibrating remote control cock rings) may help her fall in love with your penis a little more. But if that's too high-tech for you, try a simple rubber ring with a strategically placed nubbin for her. If you're selfish, rotate it 180 degrees for extra ball attention. These textured types of rings can be used on dildos or wrists (during fisting) for extra sensation for the receiver.

Rubber dick rings are really cheap and flexible, but porous (i.e., can't be sterilised) and therefore shouldn't be shared with multiple partners. They may not be tight enough, either. Leather is bad-ass, but gets pretty skanky pretty fast. And we think metal is just plain bad, because although you can sterilise it, you can't get it off in a pinch. (If you're reading this section because you've currently got a metal cock ring choking your chicken, ice it down — it should eventually slide off. If the ice just makes your dick cold, head to A&E.)

Here's how to put it on: start flaccid or semi-erect. Tuck the twins through one at a time, followed by their floppy father. But maybe you want to make it Daddy's night out, in which case just wrap the ring around the base of the shaft. Get one with a textured surface to give Mummy a treat too. If the ring pulls on your pubes, a trim might be in order. And for novices, remember the five golden cock ring rules:

1. Don't attach the ring too tightly.
2. Don't use a ring you can't adjust or remove easily (i.e., use one with Velcro or poppers).
3. Don't leave it on for more than 20 minutes at a time (no more than ten minutes the first time) — you are messing with blood flow to and from your pride and joy, after all.
4. Take it off if it hurts (duh).
5. Don't fall asleep or pass out with it on. Or else your dick might fall off. (OK, it probably won't fall off, but it could suffer some permanent damage.)

Other Toys for Boys

Vibrators aren't just for women. We know plenty of men who've 'accidentally lost' their girlfriends' favourite vibes or misappropriated a penis pump (see page 248). Now they even make toys specially designed for rods; these are usually vibrating 'sleeves' you stick your dick into that try to replicate a body cavity. The selection for dudes is still pretty limited and technology still has a way to go — so you'll need to close your eyes and use your imagination real good. French ticklers (sheath devices that resemble a rubber porcupine with a weight problem) don't do much for either partner, but those funny-looking nubbins will give your member a makeover, which may detract attention from your, uh, shortcomings. If you really want to have a porn-star penis for a day, try extenders made of thermal plastic or 'Cyberskin' (see sidebar). They'll add length and girth, but might detract from your own pleasure. And don't expect your girlfriend or boyfriend to be that excited about having their cervix rammed or their colon jammed.

A Few of Our Favourite Things

On the next few pages you'll find some of the best, most popular sex toys around, available from quality online sex shops like Love Honey (our favourite with the best prices: at lovehoney.co.uk), Paramount Pleasure at paramountpleasures.co.uk, Passion Online at passiononline.co.uk, Adult Sex Shop at adultsexshop.co.uk, or Blushing Buyer at blushingbuyer.co.uk. Better still, check them out in person from your local Ann Summers, who've recently gone upmarket.

Some of these toys are born in the USA and a little harder to find in the UK (although by no means impossible). Watch out for different voltages on US products; you'll need an adaptor, or you may get a nasty surprise. If our favourite toys are nigh on impossible to locate in the UK, we've suggested some alternatives, which get our thumbs-up. All toys or their UK alternatives are available from Love Honey, unless otherwise noted. All prices are approximate, and vary from shop to shop.

For BDSM-related toys (e.g., restraints and whips), plus other props and outfits for fantasy and role-playing, see the 'Kink' chapter on page 135.

type	size	description
Hitachi Magic Wand Vibrator (plug-in)	12 ins (30 cm) long, 2½ ins (6ish cm) diameter	A best-selling, two-speed 'back massager' with a hard plastic handle and a spongy acrylic head; it provides external genital stimulation so strong you can feel it internally, too.
Fukuoku 9000 Vibrator (battery)	2¾ ins (7 cm) long	This rubbery thimble fits on your finger like an extension of your body, comes with three interchangeable textured finger pads and a carrying case.
Smoothie Vibrator (battery)	6–6½ ins (16 cm) long, 1–1¼ ins (3 cm) in diameter	A 'traditional'-looking, quiet, plastic vibe for penetration or external stim available in multiple colours, animal prints or waterproof 'iMac' versions.
G-Spot Vibe with Tickler Vibrator (battery)	8 ins (20 cm) long	The firm curve and blunt end of the jelly rubber shaft pinpoint your G, while the nubby-ring around the base gets the vaginal opening.
Wahl 7-in-1 Vibrator (plug-in)	6½ ins (16 cm) long	Long-lasting, super-quiet, electric, plastic vibe with seven different attachments, including a suction cup that turns any lifeless dildo into a hummer.
Rabbit Pearl Vibrator (battery)	5 ins (12.5 cm) long, 1½ ins (3.75 cm) in diameter	The vinyl shaft swivels at an adjustable angle for the G, plastic pearls tumble in the rotating midsection for tickling the outer third of the vagina and two rabbit ears flutter against the clit at variable speeds.

pros/cons

apropos occasion

damage

Pros: Lasts for decades and can be transformed into a penetrator with a cheap vinyl attachment (e.g., the G-Spotter, £8).
Cons: It's wake-the-neighbours loud, not very sexy-looking and could feel too strong (if there is such a thing). You'll need an adaptor for the plug and the voltage.

You're home alone and in need of a sure thing.

about £30

Pros: It's discreet, lightweight, cordless and great for clit stim during any kind of sex.
Cons: There's only one speed and one finger attachment with this version, but you can get the Fukuoku Power Pack with three vibrating fingers or the Fukuoku Waterproof Glove with five vibrating fingers and variable speeds.

After watching one too many episodes of *Star Trek*, you need to play out your Cyborg fantasy.

£20

Pros: Won't scare your kids when they find it in your drawer.
Cons: No helpful curves or clit attachments, as if built by a guy to make sure it wouldn't compete with his thing. Not easy to find in the UK. We recommend the Perfect Pencil Vibe (£10) on Love Honey, or the Aerotech (£7) and the Waterproof (£10.99) on Passion Online.

You're a sex missionary trying to convert someone who's scared of toys.

£10

Pros: Many toys sold for G-spot stim are too floppy to please — but not this one!
Cons: May be a little too long for some women to get both their G and their clit.

You've put the vinyl cover on the bed, emptied your bladder and are ready to impersonate Old Faithful (p. 103).

£15

Pros: You'll never get bored.
Cons: It looks like a kitchen appliance. You'll need a voltage and plug adaptor in the UK, so save yourself the trouble and go for the Tender Touch Massage Kit (£30).

You're home alone and in need of a sure thing — and your walls are very thin.

£35

Pros: Because it's Japanese, it's built better.
Cons: Because it's Japanese, the phallic tip is a creepy face.

Your lover has recently broken your heart, you've just watched *Steel Magnolias* on the DVD and you've eaten a pint of Ben & Jerry's — soon, everything will be all right.

£25

	type	size	description
Aqua Allstar	Vibrator (battery)	5 ins (12.5 cm) long (insertable portion), 1³/₄ ins (4 cm) in diameter	The soft rubber shaft and protruding rounded nub both vibrate for simultaneous internal and external stim, respectively.
Hello Kitty Vibe	Vibrator (battery)	5¹/₂ ins (14 cm) long	Kitschy, well-made, one-speed, plastic, external stimulator with medium vibes.
The Butterfly	Vibrator (battery)	2³/₄ ins (7 cm) long, 2 ins (5 cm) wide	Wearable, butterfly-shaped, plastic vibrator with elastic leg straps that provides clit stim during intercourse (or other play). Other vibe options include daisy, dolphin and dragonfly.
Platinum Vibe	Vibrator (battery)	6¹/₂ ins (16 cm) long, 1¹/₂ ins (3.75 cm) in diameter	Strong, sleek, metal stimulator/penetrator that's ridged like the top of a soft ice cream cone.
I-Vibe Pocket Rocket	Vibrator (battery)	4 ins (10 cm) long	Quiet, pocket-sized, plastic, external stimulator with interchangeable, textured tips. (The waterproof version is called the Water Dancer.)
Vibrating Duo Balls	Vibrator (battery)	Each ball is 1¹/₂ ins (3.75 cm) in diameter	Two connected vibrating balls with variable speeds for G-spot stimulation and kegel exercises.

Pros: Of all the less-expensive dual vibes, this one gives you the biggest bang for your buck — plus, it's waterproof!
Cons: No gimmicks or cool tricks to show off to your friends. Not widely available in the UK. Why not try the Water Bunny (£17)?

You're in the hot tub at your ski villa in Switzerland with your two private ski instructors and a bottle of Dom. (You can dream.)

£20

Pros: Naughty schoolgirl factor.
Cons: Naughty schoolgirl factor. Another novelty item in the UK. Our best alternative is the Royal Guard Vibrator (£11). Think Buckingham Palace!

You're searching for the perfect back-to-school accessory. Or you're a royalist.

£18

Pros: It's so cute, it's like a fashion accessory for your clit. And then there's that whole clit-stim-during-intercourse thing.
Cons: If you're the kind of chick who hates shopping, you might find it too girly. In the UK, the best alternative is the Venus Butterfly Strap-on (£20).

The hen party invite says 'bring lingerie' but you really want to bring a sex toy.

£30

Pros: Industrial chic aesthetic.
Cons: Industrial chic aesthetic. Hard to locate in the UK, but there are a few lurking. Worth the hunt, though. The closest UK alternative is the non-vibrating Heavy Metal Dildo 6 Inch Ribbed (£30).

You escape to a bathroom stall at a late-night rock concert after some serious body-rocking in the mosh pit (assuming you can get the vibe past security).

£40

Pros: It'll make your boyfriend feel really big.
Cons: There are none. Now go out and get one.

Anytime, anywhere.

£20 (with Doc Johnson Lube)

Pros: If you like the idea of Ben Wa balls, but know they don't do jack, now there's something meatier.
Cons: They're kind of retarded.

Your sensitive ponytail boyfriend named Ian gave them to you as a 'just because' present.

£13

type	size	description
Little Flirt 	Butt plug	3¼ ins (8 cm) long, 1in (2.5cm) in diameter	It's like a (very) mini bowling pin made of firm silicone with a base.
Large Jelly Love Beads 	Anal beads	10ins (25 cm) long, 10 beads of incremental size	Soft, smooth Jelly beads on a flexible stem for anal insertion and removal.
Spiral Plug Kit 	Butt plug, vaginal plug and/or clit stimulator	3¾ ins (9 cm) long, from ⅞ ins to 1⅜ ins (2–4 cm) in diameter	The spiral ridges of this harness-compatible, silicone plug provide sensation and help keep it in place once inserted; you can use the hard, plastic, peanut-sized Itty Bitty Vibe separately or inserted into the base of the plug.
Fleshlight	Masturbation sleeve	10 ins (25 cm) deep inside	Comes in three shapes: mouth, vagina, or anus. You stick your dick in its Cyberskin and pump up and down.
Gummy Bear Ring 	Cock ring	Stretches to 2½ ins (6cm) in diameter	Fits snugly (and easily, with a little lube) around the base of a penis or dildo with a protruding jelly nubbin for the receiver's enjoyment.
Orbit Ring Vibe 	Vibrating cock ring (battery)	Stretches to 4 ins (10 cm) in diameter	A soft jelly ring that provides quiet, external vibration (at variable speeds) on her clit or his balls during penetration by a dick, dildo, or fist.

pros/cons	apropos occasion	damage
Pros: Gentler than Johnson's Baby Shampoo. **Cons:** 'Is it in yet? . . . Is it in yet? . . . How about now?'	You're meeting your butt for the first time and you want to make a good impression.	£10
Pros: Easier to clean than plastic beads and no rough edges to file. **Cons:** What's not to love?	Your squeamish partner won't offer up their own finger but they're willing to let a third party intervene.	£10
Pros: It's the only cordless, vibrating silicone butt plug available in the US. UK readers, look for the Ass Shaker. **Cons:** There are separate cleaning instructions for the plug and vibe. High-maintenance dates suck.	You're a butt-play pro with a really boring office party to attend. (If you don't want to blow your cover, leave the vibe part at home.)	£22
Pros: Makes for good dinner party conversation. **Cons:** It requires a lot of imagination.	You've got a broken arm.	£45
Pros: Cheap, easy and non-intimidating. **Cons:** It could be mistaken for edible candy. For six times as much fun in the UK, try the Magic Orgasm Ring Set (£17) – six individual stretchable rings with different shaped nubbins and protrusions.	The protruding nubbin on your own penis fell off.	£8
Pros: 'Vibrating clitoral stimulation during intercourse? Have I died and gone to heaven?!' **Cons:** It might feel like someone's holding down your dick and tickling it until you scream mercy. In the UK, your best alternative is Dual Clit Stim Ring (£10).	Your new girlfriend has never come from intercourse and you want to put all her ex-boyfriends to shame.	£23

type	size	description
Tweezer Clamps	Breast sensation toy	3 ins (7.5 cm) long clamps, 12 ins (30 cm) long chain	Padded vinyl clips linked by a metal chain that are easily adjustable from light to tight.
The Crystal Wand	Dildo	10 ins (25 cm) long, $7/8$ in (2 cm) in diameter	Clear S-shaped Lucite wand designed specifically to hit the G or the prostate.
Champ	Dildo	$6^3/8$–$7^1/2$ ins (16–19 cm) long, $1^1/5$–2 ins (2.5–5 cm) in diameter	A well-built and flexible silicone 'penis' with a smooth curve that works for both vaginal and anal play.
Soft Pack	Flaccid dildo (with 'balls')	$3^1/2$–7 ins (9–18 cm) long	Prosthetic male 'package' with lifelike 'skin' and scrotum made of Cyberskin you wear in your pants. Available in different colours and four different sizes.
Terra Firma Harness	Harness	Fits hips up to 56ins (140 cm)	Basic harness with adjustable straps to securely hold dildos of all different shapes and styles. Available in nylon if you're cheap, 'stardust' vinyl if you're glamorous and leather if you're nasty.

pros/cons	apropos occasion	damage
Pros: Won't fall off. **Cons:** Might remind you of going to the dentist. Lots of versions of this toy in the UK; we recommend Vibrating Nipple Clamps (a snip at £35).	You've been a very bad girl (or boy) and need a constant reminder of your naughty ways.	£10
Pros: It includes a velvet pouch and a seven-page how-to guide. **Cons:** You have to have good aim. Sometimes difficult to source in the UK, but you can easily find a variety of glass dildos in similar curved shapes on Love Honey.	You are a fairy princess and you use your magic wand on your magic spot in your special place and oh, isn't it magical . . .	£30
Pros: Because size does matter. **Cons:** It may give your boyfriend a complex. Try the Amor dildo on this side of the pond (£20).	You want that post–Christmas dinner full feeling without all the calories.	£40 and upwards, depending on size
Pros: The closest you'll get to knowing what it feels like for a boy without having sex-reassignment surgery. **Cons:** Not suitable for penetration . . . bummer. We searched, but couldn't find any UK equivalent.	It's drag king night and you want to bump and grind with the pros.	£10
Pros: Two-strap style leaves the wearer open to play, which is always a good thing. **Cons:** Incompatible with a second dildo for the wearer and there's no pouch for a little baby vibrator. If you can't find the Terra here, Love Honey offers several harness starter kits.	Your boyfriend has been a very bad girl and needs a reminder of his naughty ways.	£25 upwards, depending on material

KINK, IT'S NOT WHAT YOU THINK

BDSM for the Rest of Us

What makes great sex great? The hot pursuit? The triumph of persistence over impediments? The deliberate and planned seduction? The unexpected, the unpredictable, the unknown? The psychological drama of the moment? The breach of taboos? Yes. Yes. Yes, yes, yes, yes!

When your sex life is missing any or all of these elements, you can become bored. Perhaps a long-term relationship has lost a little of that once bright and shining spark, or you yourself have become a creature of habit, sinking into a familiar rut with partners old and new. But what if we said you could get back all the excitement you once knew and then some? What if we said you could make your fantasies a reality, safely and discreetly, with just a little effort and no money down?

Forget everything (you think) you know about BDSM (i.e., bondage & discipline, domination & submission and sadomasochism). No, you don't have to join a weird club or learn the Trekkie-esque lingo or have a diploma in theatre to enjoy them. You don't even have to like pain or gimp outfits. This chapter is not about giving up 'normal' sex, adopting a new 'lifestyle', joining a 'community' or becoming a 'freak'. It's about making sex hotter. It's about giving voice to your darker, maybe even slightly disturbing desires by exploring new sensations, using restraints, dressing up (or down), playing make-believe and other mind games — with or without actual intercourse. It's about making kink a part of your everyday sex life . . . OK, maybe just your weekend and holiday sex life.

Take from this chapter what you will. Some people favour the physical aspects of BDSM, others are more into the mental side of it. There's no right or wrong way to play (except, of course, when it comes to safety and consent) — if it turns you and your partner on, that's all that matters. Don't worry about what anyone else would think, or what they'd call it. Just because you like something a little kinky doesn't mean that you're damaged goods or you suffered some childhood trauma. Just because you like to be tied up, spanked and called 'bitch' doesn't mean you're a bad feminist. Just because you want to play-rape your boyfriend doesn't mean you have criminal tendencies.

Pushing your boundaries to push your buttons takes some planning. It also requires trust, communication and a little love (you can't brew its opposite — a little sadistic hate — without it). That's why experimenting with comfort zones is easier, safer and usually more satisfying when you're in a long-term relationship. So we're not going to give you a tour of anonymous power play or SM nightclubs here. (That's what late-night PPV flicks are for, right?) Read this chapter with a luvva and then figure out who's going to service whom tonight.

Power Plays

Thomas Jefferson said, 'Power is not alluring to pure minds.' But who wants to be pure? OK, so Tommy J was right: extremes of power — whether wielding it absolutely, or giving it up completely — don't really fly in a democratic society. But power plays and shifts are givens in any relationship, especially sexual ones. We spend so much time trying to stabilise them outside the bedroom that to emphasise or even distort them in the bedroom can be pretty thrilling. It's OK to enjoy the abuse of power there, privately. You can be bad, or heaven forbid, weak — we won't tell.

Explicitly playing with power goes beyond simply being the initiator or literally the one on top. It's like this: one person, traditionally referred to as 'the top', takes total control; the other, known as 'the bottom', relinquishes it. Totally. Perhaps the top ties up the bottom, teasing them mercilessly until the top is ready for them to come. Or maybe the bottom's been very, very bad and needs to be punished with a good spanking over bended knee. Or the top could decide to make the bottom their love slave, one who is responsible for servicing their every need and happily honouring all their sexual whims, without question or hesitation. None of these scenarios needs to be terribly hardcore — for example, if you're the boss, you could simply decide to have your partner draw you a bath, gently wash your hair, feed you grapes and deliver French kisses whenever you ask. Then again, you could hog-tie your buddy with nylon rope, slap a blindfold on them, shut them in the closet, occasionally open the door to bring them close to orgasm with a gloved hand, only to close the door again and leave them longing in sweet, sweet misery.

Why Give Up?

To be dominated is to give yourself over to another completely (that even sounds sexy). You offer up your body as an instrument of your partner's pleasure. But that gives you pleasure, so it's a two-way street, really. Being submissive makes the responsibility, guilt and hang-ups melt away — you perform whatever sexual acts come up, not because you necessarily want to (wink, wink, nudge, nudge), but because you have to. What freedom! You're a puppet, but you're also the centre of attention — pure heaven for a repressed prima donna. If you kinda like being held down and tickled, why not take that to a whole 'nother level? You can get caught up in the moment. You don't have to think. You don't have to do anything, only what you're told. Which is not to say that you're passive; you are receptive, responsive, appreciative, grateful. And no, there's no correlation between social, economic, or mental status and your power preference. Being dominated isn't demeaning; it's fun!

Why Take Over?

To dominate is to take full responsibility for what happens when, where, how often and to whom. You take control because you know exactly what you want or exactly what your partner deserves — and you don't want them getting in the way of your plans. You can embrace all those character flaws that won't win you any friends in the real world, like greed, pride, gluttony, lust, sloth, wrath ... pretty well all of the seven deadly sins (except for maybe envy, because you envy no one, especially not your plaything). To hell with Elvis: be cruel! Use them, abuse them — in this safe and controlled sitch, it's OK. You don't even have to do anything; just torture them with denial, making them talk dirty or admit to their deepest fantasies or expose themselves or beg. Ironically, while you can do as you please, you've always got your partner's pleasure in the back of your mind because, after all, complete trust is a precious gift. So it's always a two-way street, you see?

Why Choose?

You don't have to be one or the other — everyone has a bit of bully and wimp in them. The power dynamic usually switches throughout a single bout of good old traditional boot-knocking and so can it throughout your relationship with BDSM. (In fact, they say in the biz that the best tops were once bottoms.) But why not decide to make it all one-sided for a night? It'll help keep things on track and running smoothly; plus you won't have to do any quick emotional maths to keep up (always a drag during any kind of sex).

C·o·m·m·u·n·i·c·a·t·i·o·n

Of course, the irony of all this power play is that it's completely consensual. Sure, the bottom gives up control, but as the guys at the Gas 'n' Sip in *Say Anything* would say, they do so by choice, man. The exchange of power has to be mutual, among equals and without pressure or manipulation from either side (all that good stuff happens within a planned date). Bring it up casually but confidently. If you're not reading this chapter together (like we told you to), have your partner read it and see if a lightbulb goes off.

Communication is the cornerstone of all relationships — a kinky relationship is no exception. Partners need to figure out what they want, what they don't want; what they're willing to do and what they would never do; how they'd like an evening to begin and more importantly, how they'd like it to end (with a bang or a whimper?). The more specific you are before you get down to business, the less chance there is for confusion and disappointment during or after the business. Some people fear such frank discussions take the spontaneity out of it all — they think that hot, wholly satisfying sex should just happen. But what could cool down a moment more than your partner strapping a collar on you and making you eat a can of cat food when you are decidedly a dog person? The whole point of this kind of sex is to be able to relax, get caught up in the moment and live your fantasy without any annoying distractions or discomforts (at least unplanned ones) to bring you back down to earth.

Look, we're not talking about sitting down and drafting an 80-page script complete with stage directions and production costs. Make the planning part of the fun: exchange dirty e-mails, explicit letters, or do/don't lists; use erotic books and videos for inspiration; buy all the props you want used, instead of hoping your partner will read your mind. Compromise, but never cave. Once you get to know each other's preferences and develop a rhythm, you won't have to outline a game plan every time. Perhaps you'll develop a secret code that means 'hot kinky sex tonight!' — a particular outfit, a hand signal, or a voice message simply saying 'Hot kinky sex tonight!'

Emotional Safety and Responsibility

We said it before, we'll say it again (though we hate making the acting analogy): know your motivation. Make sure it's self-affirming, not self-destructive. Don't use kink to work out a dysfunctional relationship — that's what therapy is for. While some abuse survivors find SM helpful to their recovery, this is dangerous emotional territory that should only be traversed with a loving, long-term partner and an understanding counsellor waiting in the wings. Got anger issues or insecurities? Then get out. Even if you're mature and well adjusted with loads of self-esteem and confidence, dabbling in physical and psychological power plays can be intense, scary even. It can expose hidden fears or dark sides. It can make you feel helpless and emotionally vulnerable (especially when it's done well). That's some heavy shit. But that's what makes it so good.

Fools rush in where angels fear to tread, but you're no angel and you're no fool, either — so be thoughtful, respectful and careful. This means you're not drunk or high. (A glass or two of wine might help get you in the mood, but sloppy drunks and Japanese rope bondage don't mix.) If you're the bottom, it means you trust the top to stop; and if you're the top, you know when to stop. You need to be prepared for things not to go exactly as you planned or hoped; if boundaries get accidentally crossed, follow-up care must be provided — and a post-game chat and cuddle are requisite.

The Golden Rule of Kink: only play with people who will play nice, 'cause the ex who caught you cheating and now has you cuffed and blindfolded ain't comin' back.

The Only Time No Doesn't Mean No

Power play wouldn't be power play if you couldn't tell your partner to 'Please stop, oh god, no more!' and not mean it. That's why you need a 'safe word' — your escape route for when things get too heavy. Everyone needs an out, no matter how much you trust your partner. In fact, it's got nothing to do with trust — it's about how the noises and faces you make when you're having an orgasm are the same noises and faces you make when you stub your toe. (Playing without a safe word is known as edge play — call us sissies, but we're not down with that.) Common safe words are 'red' (with the corresponding green for 'more' and yellow for 'chill out a bit, please') and plain old 'safe word'. But we prefer 'seriously' as in 'Dude, seriously'.

Bondage Basics

Bondage — the word immediately evokes images of angst-ridden goths with bad eye make-up, pasty skin and crucifix jewellery. But using restraints is one of the easiest, cheapest and most versatile ways to add the unexpected to one of nature's more predictable acts. Whether you like Siouxsie and the Banshees or not.

Depending on who's doing the tying, bondage can give you control and responsibility, or render you helpless — but in both cases, assuming everyone's happy with their role, each partner's selfish desires are met. Elaborate, Houdini-proof restraints up the ante on the power dynamic, but often the simple, more symbolic act of tying off a pair of wrists with a sturdy but admittedly escapable bind is rush enough. You may not even need any physical restraints, just an authoritative voice commanding, 'Don't you dare move an inch!'

If you tend to find it difficult to reach orgasm — either because you put too much pressure on yourself or you feel greedy when your partner spends too much time on you and you end up psyching yourself out — then being on the bottom, metaphorically, is for you! Just lie there and take it. The physical constriction can also feel good for its own sake, like a heavy blanket in winter or the Velcro blood pressure strap at the doctor's. Sometimes a futile struggle against the restraints adds drama. Sometimes bondage is just a matter of aesthetic appreciation — there's a reason those thick leather cuffs are so popular with the MTV crowd these days. Other times it's a matter of arts and crafts, with whole systems of loops and knots more tricky than your grandma's county-fair prize-winning needlework. Bondage also goes great with role-playing — and pasta.

Materials

Rope — so classy, so elegant, so versatile, so available. Pick some up at any DIY shop; if you want to get fancy, visit your friendly neighbourhood yacht chandler. Soft, shiny, twisted (or braided) nylon is strong, comfy and non-chafing. It stays clean, lasts longer and is easy to loosen (though maybe too easy in some cases). Keep the ends of nylon from unravelling by carefully melting them with a candle flame. (Save the candle for hot wax play later — see 'Sensation(al) Play' below.) For a more rugged look and feel, try cotton cordless clothesline — it's pliant and knots tightly (sometimes too tightly, see 'Safety Tips'

the truth about handcuffs

When your luvva needs to be cuffed and booked, don't reach for that pair of police-issue handcuffs you swiped after getting arrested in Alabama for taking it up the bum. The average set of cuffs is designed not with coital pursuits in mind, but rather in-transit prisoner restraint — hence, their high pain-potential quotient. For this reason, even the most hardcore bondage practitioners only use them for form, never function. If used in a struggle or any situation in which there is pressure on the cuffs, handcuffs can cause more than discomfort: they can lead to nerve and bone damage, sometimes irreparably. But if your outfit just wouldn't be complete without a pair of these silver bracelets, obey the following laws: make sure they aren't too tight (the wrist should be able to move freely), avoid creating tension in the cuffs (they aren't a leash), don't put any weight on them (lying on your back with your hands under you = no-no) and splurge, you cheap slut! Don't buy a pair with cloverleaf keys, as the motion of the ocean can cause the cheapo sliding lever of the 'double-lock' mechanism to slip and the cuffs to tighten or release. Quality brands have a pin-point that fits in a hole after the cuffs have been put on to secure the size, thus ensuring safety and fun.

below). Keep the ends from fraying by dipping in glue or nail polish, or wrapping with duct tape or twine. Hemp rope is sturdy but scratchy on the skin. Whichever material you decide on, get about 30 metres so you can cut it into several shorter pieces, varying from about three to ten metres; shorter lengths are good for tying ankles and wrists together, longer lengths work well for full-body binding. The thicker the rope, the less likely it is to cause circulation problems: stick with something between one and two cm in diameter.

PVC (vinyl) tape, medical tape, or duct tape can also be used like rope — use old ripped clothes, sheets, or plastic wrap as a buffer between the tape and the skin (except with the PVC tape, which is soft, shiny, reusable plastic that sticks to itself, not your skin or clothes). Tape will increase body temperature, especially when using plastic wrap, so make sure the bound one doesn't overheat. And keep medical scissors (with the blunt ends that won't scratch skin) nearby for quick release.

Purpose-made cuffs are straps usually made of leather or fabric that wrap around particular body parts (e.g., wrists, ankles, thighs) and can be fastened together (e.g., wrist to wrist, wrist to thighs, etc.) or to other forms or restraints (e.g., chains, hooks) with built-in buckles or attachable fasteners like D-rings, padlocks, spring clips or karabiners and even cable ties. Thicker, softer cuffs (especially the fleece- or fur-lined ones) are obviously more comfortable, especially when you're planning on going at it like wind-up toys. Well-made cuffs are more expensive, but they're stronger, last longer and look better.

Chains provide sturdy connections between the softer restraints (never use chain as you would rope — see 'Safety Tips' below). Each link can be used as a point of anchor, so they're endlessly adjustable. Run a length of chain under your bed and attach to ankle cuffs from either side to spread-eagle your 'caged bird'. Speaking of which, 'stretchers' are long, solid objects that force body parts (like legs) apart for that open-to-the-public feel. Make your own by running a chain through a 1.5-cm metal tube cut to about a metre at your DIY shop, with the chain connected to cuffs at either end (be sure there are no sharp tube ends). Or just attach the chains or fastening devices to strong hooks in the walls or ceiling. We're not recommending any kind of suspension (way too dangerous), but the hooks should be sturdy enough to withstand some serious tugging. Follow instructions for safely installing a hanging chair for your own kinky purposes. And remember to actually hang a chair (or at least some potted plants) from the hooks whenever the parents come over for tea.

There's an endless array of other attachment points around your house just waiting to be violated: tables (make sure they can hold your weight), futons (or, even better, futon frames), staircase railings, hammocks, toilets (if you're really dirty), footstools and, of course, chairs (wooden ones with lots of struts are best). And be sure to think outside the box when positioning; for instance, the seat of an armless chair can be used as an inanimate knee to bend your brat over.

But if any of this is too high-maintenance for you, just grab a necktie, a long sock, a woven leather belt, a winter scarf, or a cotton handkerchief for more spontaneous bondage. Whatever kind of ties you bind, be sure to follow all the safety precautions below.

Rope Techniques

Below are some very basic tying techniques for 'My First Bondage Scene'. If you want to get any trickier (e.g., hog-ties, crotch-ropes, etc.) invest in a complete guide to bondage like Jay Wiseman's *Erotic Bondage Handbook* and steal your nephew's book of Boy Scout knots.

Rope Handcuffs (limb to limb): The best place to start is wrist to wrist, with the palms facing each other. Lacing the fingers together will help create a natural gap between the wrists for breathing room. Take about two metres of rope and centre it over the two limbs you want to tie together. Wrap each end around both limbs several times (at least three or four), distributing the tension evenly over the skin and leaving a bit of room between the limbs so circulation does not get cut off (at least three to five cm apart to allow for later cinching).

When you've only got about 30 cm left, twist the two ends around each other at a central point between the limbs (instead of on the side of one limb) to create an intersection with the rope. Then wrap those ends once or twice around the section of rope that's between the two limbs (you're now wrapping at a right angle to the initial binding, like a ribbon around a birthday present). Gently cinch the two ends to make everything evenly snug and tie them together with a square knot. (If there's enough space between the wrists, you can continue to wrap in opposite directions at right angles to the first set of coils until you run out of rope and then tie the knot.) To make a square knot, also called a reef knot, you twist the right end over and around the left; the end that started on the right should now be in your left hand and vice versa: take the end that's now in your left hand and twist it over and around the right; you should end up with a symmetrical loop inside a loop. (Don't confuse a square knot with a granny knot, which is the asymmetrical over-under version you probably tie your shoelaces with and that has a tendency to come undone.) When you're finished, there should be enough room between skin and rope to easily slide a finger through. All of the above goes for ankles, too (see illustration).

The Double-Rope Handcuff: Double (or fold over) several feet of rope so the cut ends are aligned and there's a folded loop at the other end (that's called a Lark's Head). Wrap the doubled-up rope around the limbs once. Bring the two cut ends through the Lark's Head at a point between the limbs (rather than to the side of one) and pull the two ends back in the direction they just came from and start wrapping (still keeping the two cut ends together). After several coils, when you only have about 30 cm left, bring the two ends through the Lark's Head again. Then pull each end in opposite directions (at right angles to the first set of coils) and between the limbs. Wrap until you run out of rope and tie off with a square knot (see illustration).

Where Do You Think You're Going? (limb to object): The simplest method is to use two lengths of rope: one to wrap the limb(s) and the other between that wrap and the object. For instance, tie a handcuff with one piece of rope; slip the other piece up through the handcuff, then take both ends of that rope and tie them around or to the object. Or, as you're wrapping a limb, put all wraps through a welded D-ring and use that as the loop for the second connector rope. Or you can wrap the limb in a large bandana or fabric and then tie a connector rope through all those wraps, making sure there's a finger's width of room between skin, material and rope. If you've tied one end of the connector rope to the limb wrap and then tie the other end to, say, a heavy bedpost, use a sturdy knot that will resist tugging from your captive but will come undone easily when you want it to (like a half-hitch with a bow in it or a double half-hitch — see your handy Boy Scout guide for that one).

Purpose-made cuffs with built-in loops or built-in extension ropes will work, too (just don't get the cheapo kinds — they tend to break). With all of these methods, your priorities should be to make sure that (a) tugging won't result in tightening around the limb and (b) the object won't fall over on top of them.

Turning Japanese: A popular Japanese technique is to tie the arms behind the back, with each hand extending towards the opposite elbow, creating a U shape with the arms. You wrap the rope around the wrists. Since you won't be using the cinching method above, wrap a little more snugly, being extra careful to distribute tension evenly and still leaving a finger's width of room. Tie with a square knot (see illustration). To help keep the hands up and out of the way of a soft, supple behind, use a longer piece of rope and after you've tied the knot, separate the two dangling ends, pulling each under one armpit, up and over the respective shoulder and then back towards the nape of the neck to tie the ends together (never pull rope in front of the neck). Any rope that passes across the shoulders behind the neck for support is called a yoke harness. Use it to attach foot ropes to (instead of the horizontal chest ropes mentioned below, which will just result in drooping harnesses).

Chest Harnesses: Double a long piece of rope and place the Lark's Head in the middle of your partner's back, between their shoulder blades. (If their hands are tied in front and they will be lying on their back at any time, position the Lark's Head slightly off to one side of the spine.) With your partner's upper arms against their sides, wrap around the chest (including the arms) above the breasts back to the Lark's Head. Pass the two ends of rope to the centre of the back and pass them through the Lark's Head and then wrap in the opposite direction below the breasts to the back and pass the two ends through the Lark's Head again. To create a yoke chest harness, bring both ends under one armpit (below the chest wrappings), up and over that respective shoulder, behind the back of the neck, in front of the opposite shoulder and under that armpit (below the wrappings) back to the Lark's Head; separate the ends and pull one through the Lark's Head, then tie a square knot. To create a bikini harness once you've got the chest wrapped, pull the two ends up and over one shoulder, down between the breasts, under the horizontal wrap below the breasts, back up and over the opposite shoulder, back down to the Lark's Head, then tie a square knot (see illustration).

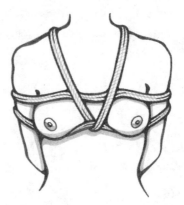

Bondage Safety

If you hadn't yet gathered from the intricate instructions above, bondage is an art form, an acquired skill, a science. Fail to follow the safety rules below and you could seriously fuck up more than just your sex life — how about your life?

● **No-no's for novices:** First of all, don't even think about suspension, crucifixion, body-piercing, branding, electricity play, etc. Those are for the professionals who make BDSM a way of life (i.e., not you, at least not yet).

- **Tying knots:** When using rope, you want to be able to untie your partner quickly. When bringing the two ends of rope together, use a simple square knot. When tying one end of rope to another object, use loops so that a quick pull of one end of the rope will immediately loosen the knot (like a double half-hitch).
- **Restraint snugness:** Don't make restraints too tight, especially on joints where there are major arteries or veins near the surface (pulse points like wrists, ankles, elbows, knees, armpits, upper arms, etc.). The harder and less flexible the restraint, the looser it should be. Whatever restraints you use, you should be able to fit one or two fingers between the bondage and skin. When binding two body parts together (e.g., wrist to wrist), make sure there is a bit of room between them as you tie.
- **Distributing tension:** Distribute the tension over a wide area to avoid too much concentrated strain on muscles or joints at a single point. Wide padded cuffs are always good. If you're working with rope, use several wraps of rope (one is never enough) spread evenly over an area, never bunched up or overlapping, keeping room between rope and skin; a single turn of rope around all the rest can comfortably and safely provide a snugger fit.
- **Circulation:** Having a limb fall asleep is usually an unwelcome distraction. The tier-upper should check for cooling or discoloration (i.e., whitening) of parts past the restraints about every ten or 15 minutes. If the bound one starts feeling an uncomfortable tingling or numbness, they should pipe up. If you fail to follow these simple instructions and a limb gets totally numb, then remove the restraints, lower the limb, massage the area to help with blood flow and cover up to help warm the limb.
- **Nerves:** If you tie someone up incorrectly, very important nerve paths can get pinched. The result is usually shooting or focused pain. Untie immediately to avoid serious nerve damage!
- **Restraint strength:** Dizziness from impaired circulation (whether from bad bondage or a sustained position) or a head rush from a particularly intense sensation can cause fainting. Therefore, make sure you use restraints that can support the weight of a person should they fall and that can be released immediately, even with their full weight on them. ('Panic snaps' — hooks to attach rope or chain to fixed objects and sold at sex shops and maybe even your local DIY shop — are made just for this.) Similarly, restraints should be able to withstand the struggling and writhing of a

wound-up, bound-up bottom; if the ties are too loose, they can chafe or come undone suddenly.

- **Positions:** 'Sensual bondage' restrains a person firmly but comfortably. 'Endurance bondage' stretches, cramps, or contorts the body safely, but with some purposeful discomfort. The latter should be done with extra care and for shorter periods of time — no longer than half an hour. With more sensual bondage and a little practice, healthy players can stay in a comfortable position for about an hour. You can extend play by varying positions often and leaving enough slack (sometimes a couple of centimetres is all you need) for the bound person to move their bod a bit to readjust when necessary. But too much slack can give them leverage to strain or dislocate something in a struggle. Prone position on a bed is the least stressful. Never walk away from anyone tied up lying facedown. Standing positions are a little trickier, because of the risks of falling, quicker numbing and joint stress. If they're standing with their arms above their head, keep their elbows bent. And don't suspend anyone from their arms or legs.

- **Restraints to avoid:** They may look good, but silk scarves and stockings have a tendency to get too tight under tension, making them unsafe and nearly impossible to untie without cutting off. Avoid thin ropes, twine, thread and phone or electrical cord, as they're more likely to cut off circulation. Leather thongs may look good, but they cut into the skin and are a bitch to untie, so take care.

- **Collars:** Never tie anything around the neck and certainly don't hang anyone from their neck. Buy a purpose-made human collar (pet collars won't work because they're designed for animals with much stronger necks). Leave room for at least two fingers between skin and collar. No pressing on the Adam's apple. In fact, there should be no pressure on the front of the neck, so don't tug on it from the back — all leading around should be done from the front.

- **Breathing:** Don't obstruct nasal passageways, or gag someone completely. Gags aren't a good idea for someone with asthma or a cold. And when you tie something in the mouth, watch out for triggering a gag reflex. Nothing like puke to put a damper on an evening.

- **Alone time:** Don't leave a bound person alone. If abandonment is part of your thing, pretend to make a dramatic exit and keep an eye on them from afar.

If they are gagged or in a particularly strenuous position, check on them up-close-and-personal every few minutes.

- **Check-ins:** Whoever's in the driver's seat is ultimately responsible for the safety of everyone present. Check in with your partner often, make sure they are comfortable, encourage them to let you know of any numbness or dizziness, feel for cooling due to compromised circulation and look for signs that they might be on the verge of really freaking out.
- **Troubleshooting:** Be aware of medical conditions like joint pain, heart problems, bad backs, asthma, sexually transmitted diseases and infections, etc.
- **Undoing:** Don't put on a restraint you don't know how to remove quickly. If you're using something with a key, place the key within arm's reach before you actually lock the restraint. Keep a pair of medical scissors (with blunt ends) handy for tape, plastic wrap and particularly hard knots or, in case of emergency, when removal needs to be super speedy.
- **Safety kits:** Put together a care package containing the above-mentioned bandage scissors, duplicates of all keys to locks and restraints, a first-aid kit, water and safer sex supplies. Keep it nearby. You may feel like you're geeking out, but everyone knows geeks make the best lovers.
- **New partners:** Never let yourself be tied up on a first date. While we're at it, don't stare directly into the sun, don't play in traffic, don't stick your hand in boiling water and don't jump off bridges.

Sensation(al) Play

You've heard of Chinese water torture, right? Sometimes the plainest of sensations, when applied repeatedly or unexpectedly, can be excruciating — or excruciatingly good. Playing with different textures and temperatures on your partner's skin is like having a brand-new set of appendages with which to grope your partner — especially when they can't move an inch. (Tell them to lie back and imagine they're doing it with Edward Scissorhands.) Alternate the sensations: a hairbrush or a snare-drum brush dragged over their back and then a silk scarf; fingernails and then fur; Tiger Balm and then ice, etc. (Just don't put ice inside any holes besides your mouth since it can damage the delicate linings.)

The MVP in sensation play is, of course, hot wax (especially when alternated with ice). Those candles you normally light for some lovey-dovey sensualist sex are handy tools for a little torturous temperature teasing, too. Just make sure you're using plain white paraffin household candles, because coloured, fragrant or beeswax candles burn at a higher temperature. And don't use a candle that's been burning on your nightstand for three hours, either, as the wax will be too hot (you're nasty, but not that nasty). Put down a towel to protect your Harrods Egyptian cotton sheets, hold the candle at least a few feet above your partner and let the wax drip down onto their skin, one drop at a time — the farther the wax has to fall, the cooler it will be upon landing. Rub it into their skin to ease the burn a little. And make sure you let the wax land on your hands occasionally, so you know if it's getting too hot to handle. Never get wax on the face or genitals. If your partner's the hirsute type, they might want to shave (the night before, to avoid irritation) so that the wax doesn't cling to their hair. And finally, once it's all over, you can fight over who gets to peel off the dried wax. Now that's fun.

Sensory Deprivation

Remember *At First Sight* with Val Kilmer and Mira Sorvino? No? Good. Val plays a blind massage therapist, and Mira falls for his magic fingers — the idea being that because he's deprived of sight, he has a superhero's sense of touch. Well, you can fake that during sex — it's called sensory deprivation. Sounds like a Psych 101 lab experiment, doesn't it? The more senses you deprive your partner of, the more intensely they'll feel whatever you're performing on them (great oral sex, if they're lucky). Mute all their senses except touch and they'll feel like the only thing that exists in the world is your mouth on their genitals.

Start with a blindfold — a tie, a scarf, an Ace bandage, one of those eye-masks they give you on overnight flights, etc. Tie the knot to one side of your partner's head so they don't have to lie on it. If you're a novice power playa, a blindfolded partner gives you the freedom to experiment (wax, hairbrush, handcuffs, spanking, whatever) without worrying how silly you look. Earplugs or headphones will muffle sound so that your partner can only hear you when you lean right into them. And gagging isn't just for gimps anymore: it forces your partner to breathe slowly and deliberately, and it gives them something

flying the kinky skies

The first rule of travelling with kinky toys is to keep them out of your carry-on. If you're not supposed to carry on a metal nail file, chances are they won't be cool with your cat-o'-nine-tails. Plus, random checks of carry-ons are made right at the gate, in front of the whole world boarding your plane. Usually, when random checks are made on checked luggage, passengers will be asked to accompany an agent or airport security guard to another location away from the line, but occasionally, inspections are made right at the ticket counter. We're guessing a seasoned security officer has seen his or her fair share of 'massagers', but if they don't know what an item is, or if it's really strange, they might have to ask you to explain its function. It's a good idea to pack the item in the box it came in so those questions may not have to be asked. If you don't have the original packaging for your goodies, go to town with your label maker. Carry them in a bag marked 'theatrical props', which as far as we're concerned is not a lie. Or better yet, ship it all via FedEx. If that's too much work, you can always visit the local medical supply store (sharp objects), the DIY depot (rope and chains), or supermarket (rolls and rolls of cling film) when you touch down, for an impromptu (and disposable) set of DIY BDSM toys.

to bite into. Plus it lets them know who's the boss of them. Just don't try to gag to the point where they can't make a peep — gagging is supposed to be more conceptual ('Cool, I'm wearing a gag') than literal ('Holy shit, I can't breathe'). `

Gag under their tongue, and don't forget to pick a non-verbal safe word, like dropping the table-tennis ball they're holding in one of their bound hands. (You can use the bat for the spanking — see below.)

Pain

You want pain? Well, pain costs. And right here is where you start paying . . . in sweat. Playing with power doesn't ever have to hurt — but eventually you may want all that bodily attention applied with a little more focus. The kind of pain we're talking about doesn't feel like pain. At least, it doesn't feel like falling off a chair or walking into a door. Pain that you want is a different beast. You don't have to feel like your life is worthless and everything is meaningless to befriend this beast. You've heard of runner's high, right? Same deal here: pain triggers the autonomic nervous system, which produces endorphins and increases your heart rate, breathing and blood pressure — all of which can both enhance sexual pleasure and make the pain feel less like discomfort and more like intense sensation. And the more turned on you are, the more pain you can take.

Ever wake up the next morning with dark purple fingerprint bruises on your inner thighs and have no idea when that happened the night before? You don't have to get a flogging to get a kick out of pain — sometimes a nibble on the inner thigh, a nipple tweak, or a hair-pulling is all it takes (or all you can take). Breathing steadily, making some noise, and relaxing your muscles will all help you take more. More, damn it. When it's all over but for the crying, make a cup of tea and cuddle together under a cosy blanket.

- **Nipple-clamps:** You can use clamps (or even just clothes pins) pretty much anywhere you can pinch skin, but the nipples are by far the most clamped body part. (It just looks sexier than pegs on the piggies.) As any third-year girl who's been in a catfight can tell you: the less skin you pinch, the more it'll hurt. And thus, the wider the clamp, the duller the sting. You shouldn't leave them on for more than 20 minutes at a time (it's easy to lose track of time because the nips will numb fairly quickly). The real pain comes when you remove 'em and the blood comes rushing back to the area — the clampee should probably exhale upon removal to be as relaxed as possible. A stream of expletives is a nice touch, too. Some clamps are attached by a chain so you can remove both with one quick tug for double the pain. For the DIY-inclined, take two sets of chopsticks, and wrap a rubber band around the ends of each pair. Connect to erect nipples and squeeze. The clamper can massage the nipples after the deed is done: it'll up the pain right at that moment, but it'll chase away the pain more quickly in the long run. Assuming you want to chase away the pain more quickly, of course.
- **Spanking:** You know you love it. Some people save spanking for role-playing (see below), because who deserves it more than a naughty schoolgirl or -boy? Or you might find that a good spanking makes a natural segue into role-playing. Others just savour the sound it makes, or the red tinge and tingle it gives the ass cheeks. Bend your partner over your knee or the back of the sofa, do it during sex, strap them down, push them into the wall. Just make sure you spank them like you mean it: nothing spoils the moment like an insecure, wussy-handed spanker. That said, you'll need to warm them up a little if you want to go long: start with medium whacks and gradually build up. Stick to the fleshy bits and avoid hitting the tailbone, spine, backs of the

knees, lower thighs or any joints. When working on guys, watch out for that spot right between their cheeks: even the naughtiest of naughty boys doesn't deserve a spank to the testicles. (Chicks, however, will probably dig this, as it'll reverberate throughout the vulva. Some have even been known to get off on it.) When you're done dishing, it's a nice gesture to follow up with some tender ass caressing; you can also alternate caresses and spanks throughout the sesh.

Face slapping is a loaded act. But 'loaded' is what makes it so hot, especially for chicks — it's the ultimate taboo. Use sparingly, and only with prior permission (whether explicit or implied). Be prepared for some serious post-slap spooning.

- **Whipping and flogging:** spanking's hard work on the hands. Why do you think Catholic school teachers used canes? That's where whips, floggers (multi-tailed whips), and bats come in. If shopping for flagellators is a little too hardcore for you, go DIY: wooden spoons, kitchen spatulas, paint stirrers, and table-tennis bats all make handy spankers. As do canes and rulers, of course. But it's worth checking out the selection at your local sex shop — some tools even come with cut-out shapes to leave cute marks like stars on the recently spanked fanny.

Think of this as a different way of touching your partner — a touch that might be gentle and teasing or hard and stinging. (And as with spanking, steer clear of joints, bones and organ areas.) The wider the bat, the more 'thuddy' the sensation will be; narrow toys and whips will deliver more of a sting. As with spanking, you should warm up gradually, easing into a steady rhythm. Pause between each stroke to let your partner regain a little composure, or alternate the heavy hits with a soothing rub (assuming that doesn't spoil your partner's fantasy that they're being punished for stealing the plums). The receiver should focus on steady breathing (though they'll be tempted to hold their breath) and relaxing their muscles. When you've made them pay, run your fingernails lightly all over their skin. Trust us, it's a nice touch.

Of course, there's a big difference between a little positive reinforcement with the kitchen utensils and a serious whipping. We're talking Conference versus the Premier League. Casual whipping is a dangerous undertaking — if you're going to spend 50 quid on a fancy leather whip or riding crop, then you should also invest a little time in learning how to wield it safely (we have neither the time nor the stomach for that here). Sex shops often offer classes — ask your friendly sales representative if they can recommend one. Or the following site: Sexual Freedom Coalition (sfc.org.uk).

Getting into Character

There it is again: that damn theatrical analogy. Don't be discouraged, though. The following is more about setting the mood and getting into a good kinky head space than it is about training for the Actors' Studio. Except instead of setting the mood with romantic candles and Kenny G, you use PVC and a potty mouth.

Talking Dirty Without Cracking Up

Who hasn't asked themselves, 'Me, how do I talk dirty without making a total ass of myself?' There's no easy answer, no script to memorise. Dirty talk is like baby talk — it doesn't translate well outside the bedroom. Word-for-word suggestions, no matter how inspired, always sound unforgivably cheesy and cliché on the page. For example: your fat, pink pussy is soooo sweet and sticky, you dirty little bitch! Just you wait: I'm gonna juice it like a hot, plump orange, my slutty little . . . See what we mean?

There's a fine line between sexy and stupid. If your partner knows you as the quiet type, suddenly spewing forth a string of obscenities that would make the Osbournes blush probably won't have the erotic effect you're going for. You gotta work up to it. But then again, you gotta start somewhere. The most basic approach is to think of dirty talk as simply talking about the sex you're having while you're having it, rather than trying to improvise a porno script. Below are some more specific guidelines for the newbie dirty talker; once you've mastered these basics, take it to the phone next time your partner's out of town.

- **Don't enjoy the silence.** We bet you moan enthusiastically, even uncontrollably, when being given a great back rub by a luvva or a platonic friend — so why not during sex? Noise can enhance pleasure, provide feedback, and stroke egos. If you can't form whole sentences at first, just focus on sounding off a little more than usual. Moan louder, sigh longer. Say 'yes' with more gusto. Say a simple, yearning 'please'. And for heaven's sake, say their name.

- **Talk about everything but the sex.** It's amusingly perverse to have a normal conversation about your day at the office while going at it like rabbits or getting a good spanking. Plus, it gets you used to talking while the show is in progress.
- **Ask your partner what they want.** This way you kill three birds with one stone: you find out exactly what they like (it's called 'communication'); you casually introduce verbalising into your sex sessions; and you find out what language they're comfortable with (see next point).
- **Speak your partner's language.** Initially, anyway. If they call it 'dick', don't call it 'hot throbbing cock'; if they call it 'yoni', don't call it 'gaping axe wound'. (In fact, don't ever call it that.) Don't worry about creative vocabulary. Stick with the basics. Once you become more fluent in the language of love, you can get more colourful.
- **Ask your partner specific questions.** If they're on the shy side, get them talking with a few yes or no questions: 'Do you want me to [fill in the blank]?' Or, we guess you could just say, 'Do you want me to fill in your blank?'
- **Narrate.** Tell them exactly what you're doing as you do it. Or right before you do it. Or, if you really want to tease them, tell them what you're going to do and then make them wait. They'll probably end up begging for it, which — hey! — is more dirty talk.
- **Ask them to describe how what you're doing feels.** Assuming you're sure it does feel good. If you're pounding your partner in the butt without lube and you ask them, 'How does that feel, baby?' they'll probably yell back, 'Like shit!'
- **Tell your partner what you want them to do.** If you happen to be the one in control tonight, this is your responsibility. Of course, you could just tell them what you want them to do is talk dirty non-stop for the next ten minutes, na na na poo poo.
- **Say it with confidence.** If you're embarrassed to say it, then your partner will be embarrassed, too. *Commit* to the dirty talk.

Role-play

If Keanu Reeves can do it, so can you. Taking on different personas or acting out various sexual scenarios is escapist sex at its best. Plus, role-playing might make all this spanking and power play feel more natural: for example, it may seem weird to beat up on Hubby, whom you're supposed to love and cherish, but what if you're the bitchy baby-sitter and he just refuses to go to sleep? Choose your personas based on what you're going for: worship, humiliation, embarrassment, service, domination, resistance, etc. Try teacher–student, president–intern, doctor–patient, cabana boy–rich bitch, bad cop–speedy driver, model–photographer, vampire–virgin, pirate–sailor, stalker–celebrity, kidnapper–hostage, Inland Revenue agent–tax dodger, etc. (You try thinking of anything less clichéd.) If you want to get really dirty, try being Daddy's little girl or Mummy's boy, or even rapist and victim (really, it's OK, just don't brag about it at the water cooler 'cause they probably wouldn't understand). If those scenarios are too theatrical, try wrestling, stripping, or a little resistance play — you know, 'You can fuck me if you can catch me'. Or maybe the only roles you need are 'person calling the shots' and 'person doing what they're told'.

Yeah, role-playing will take a little suspension of disbelief — but so does watching a romantic comedy, playing the lottery or getting married. Tell a story together, dress up, use props. If that family picture on your chest of drawers keeps reminding you of who you really are, get a hotel room. Go out in public in character to make things really interesting (just be courteous of your fellow citizens). For example, a little cock-and-ball bondage under the clothes can keep a slave boy perpetually aware of his lowly status; or if you're out at a bar, send your partner to the loo to ice their nipples with a cube from their gin and tonic and demand visible results when they return. The role-playing can last for minutes or days (kind of like some marriages). If you feel silly (oh, you will), try starting the story in the middle of a good spanking — sometimes the role-playing springs more naturally from the physical activity, rather than vice versa. If one of you feels particularly silly, you might find that a little sensory deprivation (see above) helps you get in character.

Playing Dress-Up

You know how all the secretly slutty posh girls love tarts and vicars because they get to wear fishnets and bunny tails? That's kind of what dress-up is: an excuse to indulge your inner 'ho. It can be part of a role-playing scenario, or just a way to get in the mood for kink. Some people call it fetish clothing, which basically means that putting it on (or seeing your partner don it) helps you get off, whether 'it' is a pair of heels, a latex bustier, or a school tie. Dress-up is not always about power play, of course, but the two are frequent bedmates. The most common clothing fetishes include leather, latex, PVC, fur, heels, boots, gloves, corsets and lingerie — items and materials that variously constrict, caress, reshape, redefine, lift and frame the body. If your fantasy involves ripping said clothes off your partner's body, scour the thrift stores for cheap, disposable wear. Keep a particular eye out for uniforms of all varieties — who knows, fucking your postman may not be so far-fetched after all.

part 3

READ THIS CHAPTER

Sexually Transmitted Diseases
You Could Have Right Now!

Don't even think about skipping this chapter, because whatever you know, it's not enough. Our sex-obsessed nation suffers from a collective case of denial — we've got one of the highest rates of sexually transmitted diseases and infections (STDs) of any industrialised country because we've quarantined the hot, wet, steamy fantasies away from the cold, harsh, health realities. But the two go together like tea and biscuits. Stigma, shame and stupidity keep people from talking openly about sex and from taking care of their own health and the health of their loved/lusted ones. But if one in five people currently has an STD, then that snarky remark you just made about the clap to a group of friends could inadvertently hurt someone's feelings. And if one in three will contract an STD at some point, then that snarky person you just fucked could inadvertently hurt your genitals.

You know why flings are called flavours of the week? Because each one might have a different STD. With over 30 flavours to choose from and millions of people infected, sex ends up being a numbers game: the more people you shag, the more likely you are to be exposed to an STD. But that doesn't mean you couldn't get something from your very first partner. So basically, when you fuck, you're fucked. Look, unless you're planning on having sex with your virgin school sweetheart for the rest of your life, you *will* be exposed to an STD if you're not careful. Hell, you can be exposed even if you are careful, because condoms can't protect you from everything (including some viral stuff like herpes and

HPV, which can be treated but have no cure). Even kissing, that most innocent and intimate of sex acts, can transmit the herpes and hepatitis viruses. That's why it's called saf*er* sex: there's no such thing as safe sex. (Except for maybe cyber sex and circle jerks.)

If we may be so bold, we're going to say that if you're sexually active then you've probably been exposed to something, whether you know it or not. You might not have anything right now, but then again, you might (which is why you should get tested). So what if we're being over-the-top, fatalistic, melodramatic, inflamed — it's not going to stop you from having sex, is it? Didn't think so. But maybe, just maybe, it'll make you reconsider wrapping the sausage and asking the awkward questions.

Did you know that most STDs have absolutely no symptoms? NONE! So no more of this 'I've never had any problems so I'm "clean"' line of BS. Here's another one to grow on: most STDs increase the chance of HIV transmission. Here's another: if you've got more than one infection at a time (oh, *it happens*), they can make each other worse. These babies aren't like the chicken pox either. You can get most of them more than once.

Here's another from the All's-Unfair-in-Love-and-War department: women are more likely to develop serious medical problems and suffer from chronic conditions caused by STDs, while guys often just carry the infections, without symptoms or complications — apparently a twig and two berries is a lot less susceptible than a whole bush. But while men may not have to worry about their dicks falling off as much as women have to fret about their reproductive organs malfunctioning, they need to take responsibility for the havoc they may be unintentionally wreaking on vaginas out there. Hey, this is tough love, people.

STDs don't have to mean the end of a relationship, but the way they're dealt with can. Whether it's denial, or ignorance or a series of rationalisations, people find all sorts of reasons to conceal STDs. Maybe you think the risk of transmission is so low in your case that it's not worth mentioning. Maybe you don't want to risk losing your new honey. Maybe you think you're using enough protection that it's not an issue. Maybe you think it's your partner's responsibility to ask. Maybe you just don't know what you've got. None of these excuses holds up in the court of love — at least, not the one we preside over. But there is a difference between not telling someone you have herpes (which you carry for life) and not telling someone you had a bout of chlamydia ten years ago that was cleared up with antibiotics. (Read each infection's section for more details.)

As far as interpersonal interactions go, be sure to have that awkward and painful discussion about sexual history with any potential partners *before* you get too frisky, because it can be much more awkward and painful after the fact. Your mind has an amazing ability to rationalise away all concern when your body is turned on. And your judgement and self-control are both further impaired when your body's loaded with booze and drugs. Stay in charge, be the boss and have control issues. Because no matter how sizzling hot you think that tryst with the twins could get, it's not worth catching something that sets your groin on fire permanently. So ask. And if you've got something, then tell. (Many clinics offer an anonymous partner notification service if you discover an STD after the dirty deed and can't bear to go back.)

We may be dreamers, but we recommend getting tested together first, too. Just because you feel like you know someone, that doesn't mean you can tell whether they're hiding an STD with your superhuman STD-vision. If you're sexually active, you should be getting tested once a year — even twice a year — for STDs. And this doesn't just mean an HIV/AIDS test and a cervical smear (the latter only checks for pre-cancerous and cancerous growths that may be caused by HPV, but not for any other specific STDs). Some doctors won't volunteer testing suggestions (especially for the young-uns they see — it's not just your parents who refuse to believe that teens like to do it), so do your home-work, know what you may be at risk for and ask to be tested for specific infec-tions by name when you visit your GP or local STD clinic for a check-up. If you're sexually active and not in a long-term committed relationship, we re-commend getting tested at least once a year for HIV, syphilis, hepatitis B, chlamydia, gonorrhoea and herpes simplex virus 2; the ladies, whether in a committed relationship or not, should also get a cervical smear to check for any abnormalities (abnormalities that are often caused by HPV), as well as a test for trichomoniasis (see the trich section in 'Ladies' Night', page 233). Any of the following may be involved: visual exam (the doc plays peekaboo with your groin, maybe using a special magnifying glass), swab test (long cotton swab inside a woman's vagina and cervix and inside a man's urethra), urine sample (pee in a cup), a saliva sample (throat culture) and a blood sample (needle in your arm). The temporary pain of the dreaded urethral swab is what keeps a lot of guys from getting tested, but for the most part swabs have been replaced with painless urine tests. If you know for sure you've been exposed to an STD, get thee to the doctor asap — the sooner you catch a problem, the better it can be treated.

The bottom line is this: if you're lucky enough to be fucking, then you need to get the skinny on any infections you or your partner has, or could have. This book is a good place to start. But we only have room for the most popular, the most infamous, the most dangerous STDs. For much more information, contact the HIV & STI Division at PHLS Communicable Disease Surveillance Centre on 020 8200 6868, or visit their website on phls.co.uk. Other nice helpful people, who can offer advice and direct you to a local STD clinic for anonymous, free help, include National Aids Helpline (they offer confidential advice, informa-tion on sexual health, STDs and AIDS – 0800 567 123; available 24 hrs), NHS Direct (help and advice on all health issues plus local family planning and STD clinics – 0845 4647; 24 hrs) and FPA Health (information on family planning and sexual health issues – 0845 310 1334; 9am–7pm Mon–Fri, Weekends 8am-6pm). Knowledge is power and power is sexy.

Viral Infections

If you're going to get an STD, try not to get a viral one — they have no cures, no vaccines and like family, you're usually stuck with them for life. But if you do, it's not the end of the world, or even the end of sex. Through various treatment options and lifestyle changes, you can manage it; hundreds of millions of people already do. The first three sections focus on the most 'popular' viral infections: HPV, herpes and HIV. These are the biggies that often have the most confusing and contradictory information on them out there. We close out the viral section with hepatitis.

HPV (Human Papilloma Virus)

HPV is the most common sexually transmitted disease in the West! One in four women has this virus and it's estimated that *more than 75 percent of sexually active people* (that's you, sunshine) will have an HPV infection at some point in their lives whether they know it or not (with most women contracting their first case with one of their first three sexual partners). But ask people what HPV is exactly and you'd mostly get shoulder shrugs and raised eyebrows. Ask them if condoms will keep them totally safe from it and they'd probably say yes — but they'd be wrong. Ask them if they've ever been exposed to HPV and they'd probably say no — but again, more likely than not, they'd be wrong.

Human papilloma viruses come in more flavours than jelly beans (about 100, if you must know). While you can get different types of HPV at the same time, it's unlikely that you'd ever get re-infected with one you've been previously exposed to, once your body has had a chance to develop immunity to that type.

Some types of HPV are not sexually transmitted and don't affect the genital area at all, like the kind that cause plantar warts on the feet or common hand warts. But about 30 types can be spread through sexual contact and end up on the vulva, vagina, cervix, rectum, anus, penis, or scrotum. Of these, some cause visible, (mostly) external, genital warts — these are most often caused by 'low risk' types of HPV, since they usually have no serious long-term effects. But the more serious of sexually transmitted HPVs are invisible (to you, anyway), causing abnormal cell changes — these are considered 'high risk' because they can occasionally lead to cancer of the vulva, the penis, anus or (in most cases) the cervix: women with HPV are ten times more likely to develop cervical cancer. (And while cancer of the penis is very rare, HPV is responsible for about a quarter of all cases.) We're going to focus on the two varieties of HPV that are sexually transmitted (this is a sex book, after all) — the ones that cause warts and the ones that cause abnormal cell changes.

The tricky thing about HPV is that it's friggin' impossible to track. Most infected people show no symptoms, don't know they have it, go undiagnosed (even after check-ups) and then pass it on. And on. And on. The incubation period is usually a few weeks to six months, but the virus can remain dormant in your skin for years before (if ever) it sprouts into a wart or starts causing cell changes. So it's often impossible to tell who you got it from, or how long you're going to have it: HPV may stick around for life, or it may clear spontaneously through your body's own immune response; it could be completely dormant and non-contagious at one point and then be 'reactivated' and contagious but without any of the symptoms at another point. And unfortunately, there aren't any tests you can take when you're asymptomatic to know for sure.

So don't be one of those wishy-washy shoulder shruggers; read on. And call one of the agencies above for more information and listings of support groups near you.

HPV: Genital Warts

Warts — there's just something about that word that's so . . . *unsexy*. Maybe it has to do with frogs and witches. But really, they're not so bad: harmless little flesh-coloured growths that usually don't hurt and won't give you cancer . . . Every cloud has its silver lining, right? (The strains of HPV that can cause cancer are covered below in 'HPV: Abnormal Cell Changes'.)

Genital warts are caused by only a few types of HPV, but those few types get around — there are hundreds of thousands of new cases a year! They're super-contagious, with about two-thirds of people who are exposed to warts during sex developing warts of their very own (often within three months). As usual, they occur less on men than on women. And while they may eventually disappear of their own accord, there's no way of knowing which ones will stay and which will go, so it's probably best to get them treated asap to reduce infectiousness.

Symptoms: Genital warts will blossom into raised or flat, smooth or bumpy, small or large, soft or hard, flesh-coloured or whitish, usually round growths. Sometimes they look like miniature cauliflower florets (cute, huh?). They can grow alone or in clusters and often show up in more than one locale. Warts don't usually cause pain or burning, but they may itch a little.

If you're a dude, you can get them on your penis, balls, or even in your urethra. If you're a dudette, you can get them on your vulva, in or around your vagina and on your cervix. Equal opportunity employers of warts include the general groin area and in or around the anus. In some very rare cases, the mouth, throat, lips and tongue aren't even safe.

You can usually see or feel warts, but remember, not all bumps are warts. Some bumps are actually secondary syphilis, haemorrhoids, skin tags (benign skin growths), skin cancers or certain penile conditions with fancy names too hard to spell. So don't decide for yourself; see a doctor.

It Gets Worse? Not always. Sometimes they go away on their own. Sometimes they stay the same as they ever were. But sometimes, while you're wishing them away instead of getting them treated, they can grow to block the openings of the vagina, anus, urethra or throat, causing pain and even bleeding (which can increase the risk of contracting HIV).

Fortunately, most types of HPV that cause most genital warts don't cause cancer. But don't get too excited: you can have more than one type of HPV infection at a time; in fact it's not uncommon to be infected simultaneously with both low-risk and high-risk HPV types. Your genitals aren't picky and they aren't exclusive, either.

A weakened immune system is like water and good sunlight to warts — diabetes, HIV/AIDS, chemotherapy, Hodgkin's disease, even poor diet and stress can all trigger a growing spree.

How It's Spread: Direct skin-to-skin contact during vaginal, anal, or (very rarely) oral sex with someone who has this infection. And by 'sex' we don't just mean penetration; simply bumping uglies can be all it takes. And condoms may not protect you if your partner's infection is on the base of the penis, balls, labia or groin. Plus, while your fingers and toys won't start sprouting warts, they can be shuttle buses for the infection between you and your partner.

Genital warts are most likely to be transmitted when symptoms (that'd be warts) are actually present, since an outward manifestation means the virus is definitely 'active'. But that doesn't mean they won't be passed when they're not visible. Check it out: it's a lot harder for genital warts to grow on an open-air penis than on a cosy, moist vagina or anus. Remember, the wart itself is not the virus, but just the body's reaction to it. So the infection might live on his willy, but not show its face until it finds a better home somewhere on *you*.

You usually can't get genital warts from warts on the hands or feet and vice versa — they are different types of viruses that are very picky about the type of skin they attack. They don't switch-hit.

Knowing for Sure: The big bummer is that there is no blood test to diagnose the viruses that cause genital warts. Oh, if only things were that simple. Unless you have visible genital warts, then you won't be able to tell if you have the HPV that causes them. And like we said before, even if you have them showing, only a clinician can confirm that they are in fact warts (and not some other skin condition). Here's what to expect:

- First, a visual determination is made by the doctor — usually during the pelvic exam for women and usually never for guys. Unless the male patient mentions he might have been exposed or has a cluster the size of Ireland growing on top of his ridge, it's just not done (for some completely incomprehensible reason), *even if he asks for the standard STD tests.* So men, be specific: if you think you've been exposed, say you're concerned about HPV and want to be examined for it.
- Then, in order to see them better or to see the ones that haven't yet blossomed (i.e., if you think you've been exposed to warts but aren't showing), the doc swabs the skin with a diluted vinegar solution (acetic acid) for five minutes and then looks for white spots with a magnifying lens and a lot of light. Don't worry, this doesn't hurt a bit.
- If there's any confusion as to whether or not the growths are

genital warts (i.e., if they are weird-looking or discoloured), the doc may want to take a biopsy (cut a snippet off) of the spot. This is a simple, normally in-the-surgery or clinic procedure requiring only a bit of local anaesthetic. It may be a little uncomfortable, but nothing you can't handle.

- If you think you've got them on the outside, make sure the doc checks inside as well: vagina, anus, pee hole. Like teens and bikers, warts prefer to travel in packs.

Taking Care: It's a virus, so you know how the story goes: there's no cure. Your own body's immune system may kick the warts' asses on its own and even scare them away forever, but then again it may not. There are several treatment options available to remove visible genital warts, get rid of symptoms and reduce the risk of transmission. The treatment given depends on the size, number and location of warts, as well as convenience and potential adverse effects. With treatment, warts often clear up for good. On the other hand, some people (especially smokers and the HIV-positive, with their depressed immune response) continue to get outbreaks for what seems like an eternity. Most people will clear warts on their own within 12 to 18 months. Some warts just stabilise in size and hang around forever.

Surgery is a common treatment, especially for warts that are everywhere, warts that are hiding inside and thus hard to reach with chemicals, or warts that are stubborn and recurring. They include: freezing the wart with liquid nitrogen (cryotherapy); removing the warts with a small surgical instrument, like a scalpel (excision); burning the warts with an electrical current (electrocautery); and zapping the warts with an intense light (laser therapy). These surgical procedures require some form of anaesthetic (from local injection to full general anaesthetic) and are thus painful. But they're usually performed fairly quickly, right in the clinic or surgery. Topical treatments involve the physical destruction of the wart: various chemicals prescribed by a doctor are applied directly to the affected area, gradually removing the wart. This method can be extremely painful and/or irritating to skin. Finally, there's immunotherapy, which involves drugs that call your own body's immune system to action. Immuno-therapy has the fewest side-effects, is painless and results in fewer recurrences than the other treatments, which is why it should be the first line of attack for warts, when possible. *Important Note for the DIY-Inclined:* over-the-counter wart treatments should never be used in the genital area.

Fighting the Good Fight: The bottom line: if you have sex, you could be exposed to the viruses that cause genital warts, whether or not your partner has visible warts or you use a condom. The more partners you have, the greater your chances of bumping into HPV strains. But are you going to stop having sex altogether? We thought not. So there are several things you can do to reduce the risk of transmission of genital warts:

- If someone has visible genital warts, then don't fuck 'em. Wait for the warts to be successfully removed in order to reduce the risk.
- Use condoms before any skin-to-skin contact to protect the skin that is covered by the condom. Your other skin is still fair game for a virus — but at least any infectious areas on the shaft will be well wrapped, and that's a lot better than nothing. A female condom may better protect a woman as it covers some of the labia area.
- Some people think that if you've had genital warts in the past, but not lately, you don't have to tell prospective fuck buddies — but we think that's wrong with a capital W. Be honest; it's not a big deal, especially considering how common HPV is but let people make up their own minds.
- Pump up your immune system with a healthy lifestyle so HPV infections don't have a fighting chance.
- On that note: don't smoke. Buttheads are more likely to develop warts and have recurring outbreaks because of a depression in their cell-mediated immune response to the HPV.
- Washing with soap and water after sex may reduce your chances of infection, but it certainly does not eliminate the risk.

HPV: Abnormal Cell Changes

The 'high-risk' strains of HPV that cause subclinical cell changes are even more sneaky because you can't see them (that's what subclinical means: invisible). A few are even sinister, with the potential to cause cancers of the genitals; for all intents and purposes, when we talk about HPV and cancer, we're pretty much only talking about cervical cancer in women (men *rarely* develop health problems, such as penile and anal cancer, as a result of these high-risk types of HPV). While some of these early subclinical infections go away on their own, with people developing their own immunity to them after a few months, others lead to long-term infections — and no one knows why. Fortunately, it usually takes years for these abnormal cell changes to become cancerous, so annual smears can throw up warning flags for treatment long before things get out of hand.

Symptoms: There are no visible symptoms and nothing hurts. That's why it's so popular with the kids these days.

It Gets Worse? In women, HPV often causes abnormal cell changes on the cervix (aka cervical dysplasia or pre-cancerous cell changes), which produce abnormal smear results. If left unmonitored and untreated, those cell changes could lead to the big C — cancer — and that's what you've got to worry about. There are a few other serious genital problems that could become an issue, but they're rarer than steak tartare. People who have anal sex (or in some cases, women with severe cervical dysplasia) are at a greater risk for developing HPV-related anal dysplasia and anal cancer.

How It's Spread: Direct skin-to-skin contact during vaginal, anal and maybe oral sex with an infected person is the best way to get it. (Again, our definition of 'sex' here is very broad — naked rubbing counts.) Most people having these kinds of 'sexual relations' will be exposed to subclinical types of HPV at some point in their sex life, but not everyone who is exposed will have abnormal cell changes (especially dudes). Some experts believe this kind of HPV is less contagious than visible genital warts. And some believe most of these infections are cleared by one's own immune system before they ever become a problem (hope, hope). But at that point, there's no way of knowing whether the HPV is totally gone or just latent and undetectable.

Knowing for Sure (If You're a Woman): If you're over 17 or if you're sexually active (whichever comes first) and you've got a vagina, then you must, you must, you must get annual smear tests. You know the drill: put your legs in the stirrups and try with all your might to relax while your GP inserts a sterile speculum into your vagina to open things up a bit so she (or he) can gently, oh so gently, swab the cervix with a small spatula or brush to collect a cell sample. Whew!

Then those cells are sent to the lab for tests. The smear can't point out by name particular HPV infections, but it can detect cervical cell changes before they have a chance to go sour (i.e., become cancer). Analysing samples is a tricky biz, because existing abnormalities are (a) not always collected in the sample and (b) not always that easy to spot. If the results look suspicious but the diagnosis is uncertain, a relatively new test, called Hybrid Capture II, can be used to check fluid samples for the genetic material of HPV in cells in order to determine whether those borderline cell changes are in fact HPV-induced and therefore potentially pre-cancerous. But remember, even a positive test doesn't necessarily mean there are any serious health risks: you can have HPV but never have an abnormal smear test, in which case further treatment is unnecessary (though you may potentially be contagious — aaaarrgh!).

When smear results unequivocally find pre-cancerous changes, no Hybrid Capture II is done because it's automatically assumed that HPV is the cause, since, um, it usually is. If the dysplasia is mild, your doctor may just have you come back in a few months for another smear to give those abnormal cells a chance to succumb to peer pressure and become normal again. (More than 80 per cent of low-grade dysplasia will resolve spontaneously over 12 to 18 months. And it's usually safe enough to wait since it usually takes years to develop cervical cancer.) Or they may have you return for a colposcopy, a procedure in which they take a peek at your cervix under a special magnifying glass to see where those abnormal cells have marked their territory. During the colposcopy, they'll usually do a biopsy (a slightly uncomfortable procedure in which a small amount of tissue is cut from the cervix) to confirm the first smear findings and rule out cancer.

Knowing for Sure (If You're a Man): There's really no easy way of knowing for sure. A biopsy is the technique most often used. But because penile cancer is so rare, because it's a bitch to get a good cell sample from the thick penile skin and because HPV tests often return false-negative results (i.e., you have HPV, but the test says you don't), the test is often just skipped.

Taking Care: We hate to say it again, but there's no cure for HPV. However, we're happy to report that there are a few treatments for moderate to severe HPV-induced cervical dysplasia. (Boys with dysplasia are out of luck, but again, they won't even know they have it and they won't suffer from it — ignorance is bliss; pity their girlfriends.) The following procedures can remove the abnormal cells before they ever become cancerous. They might also happen to remove all the cells with HPV in the process (keep your fingers crossed) and will probably reduce infectiousness, at least for a little while. Which particular treatment you can call your own will depend on a variety of factors, such as the location, size and severity of the dysplasia, your age, health history, prior treatment, yadda yadda yadda. The following treatments won't feel so great and require quite a bit of time to heal (meaning no sex for several weeks), but they are all a lot better than cancer: excision of part of the cervix with either a hot wire (LEEP) or a scalpel (conisation); freezing the cells with liquid nitrogen (cryotherapy); burning the problem tissue off with an electric current (electrocautery); and zapping the area with a laser. But if you have mild dysplasia, your doctor might choose to just leave it the hell alone since those abnormal cells may right themselves independently.

Fighting the Good Fight: You fight these strains of HPV much like you do those that cause visible genital warts: use condoms, don't smoke and . . .

- If an examination has revealed any kind of abnormal cell changes in the genitals, you can be a saint and not have sex until they've been treated or until another examination has confirmed that they've gone away on their own. However, many doctors believe this isn't a practical approach in most cases: if you're in a stable relationship, it's most likely your partner has the virus already; it can take months of observation for cervical dysplasia to resolve spontaneously or for you to go through full evaluation and treatment; and it's so hard to tell who has it and if they're contagious anyway. The most that many doctors expect is that you wear condoms and limit your partners.

- Some people — even some doctors — think that if you've had abnormal cell changes indicative of HPV in the past, but not lately and not now, then you don't have to tell prospective fuck buddies — because this kind of HPV is so pervasive, it's almost to the point of being unavoidable. But again, we say let everyone think for themselves. Besides, the more we all get used to having the tough conversations, the less tough they'll be.
- Pump up your immune system with a healthy lifestyle so HPV infections don't have a fighting chance. Especially good for intimidating cervical cancer is a diet high in beta-carotene and the vitamin B known as folic acid: yellow and orange fruits and vegetables (mangoes, corn, marrow, tomatoes), dark green, leafy vegetables (broccoli, kale), whole grains, beans and peanuts.
- Finally, if it's any consolation (and we think it is), understand that most people are exposed to one or more strains of HPV during their sexual travels and most will never even know it because they will not have visible symptoms or any serious health problems. So even though it's a big deal, it doesn't have to be a *really* big deal.

Herpes

Got herpes? You might. More than one in ten Brits is infected and three-quarters don't know they have it: one in four will have no symptoms; two in four will have only mild symptoms and are unlikely to be diagnosed; and only one in four will have more noticeable symptoms and will be diagnosed. Still sure? What makes you think you're so special, huh? We bet you swore you'd never patronise Starbucks, too, didn't you? At least you're in good company: some of our best friends are in the herpes clan (and some of them even drink Starbucks).

Herpes is a virus that can cause contagious, painful, oozing, sores, on either the genitals or mouth, on a recurring basis. There are two brands: herpes simplex virus 1 (HSV-1), which is usually found from the neck up (lips, mouth, face, eyes) and herpes simplex virus 2 (HSV-2), which is more at home on your genitals. But they have no qualms about invading each other's personal space: HSV-1 can also show up in your nether regions and HSV-2 has been spotted way up north. (HSV-1 is about four times as popular as HSV-2.) Sores below the waist go by the name genital herpes and sores above the neck are more commonly known as cold sores or fever blisters, but can also be referred to as oral herpes (especially if you're going for shock value). Experts blame the inter-breeding of the two kinds on rampant oral sex (as a national pastime it ranks right up there with footie).

Once you've contracted herpes, it considers itself family. No cure, no vaccine — everyone's a lifetime member (except you don't get a card, a funny hat or any special discounts). But unlike some of your in-laws, herpes can be taught manners: with a little practice, patience and prescription drugs, you can temper the severity and frequency of attacks and learn how to avoid 'over-sharing' (at least when it comes to the virus). And if you're lucky, like many people, your own immune system will prevent further outbreaks after the first one.

The Herpes Viruses Association (HVA) can be reached at 020 7609 9061. Visit their website at herpes.org.uk.

> Symptoms: The first sign that you've been bugged is a tingly, itchy feeling and then a burning sensation at the point where the virus made con-tact (e.g., vagina, labes, cervix, penis, balls, perineum, mouth, anus) — this usually happens within two to 20 days of exposure to the virus, but sometimes it can take years, especially in guys (herpes is a patient little fucker). Within a day of the tingles, the herpes sores come a-knocking. The sores begin their life as small blister patches; when the blisters burst (ooh, fun) they turn into weeping ulcerations and then scab over. Tingly to crusty usually takes about a week; it may take up to three weeks for the sores to get the hell out of Dodge (with or without treatment). As long as you don't pick, there should be no scarring.
>
> During the first outbreak (and any other severe attacks, though the first occasion is usually the worst and takes the longest to heal), you may experience fever, swollen glands near the infected site, and general pain in the whole infected area. If you've got a genital

case, you might experience painful peeing and urethral discharge, whether you're a gal or a guy.

News flash: Herpes symptoms hit women harder than men, though no one seems to know why. When chicks get a dose of herpes in the genital area, they'll often get sores on the cervix, too, but only during the first outbreak.

It Gets Worse? For some, herpes can be the gift that keeps on giving: about half of the people who have an outbreak of herpes will get recurring outbreaks for years, although the attacks usually get less frequent and less severe over time. The nastier the initial outbreak, the more likely you are to get reruns. And HSV-2 is a worse repeat offender than HSV-1 in the genital area. For individuals destined to have recurrences, the second outbreak usually happens within three to 12 months after the first, and on the same area of the body. (However, because all the nerves are connected down there, genital sores may spread their legs a little during recurring attacks — to the ass cheeks or inner thighs, for example.) You could get monthly (or, god forbid, more) outbreaks in the first year; after that, you'll probably get about four to five attacks per year, depending on how much effort you put into prevention (see following). Most people will stop having any recurring outbreaks about five to six years after contracting the virus.

After the first outbreak, the virus is called 'latent', even though you mat still be contagious and liable to have an outbreak at any time (which, if you ask us, doesn't exactly sound latent). And if you're really lucky, you may never get a second outbreak, although again you'll still carry the virus with you for life. Whether that means you can spread it, well, that depends (see below).

How It's Spread: Herpes comes from the Greek word for 'creep'. And does it ever. Herpes can be passed on whenever a sore touches a mucous membrane (e.g., eyes, mouth, anus, penile head, labia, vagina) or whenever a finger or toy acts as a conduit between a sore and a mucous membrane (assuming that finger or toy goes directly to a mucous membrane without passing Go — the herpes virus can't survive for longer than a few seconds in the real world). Herpes can also spread if an open sore makes contact with broken skin (e.g., if there's a cut, a rash or chafing). So you can get it from vaginal, anal or oral sex, nekkid grinding, or even kissing (depending on where the virus lives on its host). Pretty much anything more than a handshake can do it. So don't take sweets from strangers, and don't take tongue, either. But, there are no documented cases of anyone catching the virus from shared inanimate objects like toilet seats, hot tubs, towels, toothbrushes, lipsticks, etc. (thanks to the virus's short shelf life after it leaves a warm body).

But HSV has a couple of little secrets. First: more than half of the people who test positive for HSV will never have an outbreak. Here's another: a study from 2000 found that 62 per cent of patients failed to recognise symptoms when they occurred. And one more for you: recent studies have shown that some people can be contagious a few days each year even when they don't have sores (it's called asymptomatic shedding). Of course, there's no way to tell when those few days are — that would make things way too easy. During these few days when you're contagious but don't have symptoms, the virus is most likely 'shedding' from the places where your sores normally sprout (e.g., penis, labia, etc.). However, it could be shedding from anywhere in that general vicinity — the research is still coming in on this subject. During these random shedding days, the virus can spread the way it normally does during outbreaks, that is, when any of these areas touches someone else's mucous membrane (mouth, genitals, etc.).

So it seems asymptomatic shedding, as well as outbreaks so mild the carrier doesn't even *know* they're outbreaks, could be the reasons why most transmission occurs unbeknownst to both parties. Think about it: when you have active sores, the last thing you're in the mood for is rubbing parts with somebody, unless of course you're Satan. But somehow, herpes still manages to get around like a Jehovah's Witness on a scooter. Some research suggests that asymptomatic shedding may account for one-third of all instances of HSV-2 transmission to another person. According to Planned Parenthood, the chance of getting genital herpes over the course of one year from an infected partner who has no symptoms is 10 per cent. And the study from 2000 mentioned in the previous paragraph also found that 3 per cent of patients with no symptoms showed signs of being contagious. Not great odds, but not entirely dire either. The good news is that the likelihood of asymptomatic shedding seem to go down after the first anniversary of your initial outbreak. The more outbreaks you have, the more often you're likely to be contagious when you don't have symptoms – but that just means the fewer outbreaks you have, the less likely you are to asymptomatically shed. Yay! By the way, HSV-1 is much less likely than HSV-2 to be transmitted when no symptoms are present, and most cases of oral herpes are caused by HSV-1. So if you're the impulsive type who sucks face with random strangers in inner-city bar loos, you're less likely to catch the big H than the impulsive type who actually screws random strangers in inner-city bar loos.

So here's some more good news: if you have oral herpes, it's difficult to 'accidentally' give yourself the genital kind (e.g., by touching a mouth sore and then touching your special place before washing your hands), and vice versa. Here's why: when the HSV is inactive, it hangs out in bundles of nerves either at the base of your spine or at the top of it, depending on whether your HSV is responsible for outbreaks below the waist or above the neck, respectively. So if you have HSV-1 living at the top of your spine (i.e., oral herpes), your genitals are pretty much protected from HSV-1 infection because the rest of your body (below the neck) has developed antibodies against it. However, HSV-1 antibodies provide no protection against HSV-2, and vice versa. So oral herpes sufferers can get genital herpes from someone else. (Some recent studies suggest that HSV antibodies may provide a little protection against their buddy virus, but it's flimsy evidence not worth risking anything for.) And remember, it is possible to 'accidentally' give your partner the genital kind if you have oral herpes (e.g., by touching your mouth and then touching their special place before washing your hands, or by taking your mouth to their special place directly).

Knowing for Sure: If you can get to a doctor within the first few days of a sore's appearance, they'll be able to take a fluid sample from it and make a diagnosis. If the sore is dried or scabbed, it may be too late to test, so get to the doc as fast as you can.

In the absence of symptoms, a blood test can tell you if you're carrying the herpes virus. Whether you've got 1 or 2 won't make a damned bit of difference how you treat it, which is why docs often don't bother to distinguish between the two — but if you've never had an outbreak, it's nice to know where the sores are most likely to show up (an HSV-1 diagnosis means you're *most likely* infected up top, and 2 means you've probably got it down below). So ask your doc for the tests that can name names. But no test out there can tell you whether you're infected above the neck or below it; you'll just have to wait for the sores to show up. Of course, they may never show, so don't waste your life wringing your hands, sitting by the phone, waiting for them to call. Life goes on.

Taking Care: Herpes is like a bad perm: you've just got to learn to live with it. Yep, there's no cure. Look on the bright side: it's not gonna kill you, and there's no reason it should kill your sex life either. Think of your outbreaks as precious me time — catch up on all those back issues of the *NME* you insist on saving, feng shui your flat, etc. And take comfort in the knowledge that herpes is a fact of life for count- less cool kids everywhere – you're not alone.

You have two choices when it comes to treatment: taking med- ication daily, or just taking it during outbreaks (what's referred to as suppressive vs episodic therapy). The former is recommended if you have fairly regular outbreaks, like six or more times a year (because nine out of ten doctors agree, monthly outbreaks suck). If your outbreaks are pretty rare, then count your lucky stars and keep the episodic medication handy. It's worth discussing both options with your doctor, since suppressive therapy may also reduce your chances of passing on the big H when you don't have any visible sores. It's the same song and dance whether you've got 1 or 2: the big antiviral drug acyclovir (Zovirax) can be taken in tablet or suspension form as either suppressive or episodic therapy, and for either oral or genital herpes. This drug speeds recovery and lessens the severity and frequency of outbreaks.

Fighting the Good Fight, Part I — Trying Not to Spread It: *Never* have sex during a genital outbreak, *never* administer oral sex during an oral outbreak, *never* accept oral sex during a genital outbreak, and *never* make out during an oral outbreak. We don't care how many condoms you're prepared to wear, just don't do it. Cross your legs and think of the Queen or something. By the way, an 'outbreak' starts the instant you get that first ominous tingly feeling, and it's not over till the scabs have fallen off and the area is completely healed (picking them off is cheating, not to mention totally gross). In fact, you shouldn't even touch your sores if you don't want to spread them farther around the general vicinity (like to your eyes if you've got oral herpes, or to your thighs if you've got vaginal herpes, etc.) — if you do touch them, wash your hands before they go wandering anywhere. Oh, and you shouldn't donate blood or sperm during an outbreak (and you shouldn't donate blood within 48 hours of taking herpes medication, either — so if you're on the suppressive therapy plan, don't donate blood, full stop).

Between outbreaks, condoms and oral sex (or dental) dams offer some protection against the sneaky symptom-free transmission. Talking purely about penetrative sex: if a woman has herpes, her male partner will be best protected by a male condom, as that protects his most vulnerable mucous membrane, his urethra. If it's a dude who has herpes, his receptive partner (whether male or female) may be better protected between outbreaks by a Female Condom (Femidom), as this provides a teeny bit more coverage over the vulnerable receptive mucous membranes: the labia, vagina and anus — and the giving guy could well be shedding the virus from his balls, bum, etc.

But there's a big difference between 'some protection' and 'complete protection'. However small you may think the risk is for your partner, you can't make that decision by proxy, so you gotta tell. (You may have been blessed with a particularly mild version of herpes, but that doesn't mean that the virus would be as forgiving with your partner.)

Fighting the Good Fight, Part II — Minimising Recurring Outbreaks:
There's no way to prevent recurring outbreaks completely, but you *can* make your body less receptive to them by taking care of yourself and your immune system. Eat well-balanced meals every day, avoid junk food, and take a daily multivitamin supplement. At

the very least, make sure you're getting enough B-complex, C, E, A, zinc, iron and calcium. And turn to vitamin E for speedier sexual healing during outbreaks. If you're into NHS-be-damned self-medication you can also take echinacea. Chocolate, fizzy drinks, nuts (especially peanuts), rice, coffee, tea, and anything that contains the amino acid arginine can trigger outbreaks, so cut them out or at least cut back. Definitely avoid anything on this list during an outbreak. And take lysine supplements (on the same shelf as the vitamins) or eat lysine-heavy foods (spuds, milk, fish, liver, eggs, brewer's yeast, beef, lamb) to help counteract the effect of arginine.

Exposure to sunlight can coax sores out, so use sunscreen and a beach umbrella. Don't scratch your genitals or remove your lipstick with too much vigour — even stubble, on the face or the pubes, might be overly irritating. Not enough sleep, stress, even menstruation can be triggers, so try to relax, like Frankie said.

Human Immunodeficiency Virus (HIV) and Acquired Immune Deficiency Syndrome (AIDS)

The biggie. The grand poobah. The mother lode. The leader of the pack. The only STD in history to get its own Broadway musical. The scary monster that really is under your bed.

Millions have died from AIDS since it was first discovered in 1981; millions more are waiting for a cure. Every year, it's estimated that at least 40,000 more Americans get infected with HIV, the virus that causes AIDS — and maybe half of those 40,000 have not been tested and have no idea they're carrying (in some cases *spreading*) the virus. The CDC (Centers for Disease Control) estimates that between 800,000 and 900,000 are living with the HIV infection in the United States — and more than 200,000 are unaware of their infection. One in 250 Americans is infected with the HIV virus; in New York City, one in every *30* adults is.

But hey, what about the UK? It's estimated that there are currently 50,000 people living with HIV in the UK, the highest number ever. Studies by the Health Protection Agency, based on blood samples taken from the general population, estimate that about a third of these people have not yet been diagnosed. Since 1982, when reporting began, 57,692 people in the UK have

the straight people myth

Worldwide, more than 60 per cent of new HIV cases are due to heterosexual sex. In the UK, sex between men was the dominant route of HIV infection until 1998, but was overtaken by heterosexual sex in 1999. And in the United States, the number of new HIV cases among breeders is rising three times as fast as the number of new cases among gay men. So get over yourselves, hets.

the lesbian myth

Not all lezzies are lifers, you know; some of them used to (gasp!) sleep with men. And some of them use drugs. And some lesbians might be less likely to see a doctor on a regular basis than straight chicks — maybe they assume the risk is less, or they can't find a doc who's down with the Sapphic persuasion, or they don't have a pregnancy scare to drive them there.

the 'getting better all the time' myth

In the late '90s, the number of new HIV cases began to rise for the first time in almost ten years. Blame it on complacency, blame it on overly cheery AIDS drug ads, blame it on bad sex ed, blame it on a sudden onset of mass stupidity — you can blame it on whatever you want, but it doesn't change the numbers.

been diagnosed HIV positive. The number of people living with diagnosed HIV in the UK is set to increase by 47 per cent between 2000 and 2005. But you knew that all that, right?

Unfortunately, old news usually means new nonchalance (those cute little red ribbons already seem to be a Hollywood fashion statement of the past). More people may be living with AIDS than dying from it these days, but that's no excuse for reckless behaviour. If AIDS doesn't grab the headlines (or you by the balls) as often as it once did, that's more to do with lack of significant progress than lack of bad news. Of course, we'd be delighted if this section became outdated faster than our publishers could update it — check in with the resources listed below for the latest on research, drug trials, etc. But don't hold your breath.

This section is barely more than an *I See Sam* for HIV and AIDS; if you test positive you'll need more help than we have room for. The Terrence Higgins Trust AIDS Hotline is 0845 1221 200, or try the National AIDS Hotline on National AIDS Helpline 0800 567 123. To find out about the latest drug trials, contact the Medical Foundation for AIDS and Sexual Health (a charity supported by the British Medical Association). Their website is at medfash.org.uk, or you can contact them on 020 7383 6345. In the UK, the sale of any type of HIV testing kit for private use is illegal.

The following section is what everyone should know. In fact, this is what everyone should *already* know — think of it as a refresher course. If you're hearing it for the first time, then consider crawling out of that cave more often.

HIV and AIDS 101

You've seen the heart-wrenching made-for-TV specials and Oscar-winning movies, so you know the deal: the human immunodeficiency virus (HIV) weakens the body's ability to fight disease and can cause acquired immune deficiency syndrome (AIDS) — the last stage of HIV infection. HIV infects and destroys T cells, which are a type of white blood cell the immune system can't live without. (Hence a T-cell count is used to determine how far the disease has progressed, and how much damage has been done to the immune system.) As the immune system crumbles, the body becomes vulnerable to 'opportunistic' infections and diseases (the same thing happens to people who undergo chemo, and girls who drink too much and pass out at parties). AIDS is a viral syndrome, that is, a group of diseases, and it's these AIDS-related illnesses (like pneumonia, various cancers, and the number-one culprit, tuberculosis) that kill you in the end: your beleaguered body just can't fight them.

> Symptoms: Like many other viruses (e.g., herpes), HIV remains in the body for life. The average time it takes for symptoms to show is *ten years*. Ten years! That's a lot of fucking. And you're contagious from day one. Early symptoms — including slight fever, headaches, fatigue, muscle aches, and swollen glands — may only last for a few weeks, and you might well miss them (or mistake them for an extended hangover, or a nasty case of the flu). Other symptoms that may develop over time include: sudden or consistent weight loss with no explanation; long bouts of diarrhoea; loss of appetite; ongoing flu-like symptoms; thrush (yeast infection in the mouth or on the tongue — it will show itself as a thick, white coating); bad breath; severe, recurring vaginal yeast infections; chronic PID (see page 194); and swollen glands. Or you might be *completely symptom-free for years*. More long-term symptoms of HIV include: skin rashes; purple growths on the skin or in the mouth; easy bruising; random bleeding

from mucous membranes or skin growths; breathlessness; mental problems (noticeable change in personality or deterioration); loss of muscle control and strength; numbness or pain in hands and feet; and maybe even paralysis.

It Gets Worse? You have to ask? About half of all people with HIV will be diagnosed with AIDS — the final stage of HIV — within seven to ten years of infection. Eventually, nearly everyone with HIV will become ill in some way because of their infection. The official definition of AIDS is the presence of at least one AIDS-related opportunistic infection, and/or a T-cell count less than 200. (If you're a healthy sort, your T-cell count should be somewhere between 450 and 1,200.) No one has ever recovered from AIDS; it is always fatal.

How It's Spread: It's HIV, not AIDS, that spreads, and you can pass it on from the moment you become infected. You will be contagious for the rest of your life. Despite its tenacity in your body, however, HIV is a fragile little virus without you, and can be killed by plain old bleach and water (*outside* the body, that is, before you go downing any bleach cocktails). HIV is spread via blood (including menstrual blood), semen (including pre-ejaculate), vaginal fluids and breast milk. One of these fluids must get into your bloodstream in order for the virus to take up permanent residence. Unprotected anal or vaginal intercourse will do nicely (oral sex is possible, but much less likely — the mucous membrane in the mouth is much tougher). So will shared sex toys (as long as the bodily fluid is still wet when you pass the toy on, the infection can carry), contaminated needles, or getting any one of those fluids into an open cut or sore. Mothers-to-be can also transmit HIV to the foetus during pregnancy or birth. Before we knew as much as we know now (which, admittedly, is still not a lot), HIV used to be spread via blood transfusions. But that is blessedly near impossible these days. Other body fluids, assuming they're free of blood, *cannot* transmit it (like tears, sweat, pee, saliva and vomit). But you know what Sherlock says about making assumptions — so don't. Also, prolonged Frenching can cause little cuts in your mouth.

Here's how you *can't* get it, despite what your schizo Aunt Ethel told you when you were planning a backpacking trip to Europe:

tongue-free kissing, sneezing, shaking hands, sharing food, sharing drinking glasses, sharing the pot, donating blood (needles are used only once), insect bites, hugging, watching gay-themed TV shows. It can't be carried in air or food, and it can't survive for very long outside the body.

Knowing for Sure: There's only one way: get tested. If you've never been tested, put down this book right now and make an appointment. We're serious. And don't give us that old line about how you're afraid of the answer. That's not just lily-livered — it's the height of selfishness and irresponsibility. If you really can't bear to know, then fine, don't get the test, and *don't ever have sex again*. For the rest of your life. No head, no nothing. Yep, we thought you couldn't do it. So get the damn test already.

It's a simple blood test — the lab will examine the sample for HIV antibodies, which indicate the presence of the virus. These - antibodies usually show up within four to six weeks of exposure, though they may dilly-dally for up to six months. You'll get counselling before and after testing — if your doctor isn't the communicative type, then contact one of the services listed at the beginning of this section.

But maybe you've been seeing the same family doctor for 30 years. Maybe you'd like to have your test in privacy. Maybe you don't want the results on your record. Don't think any of this is an excuse for not getting tested: you do have options. At sexual health clinics or test sites, the test is always strictly confidential and only goes ahead with your say-so. Your personal doctor will not be told about the test — or the results — without your permission.

But anonymous doesn't mean going solo: you should never be on your own when you get the results, even if you're 99.9 per cent sure it's going to be negative. Call a friend.

Taking Care: There's no cure and no vaccine — did we mention that yet? However, the HIV infection can be slowed down with an expensive antiviral drug 'cocktail' (they make it sound so glamorous): it's a combination of protease inhibitors (drugs that block the enzyme that lets the virus reproduce) and antiretroviral drugs (e.g., the infamous AZT — infamous if you saw *Rent*, that is — that prevents the virus from replicating, though at a different stage). The cocktail drugs, which first became available in the early '90s, were a revolution of sorts because the HIV virus becomes resistant to single drugs very quickly. The cocktail can't help cells that are already infected, but it can reduce the all-important viral load (i.e., the amount of HIV in the bloodstream).

The opportunistic diseases can also be treated (though not always successfully). You can do your bit by living healthily, to give your immune system a leg up. Most importantly, you've gotta tell everyone you've ever had sex with (unless you're absolutely sure who you contracted it from, in which case you've just got to tell every partner since then). And then hope to god they all test negative.

But the good news is that there are some great resources out there – from books, to support groups, to information and research centres – that help people living with HIV and AIDS to regain a sense of hope, live healthily, manage stress and pain, and extend their years.

Fighting the Good Fight: You can't tell if someone has HIV. Shall we say that one more time? You can't tell if someone has HIV. *They* can't tell if they have HIV half the time. (Avert, the big AIDS advice and information centre in the UK, estimates that maybe one in three people with HIV is in the dark.) So, ask. And use condoms either way. Because people suck, people lie and people don't get tested as often as they should. (Diaphragms won't do shit, as the virus can enter anywhere on the vaginal wall.) And ferchrissakes, if you can't stay off the drugs, at least invest in your own needles. Also, don't share any personal items that could have blood on them, like toothbrushes, razors, tattoo needles, etc.

If you're talking about HIV (and if you're talking about sex, then you're always talking about HIV to some extent), there's no such thing as safe sex. There is, however, *safer* sex. For example, there have been no reported cases of HIV transmission via mutual masturbation, massage, handjobs, kissing, and giving head with a condom or dental dam. And there have been only the rare few cases as a result of deep kissing, unprotected oral sex, and *protected* vaginal or anal intercourse. You're really asking for it if you indulge in *un-*

protected vaginal and anal intercourse. Which is, of course, much more fun than 'erotic massage', but them's the stakes. You have to decide how much risk you're willing to take.

By the way, there is *no* evidence that nonoxynol-9 provides any protection against the HIV virus (see page 266). The CDC in the US swears it's working on a more effective topical microbicide (as such products are known in the biz); same goes for the big pharmaceutical companies in Britain. But don't hold your breath.

One last thing: even if you and your partner have both tested positive for HIV, you shouldn't stop worrying about protection. Your partner could have a strain of HIV that has become resistant to certain medications, so reinfection with this strain as a result of continued, unprotected sex could interrupt your own course of treatment. (In addition, other STDs are more harmful to those with HIV.) So, there really is no free love.

Hepatitis

The last of the famous, international viral infections, hepatitis comes in a veritable alphabet of versions: A, B, C, D and E. While each varies in terms of transmission, severity and consequences (if any), they are all viral diseases that affect the liver. The first two are usually the ones we talk about when we talk about sex, with the hepatitis B virus (HBV) at the head of the class when it comes to sexual transmission. And while hepatitis A is usually not a long-term troublemaker, hep B can cause permanent liver damage, liver cancer and even death. Hep C is another baddie like B, but rarely transmitted via sexual contact (especially when barrier protection is used correctly every time and there's not blood or trauma involved in the sex), which is why we've omitted it here.

Hepatitis A Virus (HAV)

This is the one that about 150,000 people get each year from unknowingly eating infected poop. For reals.

Symptoms: Most people infected with the hepatitis A virus show some combo of the following annoying, occasionally debilitating symptoms somewhere between 15 and 50 days of exposure, and which last up to five weeks: flu-like symptoms, pain in the gut, dark-coloured urine, and jaundice.

It Gets Worse? Actually, it very rarely gets worse; occasionally symptoms can linger for up to a year, but they usually, eventually, go away.

How It's Spread: The virus enters a person's body when he or she orally consumes anything contaminated with the stool or blood (even just a little) of an infected person. The virus can live in the microscopic traces of poop on a hand, a fork or an asshole for up to four hours at normal room temperature, which is why eating at greasy spoons (literally) and performing oral sex (especially rimming) are popular forms of transmission. Anal sex, kissing on the mouth, and sharing needles may also increase your chances.

Knowing for Sure: Get a blood test for the antibody to the virus, which appears about four weeks after the infection. Piece of cake!

Taking Care: There's no cure, but lots of bed rest and eating right can help make you feel better. An injection of immune globulin (sterile solutions of antibodies made from human plasma) given within 14 days of exposure to HAV may prevent illness from occurring. With or without it, most people fully recover within six months, if not sooner. And once recovered, a person is immune and won't get hep A again, nor can they spread it. For the record, it's as simple as a shot at your GP's surgery.

Fighting the Good Fight: Ask your doctor about the new combo vaccine, which protects against both A and B to kill two viral birds with one stone. Always use barrier protection, especially when engaging in oral or anal sex.

Hepatitis B Virus (HBV)

The hepatitis most closely associated with sexual transmission, B can cause chronic liver problems and, in about 4,500 cases each year, death. According to the CDC, there are over a million people in the United States stuck with HBV right now, with anywhere from 140,000 to 320,000 new people joining the club each year. In the UK, approximately 1 in 1000 people are thought to have the virus. In some inner-city areas, where there is a high percentage of people from parts of the world where the virus is common, as many as 1 in 50 pregnant women may be infected.

Five to ten per cent of adults and about 90 per cent of babies who contract hep B from their infected mothers (and who are not treated within the first hour of delivery) will continue to 'carry' the virus for the rest of their lives (these are the 'chronic' cases); it's the chronic carriers who go on to have the long-term problems and are usually always contagious, even when they're asymptomatic. The other 90 to 95 per cent of adults will recover completely and no longer be contagious (their infections are called 'acute').

Symptoms: Hep B has all the same symptoms of hep A — flu-like feeling, dark urine, abdominal pain and/or joint pain — *plus* hives, clay-coloured poo and/or arthritis during the early stage of infection. If you get symptoms (and that's a big if, because more than half of all infected adults never show symptoms), they'll start to appear more gradually than they do with hepatitis A, somewhere between six and 12 weeks after exposure.

It Gets Worse? Unlike hepatitis A, hepatitis B can become chronic and lead to scarring of the liver (cirrhosis), liver cancer, liver failure and death.

How It's Spread: The hepatitis B virus is *a hundred times* more concentrated in the blood than the HIV virus, which makes it that much more contagious. Transmission occurs when an infected person's semen, vaginal secretions, blood (including 'the curse'), faecal matter, or saliva comes in contact with someone's mucous membranes or bloodstream. So, in most cases, we're talking about unprotected vaginal, anal and oral sex (two-thirds of cases are transmitted sexually), sharing snorting straws or needles, being tattooed or pierced with infected equipment, and being born to an infected mum. In rarer cases, HBV can be got from rough kissing, being bitten, and blood transfusions (though current screening precautions taken by blood banks make this almost impossible). Don't worry about food, drinks, or casual contact like hugging and shaking hands.

Knowing for Sure: Another simple blood test is usually all it takes. But it may take two to eight months for HBV to show up in a test.

Taking Care: For exposure to HBV, a dose of hepatitis B immune globulin (HBIG), usually in conjunction with the hep B vaccine (assuming you're unvaccinated) is administered within 14 days of exposure to prevent illness. For acute (newly acquired) cases, there is no treatment. But acute viral hepatitis B usually runs a limited course (about four to eight weeks), then goes away for good (i.e., you won't have serious liver problems and you won't be contagious). Woohoo! For chronic (persistent) cases, Lamivudine is recommended — the first medication specifically formulated to treat chronic hep B. The antiviral agent interferon is given to help stop the replication of the hep B virus.

Fighting the Good Fight: Hepatitis B is preventable through vaccination. A person can choose to be vaccinated; in theory, you're supposed to be protected for at least 12 years, but high-risk individuals should be screened every five years to see if they need a booster shot. A series of vaccinations, and you're permanently protected.

Bacterial Infections

Here's the good news: bacterial infections — like chlamydia and gonorrhoea — are curable.

Here's some bad news: because they often occur without symptoms, they are easily and unwittingly spread; left untreated, they can permanently fuck you up. You don't hear about them in the news because the cures are quick and simple, but that doesn't mean you don't have to worry about them.

Gonorrhoea

The oldest known STD, gonorrhoea (aka the clap, the drip, the dose) is a runner-up only to chlamydia in the Miss Bacterial Infection Pageant. The most conservative estimates put the annual number of occurrences in the United States at 600,000 — others claim there may be as many as a whopping two mil. In the UK, the number of new cases of gonorrhoea diagnosed at genito-urinary medicine clinics has risen every year since 1995. Between 1998 and

1999 the number of cases in England and Wales rose by 25 per cent, and between 1999 and 2000 there was a further 27 per cent increase. Although men were much more likely than women to be diagnosed with gonorrhoea, the rise in incidence occurred in both sexes. The biggest rises have occurred among teenagers – between 1995 and 2000, the number of cases of gonorrhoea among young people aged 19 and under more than doubled. Gonorrhoea infects your urethra, genital glands, rectum, eyes, mouth, throat and/or reproductive organs.

Symptoms: 80 per cent — count 'em, *80* — of women and ten per cent of men with gonorrhoea show no symptoms. Zilch. Looking and feeling STD-free doesn't mean you are, suckers. If you're one of the lucky few blessed with any of the following symptoms, they'll probably start off mild within two days to a month of infection, and really kick in if the infection is left untreated. Women, who will often first develop symptoms during or immediately following their period, may experience yellow-green vaginal discharge, pain during sex or pelvic examination, frequent, often burning and/or painful peeing, pelvic or lower abdominal pain, swelling or tenderness of the vulva, menstrual irregularities and/or abnormal vaginal bleeding. Men, who are more likely to show symptoms, can experience a pus-like discharge from the urethra, as well as frequent burning and/or painful peeing. Rectal gonorrhoea is even more insidious: 90 per cent of people infected won't experience rectal itching, discharge and pain when going number two. Talk about sneaking in the back door. You can get it orally, but there's only something like three cases on record, ever, so don't freak at the next sore throat.

It Gets Worse? No one puts gonorrhoea in the corner. If ignored, chicks can develop pelvic inflammatory disease (PID, see page 194); cystitis (see 'UTIs', page 235); cervicitis, an inflammation of the cervix, which can cause chronic menstrual problems; mucopurulent cervicitis (MPC), a yellow discharge from the cervix; ectopic (tubal) pregnancy, which can kill you; and miscarriage. If you're pregnant, infections can lead to premature labour, eye infections, arthritis, and bacterial blood infections in the baby, and inflammation of the uterine lining after childbirth. Dudes can develop epididymitis (inflammation of the elongated, cordlike structure along the back of the testes); sterility; prostatitis (inflammation of the prostate); and urethral scar tissue that can lead to a narrowing or — god forbid — *closing* of your pissway. Equal-opportunity complications include skin lesions, arthritis, sterility, heart and/or brain problems and increased risk of contracting HIV. And about one per cent will get disseminated gonococcal infection (DGI), the spread of gonorrhoea in the circulatory system throughout the body.

How It's Spread: Gonorrhoea gets around via unprotected oral, vaginal or anal sexual contact. It's most likely to catch a ride during penetration (of the penis or tongue into the vagina, mouth, or rectum) or during the exchange of bodily fluids, but something like unwrapped naked dry-humping can get gonorrhoea where it wants to go, too. And remember, the clap is contagious from the time of exposure until treatment is complete, whether or not you have any symptoms.

Knowing for Sure: You can have it and not know it — you can be asymptomatic for months at a time — so the only way to know it is to get tested by your doctor on a regular basis. The procedure will either be a urine test (pee in a cup) or a swab test (specimens taken from the cervix, urethra, rectum or throat). If you think you might have rectal G, you'll need a specific test for that.

Taking Care: Finding out you've got it is the hard part; curing it is a cinch. A single dose of oral antibiotics (or sometimes, an injection) should have you in the clear within a week. You and your current partner(s) should get treated simultaneously and then stay off the sex for a week, or until your symptoms subside, whichever takes longer. If you discovered the clap because you had symptoms (e.g., it felt like you were pissing fire), any partner from the past month should get treated (yep, that means you *gotta* tell 'em); if it was spotted during a random check-up, you'll have to go back at least two months in your little black book — a whole year if you're a good citizen. If you're clapping in your pants, don't be surprised if you get treated for chlamydia at the same time: the two often travel together, like Torville and Dean (chlamydia's present in approximately 35 per cent of gonorrhoea cases). And it's cheaper to treat chlamydia than to test for it. The two

infections also have extremely similar symptoms, and some doctors
have the bad habit of mistaking one for the other. By the way, not all
antibiotics are created equal, so don't assume that one dose has you
in the clear for *all* bacterial infections.

Fighting the Good Fight: As soon as the dick pokes its head out of the
underwear, no matter where it's going, wrap it up with a condom.
And if you're travelling down under, pack a dental dam.

Chlamydia

No, it's not a flower. It's a bacterial STD that likes to mess with the
penis, vagina, anus, urethra, cervix, throat and eyes. Chlamydia trachomatis is
the most common *bacterial* STD in the States (perhaps as many as three or four
million cases annually) — and also the one least likely to make itself known via
symptoms. It's especially prevalent in sexually active people under 25, and
practically on a rampage among teens. (Apparently teenagers have unprotected sex. Who knew?) In the UK, the stats are pretty similar: cases of genital
chlamydia increased by 139 per cent between 1996 and 2002. The increase
in the number of chlamydia cases between 2001 and 2002 was 14 per cent,
demonstrating that the increase is continuing. Chlamydia is the most common
STD in the UK; the total number of new infections in 2002 was 81,680.
Chlamydia has been the most common STD since 2001, when it overtook
genital warts. This was the first time that a bacterial STD had been the most
common STD in the UK. More than 39,000 new cases of chlamydia were
reported at genito-urinary clinics in the UK in 2000 among 16–24-year-olds.

Symptoms: 40 per cent of infected men and 85 percent of infected
women show no symptoms at all (making it even more clandestine
than gonorrhoea). Any symptoms you *do* have will appear within
five days to three weeks of infection. Chicks may get more vaginal
discharge than normal (whatever 'normal' is for you), vaginal bleeding between periods, painful intercourse and/or bleeding after intercourse, abdominal pain, low-grade fever, painful peeing and the
urge to go all the time, nausea, cervical inflammation, mucopurulent cervicitis (MPC, or a yellowish, stinky discharge from the

cervix). Dudes may get pus or watery/milky discharge from the penis, pain or burning when peeing, or sore and/or swollen balls — symptoms are almost identical to those of gonorrhoea and typically very mild. Equal-opportunity complications include it spreading to the rectum or eyes — in which case either may become red and itchy and produce discharge.

It Gets Worse? If chlamydia is left untreated in women, it can spread to the fallopian tubes and ovaries, causing pelvic inflammatory disease (PID, see following, which can result in sterility. Chlamydia is the leading cause of PID in the West. Many women only learn they're infected when they discover, too late, that they're infertile. Women with chlamydia are *three to five times* more likely to contract HIV if exposed to the virus. While guys can become arthritic or infertile as a result of untreated chlamydia, the odds are they won't: only about one per cent of untreated chlamydia cases will lead to Reiter's syndrome (an inflammation of the joints) and about one-third of those cases will result in *debilitating* arthritis. Male sterility can result from epididymitis — a fancy medical term for big balls — which is another (very painful) symptom of progressed chlamydia.

How It's Spread: Again, chlamydia mimics its buddy gonorrhoea. It's spread primarily through anal or vaginal intercourse, though genital frottage will do it, too — the exchange of body fluids is not a requirement. Oral sex can also transmit it, as can shared sex toys.

Knowing for Sure: Same as gonorrhoea, above.

Taking Care: Same as gonorrhoea, above.

Fighting the Good Fight: Ditto.

Pelvic Inflammatory Disease (PID)

To put it bluntly, PID is like reproductive rot. It's a progressive infection that wreaks havoc on a woman's baby-making system: the uterus, the fallopian tubes, the ovaries — basically the entire pelvic area. In the United States, it's the number-one cause of infertility in chicks, with more than 100,000 PID victims becoming infertile each year. About a million new cases are diagnosed annually, but health experts estimate that millions more, mainly in chicks between the ages of 15 and 25, go undetected. In the UK, thousands of women are treated for PID each year. Around one in ten women with a mild case of PID are found to be infertile as a result of damage to their fallopian tubes. This can rise to one in two women who have more severe or repeated infections.

PID is a follower, not a leader: it's usually the *result* of an untreated STD or another vaginal infection. (The dreaded groupie.) For information on the other infections that are specific to the vagina, see 'Ladies' Night', page 233.

Symptoms: PID can be asymptomatic: you can have it, feel fine, and then one day wake up with a seriously broken bod. If you *do* have symptoms, they can be so mild that you just confuse them with the usual probs that come along with having a vagina. But in some cases symptoms can be so bad that you can't do much else but suffer from them. Here's what you can look for (pay special attention to the first, most common two): abnormal or 'yucky' discharge from the vagina or urethra; dull pain and swelling in the lower abdomen (starting on one side); pain or bleeding during or after sex; long or painful periods (more so than usual), or maybe a missed period, irregular bleeding (also known as 'spotting'), increased pain during ovulation; frequent urination, burning, or an inability to empty your bladder when peeing; sudden high-grade fever, or a low-grade fever that comes and goes, and we'll throw in some chills for good measure; swollen lymph nodes (usually in the groin area, but could be anywhere); loss of appetite; nausea/vomiting; pain around the kidneys or liver; lower back or leg pain; fatigue; lowered sex drive; and depression. Men can't contract PID.

It Gets Worse? *Way* worse: as many as ten per cent of women who develop PID won't be able to have kids because of scarring or damage done to cells lining the fallopian tubes. A prior episode of PID increases your risk of getting PID again, because your body's defences may have been screwed up during the initial bout. Ectopic (tubal) pregnancy is more likely to occur. And then there's chronic pelvic pain.

How It's Spread: Micro-organisms (there are several that are PID-related) enter the vagina and make their way up through the cervix, into the uterus, and through the fallopian tubes, much like evil backpackers through Europe. For example, the organisms associated with gonorrhoea and chlamydia can get into the vagina via sex (not necessarily penetrative sex) with an infected person or shared toys and then off they go! The organisms can also be spread via cunnilingus, though much less efficiently. Sometimes, there are organisms that naturally occur in your cooter which, for some reason or other, turn bad and decide to go on a destructive rampage up your genital tract. Using an IUD, douching and menstruation can help scoot the organisms along your upper genital tract. If you've got a vaginal infection, especially a sexually transmitted one, get it treated before it becomes PID.

Knowing for Sure: PID's a pain in the pelvis to diagnose. It can take anywhere from a couple of days to a couple of months before an infection is recognised as PID, if it's recognised at all. It can easily be confused with appendicitis, an ectopic pregnancy, ruptured ovarian cysts — the list goes on. And because PID can be caused by any number of organisms, there is no specific test for it. Its diagnosis is based largely on symptoms, history of specific infections like gonorrhoea and chlamydia, and a history of infertility. A pelvic exam or a microscopic examination and/or culture of vaginal and cervical secretions will usually lead to correct diagnosis. For trickier cases, an ultrasound, CT scan, or more invasive procedures may be necessary.

Taking Care: Antibiotics, rest, maybe a little chicken soup and no sex. Doctors can't always be sure exactly which organisms are causing the disease, so they may prescribe a variety of antibiotics (like penicillin, ampicillin and/or tetracycline), then have you come back in a few days to see if any of them worked, and prescribe something else if not. (In severe cases, about one in four, surgery may be needed to remove abscesses or scar tissue, or to repair or remove reproductive organs.) As always, any recent sex partners should get themselves tested, even if they don't have symptoms. No sex for them, either, until everyone's in the clear.

Fighting the Good Fight: Since PID can be asymptomatic, talk to your doctor about whether you should be examined specifically for PID.

But definitely get routinely screened for chlamydia and gonorrhoea, since those are usually the culprits of a PID infection. Use barrier protection consistently; that is, no skin-to-skin contact. And don't douche! (As if you needed another reason not to.)

Syphilis

Syph has been in steady decline in the US since 1990, from 135,000 cases reported that year down to 31,500 in 2000 (2001 saw a slight increase with more than 32,000 cases). The CDC says it might be possible to rid the US of it completely — but only if they all gang up on it. And what about the UK? The picture's not so groovy. Syphilis infections shot up in 2001, driven by outbreaks among gay and bisexual men in London and the north-west. With new cases rising by 144 per cent in the general population, and by 180 per cent for gay and bisexual men in England and Wales, this appears to be the fastest growing sexually transmitted infection (STI). But the number of cases remains relatively small. Only 102 woman were diagnosed with syphilis in 2001, compared to 614 new male cases.

Syphilis can have its ass thoroughly kicked by antibiotics, but left alone, the punk can remain in your body for life and lead to disfigurement, neurological disorders or death. Sound like fun?

Symptoms: There are four stages of infection, each with different symptoms, that may overlap or occur out of sequence. But for most of syphilis's life span, there will be no visible symptoms. In the Primary Phase, one (or maybe more) *painless*, pimply, pea-sized ulcer called a chancre (it's pronounced *shanker* and it gets offended if you call it *canker*, so don't) appears about nine to 90 days after infection on the very spot where the bacteria entered your vessel: the genitals, cervix, anus, lips, mouth, breasts or even fingertips. Sometimes it never makes an appearance. But once a chancre shows its face, it's incredibly, obnoxiously contagious, just jonesing to get its grubby little hands on someone else's skin. After about one to six weeks it will heal, with or without treatment, even though the bacteria is still growing and spreading throughout your body.

The Secondary Phase includes any of the following symptoms,

which may appear from three to six weeks after the sore(s) appear, and may come and go for up to two years: a nonitchy rash in brown, rough, penny-sized patches (affectionately called money spots) anywhere on the bod (especially on the palms of the hands and the soles of the feet), that contains active bacteria and can spread the disease; flu-like symptoms; hair and weight loss; and greyish-white sores in your mouth, throat and cervix.

It Gets Worse? The third phase, called the Latent Phase, occurs between other phases (or can overlap them), has no symptoms (save for maybe small bumps called tumours that can appear on your skin, bones and internal organs), and lasts ten to 20 years. After a few years of latency without any secondary symptoms, you are no longer contagious. Finally, the Tertiary Phase is when things *really* start to get fun. Two-thirds of untreated syphilis cases end up leading to no serious problems, *but* — and this is a big but — the syphilis bacteria in the other one-third continue to invade inner organs like the heart and brain, causing minor inconveniences like blindness, heart disease, crippling, central nervous system problems, mental incapacity and freaking death! But there are two things to feel good about: it's not infectious at this point, and it doesn't ever have to get to this point with today's cures.

How It's Spread: Here's how it's *not* spread: via toilet seats, doorknobs, hot tubs, shared clothing and eating utensils. (It's a pretty fragile bacteria that can't hang onto those things.) Here's how it *is* spread: via vaginal, anal and oral sex, intimate contact, kissing and pregnancy. It's most contagious during the primary phase — when syphilis-inspired sores, warts, or rashes anywhere on the infected person's body come in contact with someone else's mouth, genitals, anus or broken skin — which is why syphilis is known mostly as a sexually transmitted disease.

Knowing for Sure: There are three main ways to get tested: a blood test (incubation can take as long as 90 days); a sore sample examination (called a dark field); and if you've got central nervous system problems (poor soul), then an examination of your brain and spinal cord fluid.

Taking Care: You can stop syphilis dead in its tracks at any stage of infection, but damage already done (like heart disease or blindness) can't be undone. The favoured treatment is a shot or two of penicillin in your bum *and* your partner's bum, since the two of you can otherwise end up passing the bacteria back and forth like an evil little basketball.

Fighting the Good Fight: Latex condoms offer good protection during vaginal, anal and oral intercourse, *but not complete protection*, since those contagious sores and rashes may be anywhere on the body.

Parasitic Infections

The dictionary's biological definition of a parasite is 'an organism that grows, feeds, and is sheltered on or in a different organism while contributing nothing to the survival of its host'. But we prefer its secondary definition: 'One who habitually takes advantage of the generosity of others without making any useful return'. That's crabs and scabies for ya — those creepy-crawly things that make you itch just thinking about them. (Yeast and trichomoniasis are also parasitic infections, but we'll deal with those bugs later in 'Ladies' Night', page 233.) The good news is, as long as you're paying attention to what's going on down there, the worst they can do is totally skeeve you out.

Pubic Lice (Crabs)

These little parasitic suckers climb onto millions of unsuspecting sets of genitals every year, feeding on human blood like a bad horror movie. They like to cling to pubic hair, but will settle for eyelashes, eyebrows and armpit hair.

Symptoms: Crazy itching in the genitals or around the anus, usually starting five days after infestation begins, though some people don't itch at all; mild fever; feeling run-down; irritability (hey, you'd be pissed off too if you had tiny insects infesting your pubes); and/or lice and/or nits (small egg sacs) in your pubic hair. The eggs take about a week to hatch.

How It's Spread: Mostly through intimate and sexual contact (not just intercourse); *occasionally* via infected bedding, clothing, upholstered furniture and toilet seats (though their lice boots aren't made for walkin' on smooth surfaces like porcelain, so it's next to impossible). If a louse falls off a person, it dies within one to two days. But the bummer is that the eggs can live for about seven days. Scratching can sometimes transfer lice to other parts of the body, so resist the urge.

Knowing for Sure: Crabs is one of the few STDs you can self-diagnose — especially if you've got good eyes or a magnifying glass. If you're not sure or just can't bear to look, visit your doc.

Taking Care: Treat yourself, your roommates, and anyone who's been up close and very personal recently with an over-the-counter medicated pubic lice shampoo, even if they don't have symptoms. After the shampooing, most nits will still be clinging to the hair shafts, and can be removed with fingernails or a nit comb. Put on clean undies and clothing . . . DUH! Wash and heat-dry any clothes, bedding and towels that you've been near in the past week. Dry-clean anything that's not machine washable. Vacuum the whole place.

Fighting the Good Fight: Condoms don't protect you, so ask the hard questions.

Scabies

This contagious skin condition is caused by little buggers that favour warm, fragrant places like your private parts; they burrow under the skin laying eggs and dropping doodie as they go. They also produce secretions, which cause an allergic reaction within several weeks. After about ten days, the eggs hatch, spawning a whole new round of parasites — just like in *Alien*, only a lot smaller.

Symptoms: Mad itching, especially at night. Look for little reddish-brown bumps, like tiny bites or pimples, or small, curling lines. The rash can show up wherever the skin is warm and moist due to folds of skin, tight clothing, or jewellery. It can take up to a month for any symptoms to appear.

How It's Spread: Because it takes a while for symptoms to develop, you can have it, not know it, and pass it on. Anything from a handshake to a handjob can spread scabies, though the latter is more common. Mites can live for up to 24 hours just hanging out in your bed, towels or furniture, waiting for you (or your roommate) to come home.

Knowing for Sure: Scabies is often mistaken for eczema, poison ivy and allergies. The mites are too small to be seen with the naked eye, so don't bother trying to diagnose yourself. You'll need prescription meds anyway.

Taking Care: Pick up the prescription medicine (and make sure your partners and roommates get some, too), then do as you would if you had crabs (see 'Taking Care' in the Crabs section above). The rash and itching may stick around for up to two weeks after treatment, but that doesn't necessarily mean you're still contagious — if all infected parties have been treated at the same time, and you've descabied your living environment, a celebratory hump 24 hours after treatment should be safe.

Fighting the Good Fight: If you've got an itch, don't scratch it; go to the doctor instead.

13

PUTTING UP WALLS

Condoms, Condoms, Condoms

'You've just read Nerve's entire chapter on sexually transmitted diseases and infections–what are you going to do?'

'I'm going to Condom Land!'

There is a long-standing fire-and-brimstone tradition of public health taking a backseat to religion. Misinformation about condoms is widely disseminated by anti-choice radicals from here to Downing Street, mostly at the expense of the health of women and teens — including blatant lies like 'safe sex education encourages promiscuity' and 'the HIV virus can leak through the pores in latex' and 'condoms can cause cervical cancer'. *Ahhhbullshitchoo!*

The scientifically sound results are in. Honest, fact-based safer sex education programmes and easy access to condoms help reduce rates of disease and pregnancy among teens who are already sexually active. Consistent and correct condom use reduces the risk of HIV transmission by as much as 10,000 times (the studies that reported the HIV virus leaking through latex were done using particles 100 million times smaller than the HIV found in semen). And while condoms admittedly do not cover all the genital skin through which some infections can be passed (such as herpes and HPV), they do cover the areas of the penis where the majority of sexually transmitted diseases and infections hang out. In fact, *failure* to use condoms has been shown to be one of the highest risk factors for contracting the HPV infections that can cause cervical cancer.

By reducing the exchange of the bodily fluids most likely to carry sexually transmitted diseases (ejaculate, vaginal secretions, saliva, sore discharges), condoms are pretty much the only form of birth control that can help protect against said STDs. (Diaphragms and spermicides might help with some infections, but they don't hold a candle to condoms.) When your worries about STDs and pregnancy are reduced, you can better focus on the matter at hand: you and your partner's pleasure. Condoms are readily available, inexpensive (on average, about 90 pence a pop), disposable and cause few side-effects, if any. Plus, if you get the really thick kind, they can make sex last longer. Goooooooo, condoms!

Step One: How to Use Condoms

You must introduce condoms into the love scenario *before* any genital contact is made — bareback poking around increases your chances of catching an STD (whether through skin-to-skin contact or bodily secretions) and getting pregnant (yes, there can be traces of semen in pre-ejaculate, see page 216). If there's foreskin involved, pull it back. Pinch out the air from the receptacle end or top centimetre or so of the condom with your thumb and forefinger. Hold it against the head of the penis, leaving some space for any future fluids to collect and roll the condom all the way down the shaft to the very base — as far as it will go — smoothing out any air bubbles along the way. (Push any foreskin towards the tip beneath the condom to allow for more FS mobility.) You can add a few drops of store-bought water- or silicone-based lubricant to the outside and inside of the condom for everyone's pleasure and safety. For closer encounters of the rough and/or anal kind, go with a thicker condom. Air bubbles, a tight fit and dry friction = greater chance of breakage = bad.

In the unfortunate but unlikely event that the condom breaks, don't panic. Put on a new one immediately. The jury's still out on whether inserting spermicides after a mishap can reduce the chance of pregnancy — just don't douche, or you might actually increase that chance by pushing sperm farther up the egg trail. And as far as STDs go, while spermicides have been found to kill some bacteria and viruses, they can also cause irritation that may actually promote the spread of some infections (like HIV). Talk to your doctor within a day about emergency contraception (aka the condom's back-up method, page 227) and STD testing (page 161), because the sooner you act, the better off you'll be.

Tough Love: How to Enjoy Condoms

If we hear any more whining about how condoms are annoying, uncomfortable deal breakers, we are going to *puke*. Could it be you've been using non-lubricated, inch-thick, five-pence prophylactics from a vending machine all your life? So condoms don't figure in your full-on, flesh-to-flesh fantasy world — we get it. We're also sure that oozing genital ulcers and child-support payments don't pop up in that utopia either.

If you make putting on a condom an integral part of sex, it's inherently sexy. What could be hotter than kneeling above your luvva, staring them straight in the eye, tearing the wrapper off a condom like a mini striptease and *oh so slowly* unravelling it over the throbbing specimen in play? As Yogi Berra once said, 'Half this game is 90 percent mental.' If you think it's hot, then it will be.

Granted, sensual pleasure was not a top priority for the condom industry during most of the 20th century and very few technological advances were made. But leave it to good ol' fashioned international economic competition to finally create some innovation in the biz. About ten years ago, Japan threatened to lure customers away with their new, ultra-thin inventions, so the big Western companies finally stepped up to the plate. Today there's a whole slew of new materials, shapes and sizes designed not only to protect, but to provide pleasure. Who knew?

The key is to invest in that pleasure. Experiment with different brands. Seek out thinner varieties for a warmer, more natural feel — as long as they're government approved, they've passed the same safety requirements the thicker brands have. And if you're still having trouble getting over the hump during a hump, then practise: masturbate with a condom to condition your cock-a-doodle for 'the real thing'. Gals, don't just leave it up to your partners to provide; have an opinion on the matter — and supplies on hand. And everybody, pay a little extra, would you? These are your family jewels, after all. Don't they deserve the very best?

Shapes

Once upon a time — 1993, to be exact — a clever Indian surgeon by the name of A.V.K. Reddy thought outside the condom box and designed a prophylactic with, get this, pleasure in mind. *Ingenious*. The resulting Pleasure Plus condom has a patented, asymmetrical pouch of extra ribbed latex that lines up with the sensitive frenulum (where the underside of the shaft meets the head). More room means less constricted nerve endings; extra material means extra stimulation. The ladies even benefit from the bunching that occurs near the base.

After Reddy's company went bankrupt and he lost his Pleasure Plus rights to another condom manufacturer, Reddy had to start over. We like to think he just couldn't get rid of the voices in his head, à la *Field of Dreams*: 'If you build it, they will come.' Well, build it he did. Though the Inspiral looks like a balloon sculpture on acid, its bulging pouches spiral around the head of the penis for a looser fit and much more sensitivity. It was designed with the penis in mind, but women really seem to go gaga for it, too. It's one of the most expensive latex brands out there, but add a little lube inside the head and you'd probably be willing to pay double.

And now it seems Trojan's caught on to this whole 'pleasure' thing with their new Trojan Her Pleasure: a latex condom that balloons out *midway* up the shaft, all the way up to the tip, with 11 alternating rows of raised bars around the bottom half of the shaft. These ribs for her pleasure might actually work for once, since they line up with the outer third of the vagina during penetration — where it counts. The loose fit of the top half should help put a smile on his face, too.

Materials

You name it, condoms have probably been made from it at some point during their centuries-old history: oiled silk paper, papyrus soaked in water, fish bladders, linen, thin leather, tortoiseshell, animal horn, human muscle tissue, gourds, sheep intestines ... In fact, some are *still* made from animal membranes for those allergic to latex. Delicately referred to as 'lambskin condoms', these hoods have a natural feel and keep runaway sperm from escaping, but they are too porous to keep the HIV virus contained. So unless you're in a monogamous, HIV-negative relationship, fugghedaboutit.

Condoms became 'rubbers' when they began being mass-produced from latex, a strong and thin-pored type of rubber, in the mid-1840s. Today, it's still the prophylactic material of choice for producers and consumers, as it protects against pregnancy and HIV transmission (not to mention the fact that it's cheap). But latex is not without its faults: it smells kind of, well, rubbery; it disintegrates when combined with oil-based lubes; it can feel like wearing a thick winter sock; and it's prone to breakage under duress (e.g., too tight a fit, or not enough lube). But that's just nitpicking when you consider all the sexual freedom latex provides you.

The newest godsend in the condom department is polyurethane — cue the singing angels! — the material of the future, a Walt Disney wet dream, *plastic*. The benefits of polyurethane are myriad: much, much thinner, odour-free and tasteless, transparent and thus respectful of every erection's inherent beauty, not as sensitive to direct heat and light, compatible with any and all lubricants (including oil-based ones), more heat conductive than latex (a major factor in men's pleasure) and hypoallergenic. But — and there's always a but — it's not as elastic as latex, so it can't stretch as much before breaking (which is just another great reason to use lube — it helps reduce the likelihood of breakage). While laboratory tests have proven that sperm and viruses (including HIV) cannot pass through a polyurethane wall (it's 100 per cent non-permeable), the government health agency has yet to establish a protocol for testing the material's rates of effectiveness against STDs and pregnancy and therefore cannot wholeheartedly recommend it for such in good conscience. Still, in all the years Condomania.com (one of the leading online retail condom stores in the US) has been selling the polyurethane condoms available (Avanti Super Thin [that's Durex Avanti in the UK] and Trojan Supra), they have never received any complaints about their effectiveness.

Lube

Condoms can be lubricated, lubricated-with-spermicide, or non-lubricated. The first kind are either coated with water-based lube (aka jelly) or, more commonly, have silicone-based lube built in. Just remember that silicone lube will destroy silicone toys, so when you're swapping props, be sure to use condoms with water-based lube only. Most lubricated condoms automatically

branded a fool: how to choose a condom

Who are we to presume what you'll like, what will work for you? Well, we're Nerve and presume we will. The following are some of the best condoms available from a whole slew of legit online condom retailers. Sites like condomcare.co.uk, Lifestyles Condoms (14-condoms.co.uk/lifestyles-condoms) and Passion Online (passiononline.co.uk) offer discreet shopping, safer sex education and a huge selection. (Just be sure to do a little price comparison, because the biggest sites are occasionally the most expensive.)

- *Pleasure Plus: the forerunner of the pleasure revolution (see 'Shapes'). Twelve-packs are available in an aluminium carrying case.*
- *Inspiral: the son of the Pleasure Plus (see 'Shapes'). One of the most expensive latex brands out there, but fans say they're worth it.*
- *Trojan Her Pleasure: the latest addition to the new shape latex rage (see 'Shapes').*
- *Crown Skinless: sheer, straight-walled and lightly lubricated, Japan's Crowns are the thinnest latex condom money can buy (0.0001 cm thick) — which just goes to show, money can buy you love. Could probably benefit from a few extra drops of your own water- or silicone-based lube. Not easy to find in the UK, but we've sourced them on the Internet, so give it a try.*
- *Trojan Magnum XL: the reigning champion in the heavyweight category. Magnums are the largest condom available — they're 30 per cent bigger than 'normal' latex condoms. The base is tapered, but that doesn't mean just anyone can wear one; if you're happily average, this thing will look and feel like a leg warmer.*
- *Durex Avanti (Super Thin): the first polyurethane condom for men. Not only is it the thinnest condom available in the world (0.000015 cm thick), it's also the widest and one of the shortest. But while the Avanti boasts heat conductivity, strength and oil-lube compatibility, its crackly and crinkly texture may take some getting used to.*
- *Trojan Supra: the only other polyurethane male condom available. To one-up Avanti, Trojan used a medical-grade polyurethane formula called Microsheer that's softer, more comfortable and completely clear, making this the first invisible condom. But the helmet heads at Trojan fucked it up by only offering the Supra with nonoxynol-9. Bummer.*

come with spermicide to help prevent pregnancy — which is great if that's your only concern. But if STDs are, too, then drop the condom and walk away — nonoxynol-9, which is the condom manufacturers' spermicide of choice, has been shown in some studies to cause vaginal irritation, which can help spread infections like HIV. Non-lubricated condoms may be the best way to go, because then you can custom-pick your lube to suit you, your condom and your toys. If we haven't made it painfully obvious already, we're staunch advocates of lube — a little drop on the inside of the right condom, a little on the outside and paradise is in your third arm's reach. See 'The Importance of Lube' on page 263 for more deets.

Size

If we've said it once, we've said it once: it's not the size of the boat but the motion of the ocean. However, you've got to outfit that boat properly if you want smooth sailing. Experiment with different lengths, widths and shapes to get the right fit — a millimetre or two could make all the difference. If a condom is too tight, not only will it break more easily, it'll choke the nerve endings in the penis, reducing sensitivity. And if it's too short, it'll leave more skin exposed to possible infection and slip off more easily (though this is usually only a problem for men of the most porno proportions). Read labels: some companies use the term 'large' to refer to diameter, rather than length, so be sure you're on the same page. For more headroom and thus more sensation against the head from the loose material, choose a condom that's wider at the tip and tapered at the shaft (the different diameters may be listed on the label or it may say 'oversized tip' or 'balloon top'). Just be sure it's not too loose, or you and your pride (not to mention your partner) will be headed for dangerous waters. There are a couple of snugger brands available – try Trojan Ultra Fit, Durex Close Fit, or something strangely named Beyond Seven Ribs and Dots. That's right, there's no such thing as 'small' in the condom biz. Smart cookies.

Bonus Points: Flavas, Colours, Textures

We know you don't want to hear it, but you can give and get diseases like gonorrhoea, chlamydia, genital herpes, syphilis, HPV and HIV from having unprotected oral sex (see STDs on page 161 and Oral Sex [Dental] Dams below). Of course, licking latex is about as tasty as sucking on a rubber band (to say nothing of the spermicide that might temporarily numb your tongue). Here's when you reach for the flavoured barrier protection. Since flavoured brands are only available in latex, it'll still taste like you're sucking on a rubber band, but at least it'll have some kick: strawberry, vanilla, chocolate, orange, tangerine, banana, grape, mint, even cola. Plasticky-tasting polyurethane condoms don't come flavoured, but you can add lickable products like ID Juicy Lube, or even chocolate sauce and whipped cream, since the oil in those foods won't damage polyurethane (unlike latex). Whatever flavoured agent you use, just be sure to keep it away from sensitive vaginas to avoid infections and allergic reactions.

To go bump in the night, try textured condoms. Traditional ribbed ones look a bit like flexi-straws (OK, so you have to squint to see the resemblance); designed for the non-penetrating partner's pleasure, ribbed condoms may or may not do it for you — we think probably not, though a placebo effect may be all ya need. Trojan Her Pleasures (see 208) may work better than others, since they've got the ribs in the right place. Or try ultra-thin condoms with tiny bumps or studs on the outside, inside, or both. Trojan Extended Pleasure latex condoms are the first to contain a desensitiser — four per cent benzocaine — in the lubricant. But whatever you use, just make sure it's CE approved and has a British kitemark and not some novelty item they've been selling at the pound shop for the past 20 years.

The Female Condom (Femidom)

For the independent woman who wants full control over STD prevention and birth control (or for the idiot who would still consider sleeping with a man after he refused to wear a condom), there's the *Female* Condom. Previously known as Reality Condom and sold as Femidom in Europe, they are exclusively made by the Female Health Company. The Female Condom is a flexible, pre-lubricated, polyurethane, tube-shaped pouch. A soft circular ring is inserted into the closed end of the pouch, which is then inserted into the vagina past the pubic bone. The pouch lines the walls of the vagina and the open end, which is attached to another soft circular ring, hangs outside. When you're finished, you just twist the ring to cinch the sack and gently pull it out. It's like a bin bag for your love can!

Pros of the Female Condom

- No prescription or fitting — it's available at chemists and supermarkets in a convenient one-size-fits-all.

- You can put it in up to eight hours before you're ready to commence the boot knockin'.
- Because it's made of polyurethane, it's super-thin, strong, heat conductive, odourless and compatible with all lubricants.
- The manhood can enter the sheathed vagina *before* being fully erect (unlike male condoms, which can only be rolled onto a stiffy).
- Because there's more room to move around (it's wider than a traditional condom), it's less likely to break.
- It allows women and men to switch off the responsibility of 'wearing' the condom ('Honey, it's your turn tonight').
- The outer ring covers part of the outer labia, which means less genital skin-to-skin contact, which could mean greater STD protection.
- The outer ring may stimulate the clitoris!
- Once the penis has popped its cork, it can linger for some quality cuddle time because there's no risk of the Female Condom slipping out (like there is with a traditional male condom).

Cons of the Female Condom
- A penis with very bad aim could miss the tube and accidentally end up between the vagina and the tube, defeating the whole purpose.
- It's a little more expensive than traditional condoms, about £2 a pop.
- The polyurethane's crinkly texture may make a little noise (but your moans should drown it out).
- Having one end of a plastic baggie hanging out of your cooter may not be the most aesthetically pleasing thing in the world.

As with anything new to your vagina, the Female Condom may take some practice getting inside and getting used to (but if you've ever used a diaphragm, it'll be a breeze). Expect it to move a little during the old in-out, but not so much that it's distracting. Just be sure to add a little extra lube either inside the pouch or on the penis to prevent the thrusting member from pushing the outer ring inside. When used correctly, its pregnancy prevention rates are only slightly lower than those of male condoms. Use it on the go, use it during your period, use it when you need a change, you can even use it in your ass, female or not. (The Female Condom hasn't been approved for butt play by the health authorities, but many couples are satisfied with removing the inner ring, anally inserting the pouch with their probe of choice and going at it.) Finally, while the desire to provide your genitals with the most protection possible is commendable, there is such a thing as overprotection; don't double up the Female Condom with a traditional male condom, or they might end up sticking to each other and sliding off.

Oral Sex (Dental) Dams

Yes, people actually use them. The smart ones, at least. Like we've said before, partaking of someone's sweet succotash pie can transmit infections like gonorrhoea, chlamydia, genital herpes, syphilis and HIV — both ways. For years, sheets of latex designed for oral surgery known as dental dams have been cleverly co-opted by *love* doctors to help keep oral-vaginal and oral-anal dining disease-free. Other people have used cling film (no latex taste!), or a cut-open condom or latex glove when they're catching a quick bite. But why not do it right? Glyde Dams are *made* for licking. Glydes are thin natural rubber latex available in assorted flavours (pink strawberry, purple wildberry, cream vanilla, or black cola) that are glycerine-free, which means no risk of yeast infections. And less than a quid per sheet! Just hold the barrier firmly in place over the area that's being eaten out, using only one side per meal. (It's not like a pillow — you can't turn it over to get to the cool side.) Use it once and then throw it away — don't save it for leftovers.

See the following chapter for your other birth control options.

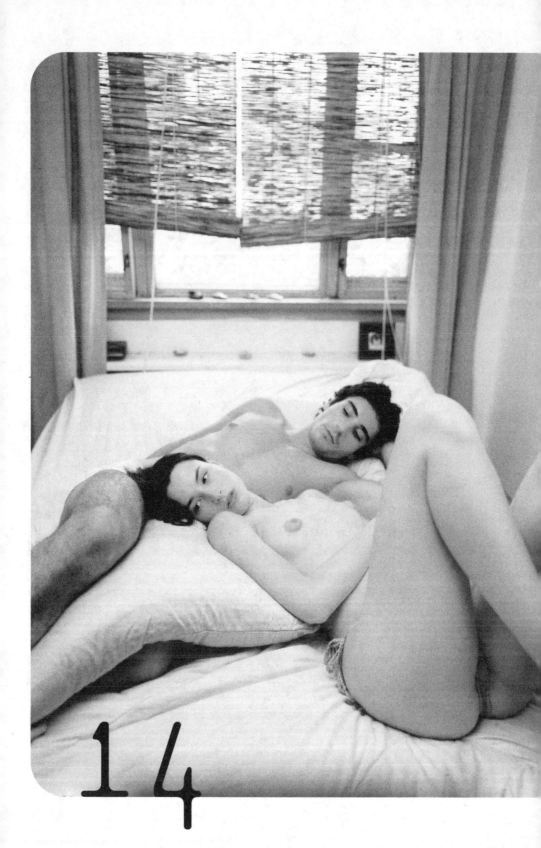

14

THE CHOICE IS YOURS

Birth Control and Emergency Contraception

Where do babies come from? The Land of Poor Planning, half the time. Each method below has pros and cons in terms of cost, side-effects, convenience, effectiveness and how well it meshes with your lifestyle. What's ideal for a young married couple may not work for a kissing bandit looking to back up her condom protection. All the options here, with the exception of sterilisation, are considered reversible birth control; that is, you can always change your mind — sometimes after minutes (e.g., a diaphragm), sometimes after months (e.g. Depo Provera).

Needless to say, this section is about het sex. More importantly, this section is not about sexually transmitted diseases and infections: one or two of the methods provide minimal STD coverage, but they should only ever be used without a condom if you're in a committed monogamous relationship and you've both been tested. If that's not you, then contraceptives should only be used as a pregnancy safety net in case the condom breaks. Most of these methods are nearly 100 per cent effective in preventing pregnancy *when combined with a condom*. Wonder Twin powers, activate! (See the previous chapter, 'Putting Up Walls', for the lowdown on condoms and oral sex [dental] dams.) If your dual action should somehow fail you, we outline your emergency contraception options at the end of this chapter. And remember, the following pages serve only as an outline of your options; reproductive decisions should be made after consulting a doctor you trust.

Note: the efficacy rates of the birth control methods listed below were taken from statistics reported on PlannedParenthood.org in December 2003.

The Nick of Time (Withdrawal)

How it works: You're going, you're going, you're going ... and then right before the man ejaculates, he pulls out.

Batting average: Since no one's perfect, there's a whopping 27 per cent chance of pregnancy. But if the guy has a great sense of timing, there's only a four per cent chance of pregnancy. Here's the whole deal on the pre-come thing: there's no sperm in the natural penile lubricant that's emitted into the urethra before ejaculation to help pave the way for the semen to come. However, there is a chance that sperm from an earlier orgasm can be left over in the urethra and thus picked up and pushed out by the pre-ejaculate during the next go-round. However, since the numbers that get left behind are so small and since they're usually cleared out with one good piss, withdrawal done absolutely positively *correctly* — which it rarely is — is actually more effective than a diaphragm, cervical cap, or spermicide. Yeah, we can't fucking believe it either.

Pros: No side-effects, no props and you get to see the money shot.

Cons: It requires superhuman self-control, self-knowledge and trust; the woman has very little (if any) control; his orgasm is tainted by low-grade panic.

£££: Free.

The ideal candidate: A married couple where each party is secretly hoping for a happy accident.

Mother Nature May I? (Fertility Awareness or 'Rhythm' Methods)

How it works: While an egg is only fertilisable for a day or so, there are several days in each menstrual cycle when a woman is conception-friendly: six to seven days before ovulation and two to three days after — because an egg can live for up to three days and sperm can live inside a woman for two to three days and, in rare cases, a week.

You work with a clinician to figure out when these 'unsafe' days are for you, using a combination of 'rhythm' methods — checking your temperature daily (because ovulation raises your body temperature half a degree), checking your cervical mucus daily (because ovulation turns it clear and slippery) and charting your period on a calendar (if you're very regular, you can better predict ovulation). On 'unsafe' days, you use one of the other methods in this section. To be extra safe, some women consider their unsafe time slot to begin with their period and end four days after ovulation.

Batting average: It's 75 to 99 per cent effective, depending on how many FAM methods you combine and what back-up method you use on your unsafe days. Studies have shown FAM to be less effective for single women.

Pros: No side-effects; no Catholic guilt (if abstinence is your back-up plan); you're getting back to nature.

Cons: Requires training, vigilance, patience and dedication; it's much less effective if you have an irregular cycle, uncooperative partners, or if your office skills suck; stress and illness can throw off your cycle or skew your readings.

£££: About a fiver for an accurate thermometer. The fertility-tracking computer will set you back a few hundred.

The ideal candidate: You're in a long-term relationship, you were editor of your school yearbook and you like to hike nature trails.

The Pill (The Pill)

How it works: The most popular contraceptive, the Pill is a dose of synthetic hormones (like those produced in a woman's ovaries) taken orally once a day. There are two versions — progestogen-only pills and combined pills — which both come in monthly packs. The progestogen-only pills contain — you guessed it — progestogen, which thickens the cervical mucus to prevent fertilisation and keep fertilised eggs from imbedding in the uterus (it may also prevent ovulation). Progestogen-only pills are available in 28-day packs, with each pill containing hormones (i.e., you have to take them all). Combined pills contain progestogen and oestrogen; they are

is menstruation necessary?

Three things in life are certain: death, taxes and menstruation. Right? That angry red curse that makes women cramp, groan, swell and cry is unavoidable, isn't it? It's normal, right? Well ... is it? Some women don't think so. Some women (including many gynaecologists) practise what's called straight-cycling — that is, they take three-week packs of birth-control pills back-to-back, avoiding the seven-day pill break and thus skipping their periods altogether. They just keep on cyclin' for months, maybe even years, without periods. Abominable, you say? A crime against nature, thou doth protest? Well, the old-school theory that there is a cleansing value to monthly bloodshed has been taking some flak lately, especially as the bleeding for a woman on the Pill can, over time, become so little as to be inconsequential. Women today actually menstruate far more often than our ancestors did, thanks to the amount of time the ladies of old spent barefoot and pregnant or breastfeeding. Going straight isn't for everyone, though. It will only work with monophasic pills (i.e., the ones that contain the same concentration of hormone in each pill, not the triphasic kind like those that control acne) — ask your doc which one you're on. And even then, some women can't trick their bodies and will spot or menstruate anyway. Also, if you're the type of gal who needs Aunt Flow for reassurance that you're not prego, this is not for you. But it's a nice option to bear in mind for that two-month camping trip, or if your period's scheduled to show up on your honeymoon. And it's often recommended for women who suffer from endometriosis, anaemia, or severe menstrual cramps and migraines. However, we must insist that you talk to your doctor before departing the Red Sea for unknown waters.

designed to thicken cervical mucus and prevent ovulation. These come in either 21-day or 28-day packs: if you're prescribed the former, you take a week off at the end of each pack to allow for menstruation; the extra seven pills in the latter are hormone-free reminders to keep you in the habit of popping. (They're often iron supplements, so don't toss them — take them, especially if you're a vegetarian!) No matter which Pill you're on, Aunt Flow will usually visit during the fourth week. The Pill is supposed to kick in within a week, but just to be on the safe side, most doctors recommend using a back-up birth-control method for at least a month. There's no need to take a break from the Pill, no matter how long you've been on it.

Batting average: Typical use (i.e., accounting for human error) of the Pill has an eight per cent failure rate. If you take it every day at the same time, that failure rate drops to about 0.3 per cent. (But only

28 per cent of women achieve Pill perfection.) If you miss a day or more, check the packaging instructions for a game plan — it varies from pill to pill.

Pros: Regular, lighter periods with less cramping and PMS; less chance of iron-deficiency anaemia and pelvic inflammatory disease; clearer skin; some protection against ovarian and uterine cancers, osteoporosis and arthritis; and if you get the Pill that starts on a Sunday, you're pretty much guaranteed period-free weekends.

Cons: Side-effects can include sore boobies, nausea or vomiting, spotting between periods, lowered sex drive, mood swings or depression. Most of these will disappear after a few months; if they don't, ask your doctor for a different brand (there are lots of different kinds).

Another common side-effect is slight weight gain or loss due to any number of factors: temporary fluid retention for the first month; the oestrogen can make you more curvy in the hips, thighs and breasts within the first few months; the hormones can affect your appetite either way for as long as you take it; the Pill can aggravate depression, which can also affect appetite. But that's nothing compared to what your body goes through during a nine-month pregnancy.

You can't smoke while you're on the combination Pill, even if you're the type who only smokes when they're drinking (it puts you at a higher risk for heart attacks and blood clots) — but you shouldn't be smoking anyway. If you 'must' puff on cancer sticks, go with the progestogen-only Pill.

Vomiting and diarrhoea, as well as some medications (check with your doc), may make both Pills less effective. The Pill may become less effective if you are taking certain other medications — particularly those metabolised by the liver. You should consider back-up contraception during cycles when such medications are taken.

By the way, the Pill does not increase your risk of breast cancer and there's no conclusive evidence to suggest that it increases your risk of cervical cancer, either. The Pill will not cause birth defects in future kids, even if you're one of the unlucky few to get pregnant while on it. Most of these worries are left over from the days when the Pill contained a much higher dose of hormones.

£££: Free on the NHS.

The ideal candidate: Any non-smoking, non-pregnant woman who has no history of liver or coronary artery disease or stroke. The risks associated with taking the Pill are way lower than those risks you assume with pregnancy. It's like flying in a plane compared to getting in a car.

The Patch (Ortho Evra)

How it works: The first birth-control patch to be approved (very recently) by the FDA in the US and the MCA (Medicines Control Agency) in the UK, Evra is a non-invasive hormone treatment. The thin, beige patch is worn on the buttocks, abdomen, upper torso (front or back, excluding the breasts), or upper outer arm. It delivers a steady flow of progestogen and oestrogen through the skin and into your bloodstream over seven days to prevent ovulation and thicken the cervical mucus. Each patch is worn for one week and replaced on the same day of the week for three consecutive weeks, with the fourth week 'patch-free', during which time you get your period. Like the Pill, you apply your first patch either on the first day of your period, or on the first Sunday after your period starts; you'll need a non-hormonal back-up method for at least a week after starting. Somehow it stays wherever you stick it, even when you bathe, swim, exercise, or wear it in humid conditions.

Batting average: It's up to 99.7 per cent effective with perfect use.

Pros: It's non-invasive and you only have to remember to change it once a week.

Cons: It only comes in beige and you're not allowed to decorate it with cute doodles. By week's end, it can get pretty grungy. In some women, there can be breast symptoms, headache, application site reaction, nausea, upper-respiratory infection, menstrual cramps or abdominal pain. On the more serious side of things, there's the small chance of blood clots, stroke, or heart attacks — especially if you smoke cigarettes.

£££: Contraception is free on the NHS.

The ideal candidate: You're an ex-smoker who thought NicoDerm CQ was a miracle cure.

The Shot (Depo-Provera)

How it works: Your doctor injects your arm or ass with a shot of the hormone progestogen every three months. Like the progestogen-only Pill, this method thickens your cervical mucus and may prevent ovulation. If you get the shot in the first five days of your period, you'll be good to go immediately. Otherwise, you'll need a back-up method for at least a week.

Batting average: It's 99.7 per cent effective.

Pros: No pre-sex routine or daily ritual to remember; great for the oestrogen-sensitive; reduces menstrual cramps; protects against uterine and ovarian cancers and anaemia, just like the Pill.

Cons: The two most common side-effects are irregular bleeding (very long and heavy periods, or no period at all) and hair loss (this can be fairly significant and seems to be more common in African women). You may also experience stomach pain, headache, depression, increased appetite, weight gain and increased or decreased sex drive (though the latter is more common). Most women don't need to take a break from Depo, but there is a very small chance you could suffer from temporary loss of bone density, which increases your risk of developing osteoporosis later in life. Women with a history of liver disease should stay away from Depo.

The biggest bummer is that Depo is a ride you can't get off — any side-effects you incur may last until the shot wears off (up to 14 weeks). And it may take up to 18 months after your last shot to get pregnant, if that's what you have in mind.

£££: Free on the state.

The ideal candidate: You're the forgetful type who's not afraid of a little period sex every now and then.

Mr T (The Intrauterine Device or IUD)

How it works: The IUD is a small, plastic, T-shaped device that's inserted into the uterus during menstruation by a doctor. Its presence prevents the sperm from getting too cosy with the egg and keeps fertilised eggs from getting too cosy in the uterine lining. It begins working immediately and stops as soon as it is removed. Once in place, a string from the IUD hangs down through the cervix into your love canal, which you're supposed to check on regularly to make sure the system's in place (if it isn't, use back-up protection and call your doc). Have a check-up after three months and then once a year, like you always do.

Batting average: The copper-coated ones are effective more than 99 per cent of the time; the progestogen version, 98 per cent of the time. Only Depo-Provera and sterilisation are more effective — the IUD even beats the Pill.

Pros: No pre-sex rituals or daily grind; it doesn't change the hormone levels throughout your bod (even the progestogen version only has a local effect on the uterine lining); and the progestogen one may reduce menstrual cramps.

Cons: Insertion may feel like severe menstrual cramps, but they go away with a little rest and pain reliever. The wall of the uterus could be punctured during insertion — but that's rare. IUDs can also cause infection, which is why your doctor may automatically prescribe some antibiotics when you start as a preventative measure. Once in, IUDs can cause more menstrual cramps, spotting and heavier periods. You shouldn't use an IUD if you have a history of pelvic inflammatory disease (PID), chlamydia, or gonorrhoea, or if your bedroom has a revolving door: a foreign body in your uterus gives all those STD critters something extra to hang on to — which can increase the likelihood that they'll blossom into a raging case of PID.

£££: Free on the NHS, but there's a cost if you get it inserted in some clinics.

The ideal candidate: It's not for the queasy. You should be in a stable, monogamous relationship where neither of you has an STD (page 161).

The Ring (Vaginal Ring, NuvaRing)

How it works: It's a flexible, transparent ring that fits into the vagina and releases a continuous low dose of oestrogen and progestogen. Once you get a prescription from your doctor, you insert the ring yourself at the beginning of your cycle, leave it in for three weeks and take it out while you have your period. Then you put a new one in and start over.

Batting average: More than 99 per cent effective with correct use. We're talking a perfect record of insertion and removal.

Pros: As opposed to the Pill, you only have to think about it twice a month (when you insert and remove it, which are both easy to do); the low and steady doses of hormones mean little spotting; ovulation returns very quickly after you stop using it.

Cons: You cannot smoke; if you have blood clots, severe high blood pressure, particular cancers or a history of heart problems, then it's not for you; the ring might cause vaginal infections, headache, weight gain, or nausea.

£££: It's new in the UK and you may have some trouble getting it on prescription through the NHS, so expect to pay a fee if you go privately.

The ideal candidate: You're not squeamish about touching your front bottom.

The Beanie (Diaphragm)

How it works: It's a dome-shaped latex cup with a flexible rim that fits into your vagina to cover the cervix, preventing the sperm and egg from hooking up. You see your doc for a fitting and s/he shows you how to coat it with spermicide cream or jelly and how to insert and remove it correctly — it's like having a personal stylist for your vagina. A diaphragm can be left in for up to 24 hours, but if it's been more than six hours since insertion (or if you're going for round two), you insert another dose of spermicide into the vagina, without removing the shield. It's a two-for-one approach: the diaphragm literally blocks the sperm in their path and the spermicide stuns them (see page 225). The diaphragm must be left in for six hours after intercourse.

Batting average: With perfect use, this method has a six per cent failure rate. But hello, people, we're talking about fitting a little rubber cup into the vagina: the real-life rate of failure is a frightening 16 per cent.

Pros: Can last for years; no major side-effects; offers some protection against chlamydia, gonorrhoea and pelvic inflammatory disease; can be inserted hours before a booty break for a smooth operation; can reduce the risk of cervical cancer; doesn't fuck with a woman's hormones; and neither partner can feel it (assuming it's been inserted correctly).

Cons: Needs to be checked regularly for weak spots or holes (hold it up to a light or fill with water); insertion is an acquired art; increased risk of bladder infection; it's not an option if you have latex or spermicide allergies; some positions (and some penises) can dislodge the diaphragm; it requires decent vaginal muscle tone (kegels!); it can get messy with all that spermicide; and spermicide has been getting a bad rap lately (see below).

£££: Another freebee on the NHS, but expect to pay a few quid for a spermicide.

The ideal candidate: You like to wear hats.

Lovin' Cup (Cervical Cap)

How it works: It's a thimble-shaped latex cup that hugs your cervix to thwart any sperm–egg nookie. Your doctor will size you and train you in spermicide application and insertion. You don't have to use spermicide with the cervical cap (since it provides such a tight fit over the cervical opening), but it's recommended for added pregnancy protection. Like a diaphragm, it can be left in for up to 24 hours, but if it's been more than six hours since insertion (or if you're going for round two), you should insert another dose of spermicide into the vagina, without removing the shield.

Batting average: For women who have never given birth, the cap has a nine per cent failure rate with perfect use and a 16 per cent failure rate with typical use (yep, that's you). But get this: for women who have given birth, the failure rate is 26 per cent with perfect use and a massive 32 per cent with typical use.

Pros: Can be inserted up to 48 hours before sex (call it 'the week-ender'); offers limited STD protection (see 'Diaphragm' section); may last for years; and has no serious side-effects.

Cons: It only comes in four sizes, so you may never find that perfect fit; insertion is an acquired art; it's not an option if you have latex allergies; it can be messy if you use spermicide; and spermicide has been getting a bad rap lately (see below).

£££: Free on the NHS, but the spermicide will set you back about £3.

The ideal candidate: You're a practised diddler with an average-sized veegee.

Goo (Spermicide)

How it works: Contraceptive foams, creams, jellies, films and supposi-tories — collectively known as spermicides — are like a stungun to sperm. Spermicide is inserted deep into the vagina at least ten minutes (but no more than an hour) before sex; it immobilises the little guys until the magic moment has passed. It later dissolves in the vagina. The foam blocks the entrance to the uterus with tiny bubbles; the creams, jellies, films and suppositories melt into a thick liquid that also blocks the uterus entrance. 'Spermicide' is also sometimes used to refer to the key ingredient in these sperm-beating products. Many lubricated condoms are also coated with spermicide for good measure. Goo must be reapplied if you want to go back for seconds; it should be left well alone for six to eight hours after sex.

Batting average: With perfect use, it has a 15 per cent failure rate; with average use, that number jumps to 29 percent. Due to this massive failure rate, it should only be used in conjunction with a condom (male or female), diaphragm or cervical cap.

Pros: It offers *some* protection against chlamydia and gonorrhoea; it's available in most chemists and supermarkets; it acts as a lube; and insertion can be one of your patented 'moves'. By the way, there's no conclusive evidence that inserting spermicide *after sex* as an

emergency measure (if the condom breaks) is effective in preventing conception. It can't hurt to give it a shot, but you should also
talk to your doctor about emergency contraception (see page 227).

Cons: Besides being slightly sloppy, it may increase your risk of contracting HIV (or giving it if you're HIV positive): new studies suggest
that nonoxynol-9, which is the key ingredient in most spermicides,
can be very irritating to the vaginal wall, increasing a woman's
chances of contracting HIV from an infected partner. Thus, you
should only be using spermicides as a method of birth control if
you're in a monogamous relationship and you've both been tested
for HIV. You might be able to find spermicides that use octoxynol-9
instead — but it's harder to track down and there's no evidence to
suggest that this ingredient is any less irritating to the vagina.

£££: Expect to pay about £5 for the applicator kit and around £3 for
refills (containing 20 to 40 applications).

The ideal candidate: You loved finger-painting as a kid.

The Final Word (Sterilisation)

How it works: For both women and men, this is a permanent surgical
procedure. In ladies, the fallopian tubes are cut at the point where
eggs are usually fertilised by sperm via intra-abdominal surgery.
Called tubal sterilisation or ligation, it's effective immediately, but
it's invasive, which is why it's usually opted for during Caesarean
sections (since the docs are already in there). It can also be done
post–vaginal delivery (through a small incision under the navel); at
other times, it's usually done with a laparoscope (a narrow tube
inserted through the abdominal wall). In the gents, the tubes that
carry the sperm from the testes to the prostate are cut. Called a
vasectomy, this fairly simple, in-office operation usually takes at
least 15 ejaculations to kick in, because of leftover sperm in the
tubes. A simple lab analysis of your semen will tell you when you've
run out. There is a *tiny* chance that each of these operations could
be reversed, but it probably won't be covered by the NHS and
there's no guarantee it'll work. So don't count on it; if you're considering this method, then consider it a done deal.

Batting average: At 99.5 to 99.9 per cent effective, this is about as good as it gets.

Pros: It's the last time you'll ever have to think about birth control. These operations can be performed on almost anyone and have no side-effects or impact on your sex life.

Cons: I-R-R-E-V-E-R-S-I-B-L-E. (Though there's a small failure rate.) There's also the possibility of bleeding and bruising right after the surgery. If a woman does conceive post-op, it's more likely to be an ectopic pregnancy (in the fallopian tubes). In dudes, there may be an infection or blood clot in the testicle area, temporary sperm leakage and hardened 'sperm bumps', all of which will need treatment. Did we mention it's irreversible?

£££: Free on the NHS, but you may have to pay for a reversal (blokes only).

The ideal candidate: No (more) kids, thank you; pregnancy may be life-threatening for you or your partner; you don't want to pass on a hereditary disease. And you're really, really sure.

Oh Shit, the Condom Broke: Your Emergency Contraception Options

Emergency contraception is not abortion — it's an after-the-fact method of birth control that can prevent both unwanted pregnancies and abortions. It's not something you should turn to on a regular basis, but in times of fuck-ups (e.g., when the condom breaks and your back-up method conks out), it's your superhero come to save the day. Just don't wait around for your superhero to fly in; seek it out as soon as possible after an accident (like within a day). It's safe, it's effective and no, Mr Anti-Choice, its availability *doesn't* make women (or even teen girls) less likely to use before-the-fact birth control.

Emergency contraception may not prevent ectopic (tubal) pregnancy, which can be fatal. If you experience the following warning signs for more than a few days after using emergency contraception, follow up with your doctor: severe lower abdominal pain, spotting (especially after a light or missed period), faintness and dizziness. The other thing emergency contraception won't protect you from is STDs. No shit, Sherlock, right? But it's easy to forget that the circumstances that led you to seek out EC may also have put you at risk for infection, especially if it was a one-night-stand kind of 'oops'.

When it comes to post-coital birth control, you have two choices (well, three if you count oh-please-god-don't-let-me-get-pregnant): the emergency contraception pill and emergency insertion of an IUD.

Emergency Contraceptive Pill (ECP) or Post-Coital Pill (PCP)

How it works: This method has been erroneously dubbed 'the morning-after pill' — it can actually be used up to 72 hours after unprotected sex – which is why it's now known as the Post-Coital Pill (PCP). It's basically a superhigh dose of the birth-control pill that prevents the egg from getting fertilised or implanting in the uterus wall. The older type of PCP contained a combination of oestrogen and progestogen. This is no longer available, but since February 2000, there has been a new PCP called Levonelle-2. This contains only one hormone — a progestogen — and it is claimed to be more effective than the old type of PCP. It is also less likely than the old PCP to cause nausea and it causes very little in the way of side-effects. Your doctor may prescribe you a PCP; you can also buy them (if you are over 16) over the counter at most chemists and even some supermarkets (with pharmacies). Family planning clinics often have them to hand. The OTC version is slightly different to the prescribed PCP, but they are taken the same way. The 'pill' is in fact, two pills. One taken immediately, the other exactly 12 hours later.

Batting average: It prevents about 95 per cent of pregnancies from developing if it is taken within 24 hours of unprotected sex. This decreases to an estimated 85 per cent if taken within 24 to 48 hours and to 58 per cent if taken within 48 to 72 hours, so it is important to take the first dose as soon as possible.

Pros: Shall we say this one more time? *It's not an abortion.* (In fact, if you're already pregnant, it won't harm a developing foetus.) If you have a super-cool doc, she may give you a prescription before you need one, to keep on hand for self-administering next time you have an oops. Pretty much anyone can use it, even women who can't take birth-control pills on a long-term basis.

Cons: The most common side-effects of the emergency contraceptive pill include a day or two of nausea (for about half of all women who take it) and/or vomiting (for about a quarter of those who take it). If it makes you sick, talk to your doctor. You may have to repeat the dosage. Other possible side-effects may include a day or two of cramping, breast tenderness, fatigue, irregular bleeding, abdominal pain, headaches or dizziness, although this is less likely with the new PCP. The pill may also affect the duration and timing (either way) of your next period.

£££: Free on the NHS, but expect to pay around £24 if you buy it over the counter. Plus, of course, the tenner you're going to spend on a box of reliable condoms that afternoon to keep in your nightstand. Right?

The ideal candidate: The condom broke or slipped off; he didn't pull out in time; you forgot to take the Pill for more than two days in a row; your diaphragm slipped; you got drunk and did a very bad thing. Or worst-case scenario: you were forced into unprotected sex.

Emergency IUD Insertion

How it works: This method can be used up to five days after unprotected sex — your doctor will insert an intrauterine device (IUD) to prevent an egg from implanting in your uterus. The IUD can be left in and used as a regular contraception method (or, if you prefer, your doc can remove it for you).

Batting average: It's 99.9 per cent effective. Now that's a statistic we like.

Pros: You have more time to get to your doctor after having unprotected sex than you do with the PCP.

Cons: If you're not the IUD type, it's a little more intense than popping a few pills. Possible side-effects include cramps, abdominal discomfort, vaginal bleeding, infection and — very rarely — uterine puncture. IUDs can increase your risk of PID (page 194), which can cause infertility. Because of this, the IUD method is not recommended for women at high risk of STDs (i.e., chicks with a lot of partners and very poor communication skills).

£££: Don't worry, the NHS will cover it.

The ideal candidate: You're *not* the ideal candidate if you have an STD (or you *might* have an STD) or you have a history of PID or other infections related to your reproductive system. Other than that, any chick who's had an oops can get it.

Further Resources

For more information about emergency contraception, call the Family Planning Association (0845 310 1334 – 9am to 7pm) or visit their website on fpa.co.uk. In a genuine oh-my-god emergency, call NHS direct, on 0845 4647. For a fee, you can contact either of the following: BPAS (British Pregnancy Advisory Service) – 08457 304030 or visit the website: bpas.org; or, Marie Stopes Clinics – 0845 300 8090 or website: mariestopes.org.uk.

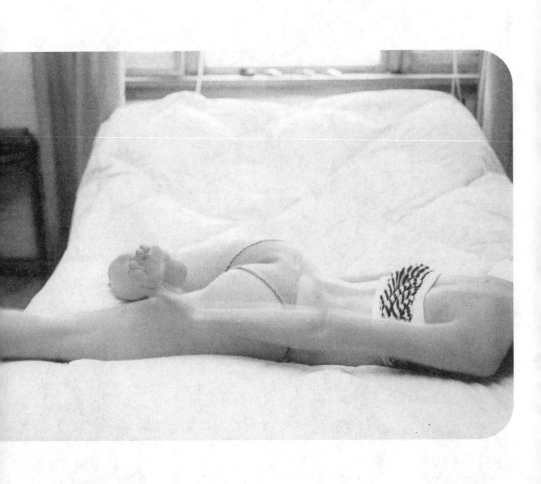

LADIES' NIGHT

Beyond Sugar and Spice:
Vaginas and Boobies

If we learned one thing from the sexually transmitted diseases chapter, it's this: when it comes to infections, women get fucked. It's the nature of the bush — warm, moist, dark caves are like heaven to microscopic creepy crawlers. It may be easier to 'dig a hole than build a pole', as they like to say in the transsexual surgery biz, but maintaining a healthy vagina takes a lot more vigilance than keeping a perky pecker. The willy is a well-oiled machine; the wilma can be — it just needs a little more TLC. Read on for a few of the things that can go wrong and some of the ways you can keep them from going that way. We follow up with a section on the two hills north of Vagina Valley, the Boobie Badlands.

Vaginitis

One of the least sexiest sounding words, vaginitis is an umbrella term for all the crazy shite that can happen in a woman's nether regions — that is, any kind of vaginal inflammation that's caused by bacteria, fungi (e.g., yeast infection), parasites or viruses. The most common varieties of vaginitis are trichomoniasis and bacterial vaginosis (other members of this dysfunctional family include vulvitis and vulvodynia — chances are, if it begins with a V it belongs). Sometimes vaginitis is sexually transmitted, other times it occurs as a result of irritation (from rough sex, smelly soaps, medications, poor diet, etc.). The symptoms all over-lap — unusual vaginal discharge and an itchy vadge are the most common — so you'll have to see your doc for an exact diagnosis. But you don't need to know any of those fancy V words to protect your tooty-fruity coochie from the whole gang (see 'Respect the Cunt' page 237).

Yeast Infections

Yeast is not evil. Yeast makes beer and bread, two of life's essentials. But in the vagina, it goes down like a fart in church. A small amount of this fungus (aka candida albicans or monilia) occurs normally in healthy vadges, where the good bacteria keep it in check. But when your system is out of whack (see 'Respect the Cunt' for examples), it grows like weeds. And then you'll be sorry. Yeast infections are most common in women under 35. Virgins and prudes aren't exempt, either: pretty much every woman will get the Big Y at least once in her lifetime and most will get it a lot more than once. What can we say? Life's a bitch. But at least there's beer and bread.

The most common symptoms include crazy itching down there; thick, white, curdy vaginal discharge (that doesn't usually smell too bad — like that's any consolation when you've got cottage cheese in your underpants); a rash on your outer labes; general soreness; and burning piss. Not all of these symptoms will necessarily be present: if it doesn't itch like a motherfucker, then it's probably not a yeast infection.

Yeast infections can be passed on during unprotected oral sex or inter-course, but a lowered immune system is the usual suspect. The pH in the vagina is normally very acidic; yeast is most at home in an environment that's only mildly acidic. So anything that makes the cooch more alkaline (e.g., semen or menstrual blood) can lead to a yeast invasion. Antibiotics are also a common culprit because they can reduce the good bacteria that normally keep the yeast in check. A warm, moist vadge is like a welcome mat for yeast, so avoid fabrics that promote moisture, such as Lycra (though if you're having trouble avoiding Lycra then you need more help than we can offer).

Most chicks self-diagnose yeast infections, because a trip to the chemist is quicker than a doctor's appointment — and who wants to hang around a waiting room for three hours with a yeast infection? Over-the-counter vaginal suppositories (i.e., any treatment you stick in) or creams both work in about three to five days. (Avoid the one-day treatments; they often don't kill the infection completely and the recurring infection can be even harder to zap.) You should see your doc if you get yeast infections regularly (i.e., every few months or more) or chronically (i.e., over-the-counter treatments don't work for you), or if they're accompanied by lower ab pain or fever. Frequent infections may indicate that your immune system is suffering as a result of an infection somewhere else in your body (e.g., cancer or HIV, or — more likely — something a little less scary like diabetes). You might also be harbouring a duplicitous and much less common vaginal infection, or even herpes, that acts like yeast, appearing to be cured by over-the-counter yeast treatments, which really just hibernates for a month before waking up again. Or you could simply have a runaway yeast infection that needs a prescription-grade zapping, plain and simple.

To help protect yourself from a yeast invasion, see 'Respect the Cunt' on page 237.

Urinary Tract Infections (UTIs)

Urinary tract infections are the worst pain known to man. Oh, wait, that's right, UTIs are mostly known to *women*. So maybe they're not the worst pain, exactly, but try telling that to a chick who currently has one (and then duck). They're usually caused by bacteria from your bumhole (e.g., E coli) that spread to the urethra and bladder and occasionally the kidneys. An infection in the bladder is known as cystitis and is the most common variety of UTI. Because a woman's urethra is shorter than a man's, she's more likely to get infected (the bacteria don't have to travel as far to get to the bladder). Her urethra is also in the same neighbourhood as her bumhole, as opposed to his, which hangs out in the schlong suburbs. Symptoms include burning, mother-of-god pain when peeing; burning, mother-of-god pain when not peeing; a near-constant urge to pee even when your bladder is empty; accidentally peeing your pants; blood or pus in urine; and maybe a fever. Talk about a dream date. These symptoms will show up a day or two after the E coli has made itself at home. If a UTI is left untreated, it can lead to lower abdominal or back pain and eventually kidney infection.

You don't have to be into scat play to spread E coli — any kind of intercourse can do it, especially a particularly vigorous vaginal sesh (with all those vaginal juices carrying things to and fro) or bum sex. And watch out for the stealth pokers who take their pinky from back door to front door without cleaning off first. Bad wiping habits may also be to blame (remember, ladies, front to back once, then again with a clean tissue). And because the vagina is an oversensitive little thing, chicks with brand-new partners are more at risk, too — if the vadge has trouble adjusting to the new bacterial environment, a little freak-out infection in the bladder may result.

It's possible, however, to get all the symptoms of a UTI (or a mild version of those symptoms) without actually having a bacterial infection — especially if you drink a lot of tea, coffee or booze, are dehydrated, have PMS, use a diaphragm (the rim might be pressing on your urethra through your vaginal wall), just took a fragrant bubble bath, recently had your G-spot (urethral sponge) or urethral opening pounded during sex, or are generally feeling run-down or stressed. These mild UTI fakers can be self-diagnosed and self-treated with over-the-counter painkillers like Pyridium — seriously, folks, taking these wonder drugs is practically a religious experience, even if it does turn your pee temporarily orange. Avoid strong spices (like curry and chilli) and drink enough to have a good pee every hour (water is best). But if the pain doesn't go away within 24 hours, see a doc. If it turns out it *is* a UTI, a course of antibiotics will fix you up good. (If you've already had a hit of Pyridium, don't worry — it shouldn't affect the results of your urine test at the doctor's surgery.)

We'd like to teach the world to sing. And right after that, we'd like to rid the world of UTIs. Every lady who makes the following tips a part of her everyday life brings us a little closer to our dream:

- When you gotta go, *go*. Pee when you have to, don't hold it. And try to empty your bladder completely every time you go.
- Pee right before and after sex. This helps flush out bacteria that could lead to a UTI.
- Drink unsweetened cranberry juice. It won't cure a UTI or ease the pain, but daily consumption for at least four to eight weeks will help protect you from future infections (it contains chemical compounds that make it difficult for bacteria to cling to the urinary tract).

- Some women who are susceptible to frequent UTIs take antibiotics to prevent infections when they have sexual intercourse. Though, extended use of antibiotics may cause recurring yeast infections, making this the *Sophie's Choice* of the vagina.
- See the following section on how to further prevent UTIs.

Respect the Cunt: What to Do When Your Rosebush Wilts

You can't do much about the havoc that hormones wreak on your body, but there are plenty more factors at play that you *can* control down there in Vaginaville. The following preventative tips will keep you smelling like you're supposed to (and that's not like a daisy or a summer's breeze), as well as helping your body ward off UTIs, yeast infections and other forms of vaginitis.

- **Know thy smelth.** Not to get too New Agey on you, but everyone has their own, unique smell and you should learn to love yours like a long-time friend. Become familiar with it (without breaking your neck) and take note of subtle changes in bouquet that occur at different times due to sexual arousal and hormonal changes. For example, during ovulation, your smell may be stronger to attract mates and your vagina may produce more mucus to protect and guide sperm on its way to your uterus. (Ah, mucus, so sexy, so alluring!) The more familiar you are with your own scent cycle, the more likely you are to notice irregularities that could indicate some kind of infection down there.
- **The vagina is a mood ring.** 'Abnormal discharge' is the surest sign that you have a vaginal infection, so you gotta know what 'normal' means for you. (One last time, ladies: there is no universal standard for 'normal' when it comes to the holiest of holies.) Discharge itself is totally normal — the vagina and cervix are lined with mucous membranes (kind of like inside your mouth or nose) that secrete stuff. Standard discharge is usually clear to slightly milky, slippery or clumpy and white or slightly yellowish when dry on your undies. Being aware of what's 'normal' for you will help you recognise 'real' abnormalities (e.g., intense pungency, itching, burning, chafing, irregular-for-you

discharge), which can be symptoms of infections and STDs like tricho-moniasis, bacterial vaginosis, vulvitis, yeast infections, gonorrhoea and chlamydia.

- **You reek what you eat.** Too much sugar, caffeine, refined carbohydrates, red meat, alcohol or nicotine can give you a funky odour. If you eat right, your partner will be more into eating you. Those baddies can also irritate the bladder and make the vadge more hospitable to yeast infections.

- **Got water?** Drink eight or more glasses of water a day and avoid soft drinks, which can promote the growth of bad bacteria.

- **You might love the '80s *Flashdance* revival but your vagina doesn't.** Tight clothing (especially tight Lycra when you're working out), tights and synthetic underwear prevent air from circulating down there, creating the perfect, moist environment for bacteria to overgrow. (That's why you may experience more infections in hot, humid weather.) They can also irritate the urethra. So while white cotton knicks may not be the sexiest, they sure are hotter than a case of vaginitis. And what better excuse to go commando or sleep in the buff? If you must wear sleek leopard-print thongs, just make sure the crotch (what there is of it) is made of cotton.

- **Don't stress.** It stresses out your vagina. So get rest. Accept back rubs. Sleep in. Practise yoga. Buy a punching bag.

- **Wash behind your lips every day.** Literally: we're talking the whole shebang, poop chute and all. Some experts recommend pure, unscented mineral oil because it's less drying than soap, but we think a mild, natural, unscented soap is more practical. Whenever you're lucky enough to get the sex, peeing and washing fairly soon afterwards can help ward off urinary tract infections.

- **Make him wash his willy, too.** While it's no cure-all, it certainly can't hurt to have your male partners give themselves a good rinse before the blessed event.

- **Douches are evil.** Unnecessary products invented by The Man to solve made-up problems and make a buck. Vaginas, like ears, clean themselves. (Cotton swabs are evil, too. We know, they feel so good! But the ear is a delicate thing and swabs can damage the canal and push the wax up even farther.) There's good bacteria in your vagina that fight off infection and when you douche, the good stuff is cleaned out along with the bad stuff, leaving your acidic and alkaline balances all off-kilter and your vadge prone to infection. Douching can also cause allergic reactions or spread existing infections to the uterus and fallopian tubes, causing more serious problems like pelvic inflammatory disease (page 194). And then how 'fresh' will you feel? The same goes for feminine hygiene sprays. Femfresh, you can take your spritzer and shove it up your own cooch!

- **Fragrances are for potpourri.** Deodorised anything is usually a bad idea down there: tampons, pads, TP, edible underwear, potpourri sachets, etc.
- **Talc does a body bad.** If you absolutely must use products (and you mustn't), avoid those containing talc, which has been linked with ovarian cancer in some studies (and why take the chance?). Some experts recommend corn flour as a good substitute (it has replaced talc in many baby powders), but others say that might cause yeast infections (and why take the chance?).
- **Wipe after you go to the bathroom.** (You'd be surprised . . .) Avoid scented or dyed loo roll. And remember: front to back, but never back again.
- **Semen sometimes overstays its welcome.** The pH in the vagina is normally very acidic; anything that is alkaline (e.g., semen) can upset this balance and make it easier for bacteria to grow there. If you're getting recurring infections, try using a condom (even if you and your partner are using another form of protection).
- **Lube with care.** Stick to sterile, non-irritating lubricants like Liquid Silk (page 267). Stay away from oil/petroleum-based products like Vaseline: all oils linger in your body longer than you'd think and they can coat the vaginal walls for days, offering a warm welcome to all kinds of bacteria. But *do* use lube: dry intercourse means chafing, which can irritate the vagina and encourage infection.
- **Be a health nut.** The vagina's arch rival is a weakened immune system. (That's why UTIs and yeast infections are so common in people with conditions like HIV that weaken the immune system.) So take vitamins. Quit smoking. Get to the gym already. Eat your greens.
- **It's just not cramps and crankiness.** During your period, you're more likely to get an infection, too, thanks to the hormonal changes in your body and all that alkaline blood hanging around. Yay menstruation! So be on your guard when you know it's that time of the month. Some experts claim that tampons let your vagina breathe more than heavy pads, while others argue that pads are less irritating to the vadge. Go with what works for you — just be sure to change your pad or tampons at least every few hours and wash your box twice a day.

- **It's not me, it's you.** If your infection keeps coming back, your partner may be re-infecting you, even if he or she doesn't show any symptoms. Try barrier protection and have your partner treated, too. (You'll probably need to see a doc for the latter, though: for example, guys can't use over-the-counter yeast treatments, so he'll need a prescription.)
- **Never mind, it's my birth control.** Some forms of the Pill cause infections in some women, as do diaphragms and certain contraceptive foams. Finding the one that's most compatible with your treasure chest is kind of like matchmaking (see page 217 for more). Your diaphragm or cervical cap should always be replaced after an infection.

One-Rack Mind: The Boobie Twins

Who would have thought that masses of glandular, fatty and fibrous tissues could rule the media, sway civilisations and reduce the minds of men (and some women) to quivering bowls of jelly? Even before girls sprout their own buds at the onset of puberty, they are well aware of the Western world's breast obsession. It can make for a complicated, lifelong relationship between a girl and her own nubbins — never mind the crazy relationship between said nubbins and the awkward, acned boys who want to grope them (the mid-maths-class boners may fade, but the mammary desire is eternal). The power of breasts — their life-giving function, their erotic potential, their squeezable softness — can be overwhelming; but too often that power is undercut by juvenile nicknames, unrealistic breast expectations and *Baywatch* reruns. So let's bow down before the altar of the teat and spend some quality time getting to know the girls.

Breast in Show

Most breasts aren't a matching set — one, usually the left, is often larger than the other, sometimes differing by as much as a cup size. Sometimes one is higher than the other, or the other points a little more south-west. Totally normal. Factors influencing the overall size include age, genetics, volume of breast tissue, weight gain or loss, pregnancy, thickness and elasticity of the breast skin, hormonal changes (especially caused by the menstrual cycle) and menopause. Though sometimes a decent bra can make all the difference.

The nipple and areola (the area around the nipple) come in all sizes and colours (almost always a darker shade of pink or brown than the rest of the skin). Most areolas have little bumps on the surface — oil glands that secrete a lubricant for nipple protection during breastfeeding (by a woman's baby, not her boyfriend). Hairs around the border of the areola are common and can increase over time or with use of the Pill. (Yes, it's true! You're not alone — and it's perfectly fine to pluck them if you don't like the look, just scrub gently with a facecloth to avoid ingrowns). The nipples themselves may be cylindrical, round, flat, or even introverted and almost all of them become firmer, possibly to the point of standing at full attention, in response to stimuli such as arctic winds, an accidental brush by, or good porn. (So to all the 14-year-old boys out there: no, erect nipples do not automatically signal horniness; in fact, some women's nipples are perpetually firm just because.) Stimulation of the nipples catalyses production of the hormone oxytocin, which translates into tingly sensations down below. As a woman gets older, her breasts become less dense (i.e., less glandular tissue, more fatty tissue) and the skin stretches and expands. You take the good, you take the bad . . .

The only breasts that *don't* have this much personality are the fake ones. Which is one of about a hundred ways that you can spot the plastic fantastics — the two biggies being immobility (even in a grade-three hurricane) and an *un*squeezable softness.

Breast Exams

From the age of 20, you should be checking your breasts once a month (during the week following menstruation when the breasts are the least tender) for lumps and irregularities. Yeah, we know you've heard that more often than you'd hear 'nice ta-tas!' on a midsummer's walk past a building site, but do you actually do it? Seriously, it's more important than flossing (you do floss, don't you?) and much more fun for your partner to watch. With one in eight women developing breast cancer in her lifetime, it's something you have got to do. If you've forgotten how, check out the Cancer Research UK's guidelines at cancerhelp.org.uk, or ask your doctor or gynae for a show-and-tell next time you're getting a check-up.

Breast Enhancement

Most men swear that in a Pepsi Challenge of Real McCoys vs Party Tits, they could tell the difference every time — of course, they're usually just trying to get ladies to lift their shirts. But if it's a hands-on kind of challenge, then we call 'no contest', because there's no mistaking the unforgiving feel of two chest knee-caps. But maybe you're not going for 'realistic'. Just promise us you'll never get implants because someone *else* asked you to, OK? And have a bit of pride: if you're going to permanently stuff your bra, at least pay for the job yourself — it'll set you back a couple of thousand. Both saline and silicone implants are health authority-approved. However, there is much debate over the long-term safety of silicone implants, and the validity of the studies that have found them to be safe. You might be better off going with saline implants — that solution can be absorbed by the body without any harm should the implants deflate (oh, they might). The procedure is relatively safe for most women, will only take one to three hours (with no overnight stay), should cause only minimal scarring and, as long as your surgeon doesn't insert the implants through the nipple, should not result in problems with breastfeeding later. Common side-effects include excruciating post-op pain, a risk of decreased nipple sensitivity to the point of numbness, and mammaries that will look and feel like flotation devices for the rest of your life. Potential risks include the implant becoming hard, deformed, and/or painful; rupture and leakage of the implant; red, thick and/or painful scars which may take several years to improve; interference with standard mammographies; and, in very rare cases, serious infection. Often, further surgery is needed throughout one's lifetime to repair botched jobs or ruptured implants, replace old implants, or improve aesthetic quality (e.g. size, shape, etc). So before you go jumping on the big boob bandwagon, weigh the decision for at least as long as you'd ponder getting your boyfriend's name tattooed on your ass. (Many chicks have regretted both.) You can look up the UK government's most updated view on flasies right here: http://www.doh.gov.uk/bimplants/ — which we'd highly recommend before going under the knife.

As for all those shifty ads on late-night TV that tout breast pumps, gels, pills, 'stretching bras' and booby-Miracle-Gro, we have two words for you: Wonder Bra. It's the only thing (besides implants, pregnancy and gaining weight) that will beef up the old girls.

Breast Reduction

We must, we must, we must decrease our bust . . . That's the battle cry of many women who've suffered from boobs too big for their body frames, whether because of breast pain, back problems, self-consciousness, or mental anguish from all the unwanted stares and cat-calling. (These are the women who tell others opting for enlargements, 'Be careful what you wish for.') If your upper deck is causing health problems, this op is usually considered recon-structive surgery (rather than cosmetic) and may even be covered by the NHS; if not, it'll set you back at the very least two grand. You may experience some decreased sensitivity and you may not be able to breastfeed afterwards. The procedure takes one to three hours and could involve an overnight stay, depending on the anaesthetic. The scars are worse than for implants (espe-cially if you're a smoker) and never fade completely — but maybe it's worth it to you. Just be careful what you wish for.

16

SELF-HELP FOR YOUR PETER

Everything You Wanted to Know About Penises and Weren't Afraid to Ask

First of all, we hate to break it to you schmucks (and we mean schmuck in the most loving, Yiddish-for-penis way): size matters. There, we said it. But in the immortal words of Einstein (and no doubt he was talking about skin flutes), it's all relative. Sure, some people have fond memories of penises past and some have particularly fond memories of nice smooth penises, or nice big penises, or penises that fit *just so*. But what's a perfectly shaped cuke to one person is a disappointing pig-in-a-blanket to another and an overwhelming meat loaf to yet another. Being nice and big doesn't guarantee that you'll become a fond penis memory and being nice and big doesn't guarantee that it'll fit *just so* either. Sometimes smaller can be better: just as penises come in different sizes, so do vaginas (or anal cavities, for that matter). Maybe every penis has a soul mate out there, the perfect fit. Regardless, most of the vagina's nerve endings are at the entrance and women are more likely to have an orgasm from external clitoral stimulation than vaginal pounding anyway. And canals, both front and back, are pretty flexible and accommodating no matter what the size — with the right tender loving care, of course. So, even though a good fit helps, what's more important is how you play with the pieces you've got.

Another thing: most straight men have seen other flaccid penises, but how many of them have seen a bunch of erect ones up close and personal? (And no, porn doesn't count.) The erection is the great equaliser; a smaller penis will often catch up with a larger one on the way up. Just because your gym shower buddy has a big limp dong doesn't mean that it'll be any bigger than yours once inflated. In case you were wondering, the average length of an erect penis is about 15 cm. The average circumference of a stiffy is about 12 cm. Apparently the smallest erection ever recorded on a man is 6.25 cm (can you believe he let someone get a measuring tape near that thing?) and the largest is 27.5 cm.

Still not feeling proud of your number-one guy? Try looking at it in front of a mirror. We're serious! When you look down on it, it looks smaller (fore-shortening, man). You could also try trimming or shaving your pubes. Some guys feel their pubic hair unfairly creates the optical illusion of a smaller rig; these guys can feel significantly more, uh, manly after trimming. (Isn't it ironic?) In the same vein, if you're a little on the tubby side, getting in shape all over will make your penis stand out. (Nothing like a little stomach flab to overshadow a handsome specimen. Seriously: for every couple of stone you gain, your gut will engulf an extra inch of your wang.) And one more thing: if other men's penises get you down, stop showering with other naked men!

But enough about embracing your penis, figuratively speaking. You want the hard facts and 0800 numbers, right?

Penis Enlargement Surgery

Penis enlargement surgery is the only way to get a bigger boat, permanently. But this usually just increases the *flaccid* length and width — and who needs that? In addition, it's expensive, dangerous and doesn't make sex any better for the penis owner. We'll spare you the gory details; let's just say that 'botched job' is bandied about a lot in this field — and at least one guy has died on the operating table. (In fact, in the US most medical malpractice insurers specifically exclude penile enlargement surgery as a covered procedure.) If you're *really* struggling with size issues, get some therapy instead: it's cheaper, more effective and won't lead to any 'gross penile malformations'. If you don't believe us, both the American Urological Association and the American Plastic Surgery Association say the same thing. So there.

Weights

Some people think that hanging special weights from your penis will make it longer. Of course, most of these people are trying to sell you the special weights. Apparently they're most effective for people who have already undergone penis enlargement surgery — to help make the surgery 'take'. But we've already made our position clear on this kind of surgery. As far as weights without surgery go: there are tribes in India that hang penis weights starting at age six; by manhood they have loooonng skinny penises that are completely useless for sex. 'Nuff said.

Nature's Helping Handjob

Some people think that taking herbal supplements will make your penis bigger. Of course, most of these people are trying to sell you the herbal supplements. If you're a pill-popper, ginko biloba and ginseng are probably your best bets. Ginko biloba is reported to help out by encouraging blood flow and muscle relaxation (which makes everything feel just a little bit better down there) and ginseng may increase the production of nitric oxide (which plays a minor role in erections) — however, no controlled studies are available on either one.

Yohimbine is an extract from the bark of the African yohimbe tree; it's made quite a name for itself by helping dudes the world over get an erection. So much so that the FDA (Federal Drug Administration in the US) decided to put the little herb through the ringer and approved it for erectile dysfunction a few decades back. However, the studies done for FDA approval were not up to present standards and most urologists don't believe it works any better than a placebo. In the UK, it hasn't been licensed for treatment of ED. That said, if you want to give it a shot, you could go for herbal preparations until the Medicines Control Agency in the UK takes heart. The health shop variety has not been standardised and may contain other ingredients that are not safe, but that's about the

run away!

Desensitising creams are meant to help you go longer by numbing your dick. And that's fun for who? The cream can spread to your partner, numbing them too (they won't thank you) and can be irritating and burning to both parties, especially if you're not using barrier protection. If you really want to desensitise things a little, go with a super-thick latex condom instead (page 203).

best there is on offer at the moment. Our advice is to wait for the official OK from the gov. You'll have a professional monitoring your dosage and side-effects (it can have some pretty serious ones if you suffer from hypertension or cardio-vascular disease, or if you mix it with the wrong stuff or overdose on it). Remember, these herbs are not meant to be a cure-all — they're more like moral support for a healthy lifestyle. And as with most 'aphrodisiacs', there's usually a hefty placebo effect at work. By the way, don't go near anything that purports to contain the infamous aphrodisiac Spanish fly. It's made from ground-up beetles (just like on those reality TV shows) and it can cause bladder irritation, permanent urethral scarring, priapism (a penis-threatening perma-erection) and even death.

Penis Pumps

So what about penis pumps? They do make you bigger — because they give you an erection, duh. They were invented for men with problems getting it up. If your erections tend to be less than fully inflated, a pump-induced stiffy might be a tad more impressive, because the contraption, which resembles a medieval torture device, violently forces blood into the penis (erections occur naturally when blood flow increases to the penile area — some just get better flow than others). But after using the pump, it's sometimes harder to ejaculate. Plus, pumps can cause bruising (ouch). And once the erection's gone, the penis is the same as it ever was, only more blue and purple and tender.

Penis Curvature

It's totally normal, dude. Call it character. Penises often curve to one side, just as many women have one boob bigger than the other — neither should adversely affect one's sex life (unless you're dating an asshole who buys into the Hollywood-cum-porno myth that all body parts are perfectly symmetrical). The only exception is the extremely rare Peyronie's disease (J-shaped erections that are virtually useless for intercourse). If you think this could be you, ask your doctor to take a peek.

Circumcision

Does it make a difference to sex? In a vacuum, no: a penis can get all its jobs done and done well, whether it's circumcised or uncircumcised. But bring societal and cultural traditions (or prejudices) into the mix and then it starts to make a difference, at least to some people (especially the ones who always order the exact same thing on the menu every time).

Research over the past 20 years has deflated the hygiene myth that uncircumcised specimens get dirtier (and not in that good, naughty way); as long as every penis gets washed properly and regularly, there should be no problems. Studies have shown that circumcision has little impact on men's day-to-day health (unless the doctor botches the snip, of course) — contrary to conventional wisdom, circumcision won't protect guys from fungal infections or UTIs. However, studies *have* shown that penile cancer (though rare) is usually found in men who are either uncircumcised or who were circumcised later in life — circumcision as a baby appears to reduce your chances of getting cancer of the penis, though no one quite knows why. Forgoing the snip may just mean that Mr Happy feels everything a little more intensely: because the hood protects the sensitive glans against underwear chafing and general wear and tear, when the foreskin does get drawn back, the head is extra sensitive. Some studies suggest that circumcised men are less likely to contract HIV and herpes. However, both the CDC (Centers for Disease Control) and amfAR (The American Foundation for AIDS Research) in the US state that there is not enough conclusive evidence in this matter to call for a national policy change — most of the studies took place among uncircumcised men in Africa and thus intact foreskin cannot be isolated as a risk factor because of other cultural or religious practices that may be associated with STD transmission rates. On the other side of the debate, some doctors say that circumcised specimens may be more likely to cause vaginal irritation (as they're missing the foreskin's 'glide' feature) and so may increase a woman's chance of contracting HIV — though little data exists to support this claim either.

As far as sex goes, we conducted an informal, in-office poll and found that a foreskin makes very little difference — when erect, the cut and the uncut are almost identical. In fact, two kosher gherkins might be more different from each other than a kosher gherkin and a hooded sweatshirt. Here are the few variations we unsheathed in our survey:

- Uncircumcised handjobs are less likely to require lube as more skin = less Indian burns (see page 33 for more).
- A foreskin may provide extra friction for the woman during extended intercourse.
- The head of a turtle dick is probably more sensitive during arousal, as it wears a protective coat the rest of the time (plus, more skin = more nerves = more . . . oh, you do the maths).

If you're concerned about someone's reaction to the state of your penis, tell them what to expect. And if a new partner asks, 'Does this come with instructions?' simply show or tell them what works for you.

Fun Spunk Facts

Though it can sometimes smell like chlorine, semen — or as we like to call it, the nectar of the gods — is made up of fructose, protein, enzymes, citric acid, ascorbic acid, alkalines, a little zinc, a little iron and about 200 to 500 million sperm per shot (though sperm only make up about one per cent of the fluid). Semen has mood swings. Sometimes it's goopy and white, other times it's clear and runny. Sometimes it's a geyser, other times it's a dribble. First of all, it's a bodily fluid and all bodily fluids are affected by diet and dehydration. Changes in your diet can affect its consistency and taste (see page 51 for more details). Other factors include the time since you last ejaculated (the longer you've gone, the thicker and gummier it'll usually be), exercise, a sudden preponderance for really tight jeans (these last two can alter your testicle temperature), age and the size of your urethral opening — the younger you are and the smaller your hole, the farther you'll putt.

Hygiene

A simple daily washing with soap and water will help ward off fungal infections like jock itch (see below). Plus, if you're planning on sharing your trouser snake with a friend, it's just plain good manners. Be especially diligent in cleaning the area just below the head: that's where secretions, called smegma ('dick cheese' to you), can build up. If you're uncut, pull back the foreskin and wash around it.

Jock Itch

Caused by the fungus *tinea cruris*, jock itch is the mean older brother of athlete's foot — and one often tags along with the other. If you're a regular victim (poor baby) you can probably self-diagnose. But, because 'itchy crotch' is a symptom of lots of other penile problemos that do need a doctor's attention (e.g., scabies, see page 200), you should probably have your first case checked out by a pro to make sure. And if jock itch becomes a near-permanent house-guest, check with your doc, too: recurrent infections can be a sign of a troubled immune system. If you're sure it's jock itch, you can buy a spray or cream over the counter. If that doesn't wipe it out, ask your doctor for a prescription for something with a bit more kick. Treatment should take about two weeks.

Don't be an easy lay — at least not for jock itch:

- Shower regularly, especially right after a work-out. And dry off properly — don't just pull on your undies and run.
- Keep it clean (we're talking the whole package). But stay away from anti-bacterial or deodorant soaps, as they can be irritating.
- If you're prone to jock itch (or you're having a bad case of sweaty balls), throw a little anti-fungal powder or corn flour down there. Feel free to reapply throughout the day, especially if you're sitting near us.
- If you're the athletic type, make sure your little outfit fits well and doesn't chafe anywhere.
- Wash your work-out clothes often; don't leave them rolled up in a damp, smelly ball in your locker or your gym bag. And dude, wash your jockstrap or box on a regular basis — for everyone's sake.
- Consuming garlic may ward off fungal infections (though this method doesn't have much more medical proof than the garlic-vampire connection). Consuming garlic capsules won't offend the hotties as much.
- Change your underwear every day. (Note: a pair of worn boxers doesn't auto-matically become 'clean' again if you haven't worn them in three days.) Change more than daily if you're a sweater.
- Go for boxers over briefs: constricting underwear can encourage fungal growth. However, the rumours you've heard of briefs killing a guy's sperm count have been wildly exaggerated. So for the sake of aesthetics, the occa-sional boxer-brief combo shouldn't be a problem.

Blue Balls

Yes, blue balls does exist. No, you're not going to die from it. BB happens when you don't get the happy ending you were hoping for and sperm leave the balls (woohoo!) but don't make it out the penis (boohoo!). The penis is congested with blood (it's called an erection) and when it doesn't get the ejaculatory signal to drain, it hangs out there for longer than you'd like. And it hurts. Real bad. The fastest relief is to rub one out — you can consider that an order. Otherwise, the blood will eventually drain out of its own accord and the pain will eventually subside. No need to mention that this is no excuse to pressure a partner into sexual favours, because we're sure you graduated from secondary school a long time ago. By the way, chicks can experience a similar ache if they don't get off — we like to call it blue labes.

Impotence

Just because the Viagra Revolution is fully under way, that doesn't mean you shouldn't do your best to prevent impotence *before* it starts (kind of like heartburn). If impotence doesn't scare the erection right off you, how about heart disease? What helps hinder one helps hinder the other. Bonus! Eat a healthy low-fat diet, exercise regularly, keep your blood pressure and cholesterol down. Here's a toughie: drink in moderation. And here's the biggie: don't smoke. Seriously, getting smashed is bad for your stiffies, but prolonged smoking is the worst, as it can permanently block the blood vessels in your penis. And if you ride your bike a lot, do your genitals a favour and invest in one of those saddles with a hole in the middle; it takes the pressure off your pudendal artery (the one that controls blood flow to the penis) and may do wonders for your sperm count and potency.

Of course, sometimes the impotence is in your head. Talk to your doctor about the various options out there — but if s/he doesn't mention couples counselling or sex therapy, then you should. Talk to your partner: you should choose a solution together. And be sure to let them know it's not their fault, or else they'll start to develop issues of their own.

Premature Ejaculation

Unlike impotence, premature ejaculation usually *is* an in-your-head problem. Thus, it's usually just a matter of reconditioning your number-one guy — and it's nothing to be embarrassed about; you'd be surprised how many adult men end up taking the expressway when they'd really rather take the scenic route. Blame it on evolution (male animals spurt superfast so they don't get caught by predators). Blame it on your parents ('Hey, sport, whatcha doing in there?'). Or blame it on plain laziness (years of rubbing one out in minutes is a hard habit to break). The official definition of premature ejaculation is coming at the moment of, or right after, penetration. More than a third of men under 25 suffer from it and about ten per cent of guys over that age do, too. And pretty much every guy suffers from it at the beginning of a relationship (nerves, stress, overstimulation) and at the sudden end of a long dry period. But if it's a more permanent condition, you're going to have to train your schlong to go long. By the way, the better you know your pelvic muscles (page 257), the more aware you'll be of your body's sexual response cycle. Combine a kegel work-out programme with the methods below. And be patient: it's not something you can fix in a matter of days, or even weeks. It'll probably take at least a few months. Think of it as reprogramming your penis after a decade of brainwashing in the cult of the quickie.

If you're currently in a relationship, you've got to tell your partner what's going on. First of all, they might be able to shed some light on 'relationship issues' that could be causing this (better to do it privately than on *Trisha*). Psychiatrists' favourites include guilt (affair, maybe?), nerves, lack of self-esteem and anxiety. You know, the little things. Second, you'll need your partner's cooperation in the exercises below. And third, you'll need to keep them in the loop so they don't become one big ball of sexual tension — it's going to require significant patience from both of you, so you should both figure out a way for them to climax that doesn't solely rely on your stick's stamina.

If you're going to retrain Mr Pokey, you need to be able to recognise the point right *before* the point of no return. And then you need to be able to figure out how to hang loose at that point — first solo and then with your partner. First, masturbate with a mission. Notice what it feels like right before you spurt. Notice what it feels like right before that moment. When you can feel that moment coming, as it were, let go and sit really still. Wait till the moment passes and then start up again. See how many times you can do this. It's going to take some practice — chances are, the first few times you'll dribble all over your thigh — but eventually you'll learn to stop and start efficiently. When you feel like you've mastered this exercise, have your partner administer the handjob under your guidance. Then try the same exercises with intercourse: holding still and/or pulling out at that moment, taking a deep breath and resuming play. In all positions, focus on keeping your butt muscles as relaxed as possible. And . try substituting your in-out thrusting for a more circular motion: it may reduce the friction on the supersensitive head of your penis.

PUMPING UP YOUR LOVE MUSCLES

Kegels for Him and Her

We don't care if you've never been to a gym in your life; you simply must work out your pelvic muscles if you want to consider yourself sexually fit. Don't worry, you won't break a sweat. You can even start working them while reading this chapter. In fact, please do.

There are several muscles in the perineal group, but two that stand out as MVPs. The pubococcygeus muscle (PC for short) runs along the pelvic floor, from the pubic bone to the coccyx (or tailbone), in both women and men. Just above it is the bulbocavernosus muscle. This one surrounds the urethra, perineum and anus in an elegant figure eight. Together, they contract involuntarily during the Big O; you contract them voluntarily when you don't want to piss your pants. (When people talk about pelvic muscles, they usually just single out the PC — but these muscles are team players.)

Until the '40s, the pelvic muscles' supporting role in sex went largely unrecognised — and then along came Dr Arnold Kegel, a Los Angeles gynaecologist. Mr Kegel prescribed a course of pelvic muscle exercises (see the work-out programmes below) to a group of women who were suffering from incontinence. After they began shaping up, they noticed a rather serendipitous side-effect (clever girls!): their sex lives took a turn for the ecstatic. Because the pelvic muscles surround the vagina, strengthening them means stronger orgasms — or maybe just orgasms, period. The exercises have been known as kegels ever since (though some docs may refer to them as pelvic muscle strengthening exercises, or pelvic floor exercises — neither of which rolls off the tongue quite like 'kegels'). Judy Blume's Margaret (*Are You There, God? It's Me, Margaret*, if you're no Blume aficionado) should have given up those futile bust exercises for something that *really* would have paid off later.

But kegels aren't just for chicks. While well-toned pelvic muscles won't take a man quite as far, they may still get him to the land of stronger erections, greater stamina, farther spurts and more intense Os (your mileage may vary). Plus, once your pelvic muscles are all buff, you can make your penis bounce and jiggle — your own stupid pet trick — which could cheer up a loved one after a tough day at the office. And making your muscles your love slaves is the first step towards injaculation and multiple male orgasms (assuming you want to chase those particular fairy tales . . . see pages 104 and 5 respectively).

Benefits that the whole family can enjoy include increased blood flow down there (which just feels good) and muscles that are better able to experience and transmit sensation. Plus, because the bulbocavernosus loops around the anus, learning how to relax it can make ass play as fun as the benevolent sex gods intended it to be. We know what you're thinking: Where have we been all your life? That doesn't matter; we're here now. So let's whip you into shape, shall we?

Targeting the Muscle Group

Chicks and dicks, next time you're on a tinkle break, stop the flow of pee for a few seconds. (Or, if you've got a good imagination, pretend you're holding it right now.) Feel those internal muscles you're contracting? Good — those are pelvic muscles. Ladies who need some extra assistance in isolating the muscles can clench their vagina around one or two inserted fingers. Or, what the hell, around a penis. Just make sure that you're not tensing your butt or abs at the same time. Once you know where those muscles live, don't be *literally* stopping the flow of pee anymore — all that holding back just isn't good for you.

Kegels for Her

Not only do defined pelvic muscles improve your sex life, they can also increase vaginal lubrication, make labour easier ('ease' being a relative concept there), prevent urinary incontinence (especially after giving birth) and help protect against prolapse of the uterus (a nasty condition, either inherited or caused by a series of tough childbirths, in which the uterus pretty much just falls down into the vagina). The exercises can also help restore vaginal muscle tone after childbirth, for a tighter fit during sex. And a good strong pelvic floor can help make your G-spot more sensitive, thanks to increased blood flow in the pelvic arena. In addition to making orgasms easier to achieve (even multiple ones), regular kegels can improve any sexual activity where control (and, more importantly, the ability to *relinquish* control) is a factor: namely, fisting and female ejaculation (see pages 109 and 99, respectively). Rifle through this book to see how many times we refer readers to this very section and you'll understand the importance of kegelling.

Your Work-out Programme

If you've never kegelled before, start slow. First, make sure your bladder is empty. Then, squeeze the pelvic muscles, hold for two or three seconds and release. Do it again, four or five more times. Repeat three times daily. (If it ever starts to hurt, back off and build up more slowly, as you would with any work-out.) When that starts to feel like a cinch, up your reps and the count you hold for: increase both gradually until you can hold the squeeze for about ten seconds, ten to 20 times in a row. Do that three times daily and you're more than halfway to paradise. If you want to get fancy (and who doesn't?) combine those long, loving squeezes with short, rapid-fire kegel bursts — three or four quickie clenches at the end of each long one. And just like in yoga class, work on keeping your breathing in sync with your squeezing: try inhaling as you contract, holding your breath while you hold the muscles and exhaling as you relax. Or inhale one deep breath while you punch out the quickies.

Another exercise that will help with the relinquishing control thing is to 'bear down', kind of like mums-to-be do when giving birth. It's like you're trying to force out the finger of your drunk lover who passed out in the middle of diddling you. If you bear down like this for ten reps, three times a day, then you deserve a golden dildo award for dedication to the field — and multiple orgasms every day for the rest of your sex life. Maintain this exercise schedule for six weeks and you should start to notice the difference in the bedroom (even if it's just you and your left hand in that bedroom).

Mad Props

To spice up your work-out, treat yourself to a vaginal barbell — which is exactly what it sounds like. You'll find them at most good sex shops. Usually made of stainless steel, they're essentially dildo-like toys that give you something to grip onto during all that squeezing. The best-selling steel weights are Betty's Barbell (designed by sexologist Betty Dodson) and the Kegelcisor (both available via Internet shopping). If you go online, you'll find KegelPro, which is a plastic device that looks a little like a nutcracker for your cooch. Of course, relying on a prop makes it slightly more awkward to break out the kegels next time you get stuck in line at the supermarket, so mix it up. Remember, there's no such thing as too many kegels.

When to Flex

Try hugging his penis next time he's in there (if you do it repeatedly it's called milking and most guys love it). Or squeeze the pelvic muscles next time you're rubbing one out. Or focus on relaxing them when your partner's going for the G. Or try to extend the involuntary contractions of an orgasm by voluntarily contracting the muscles yourself.

Kegels for Him

Regular kegel exercises are a way to bond with your penis — and who couldn't benefit from more QT with his johnson? The more adept you become at isolating these muscles (and flexing them at will), the more aware you'll be of what's going on right before and during orgasm (beyond the usual 'holy crap, that feels good!'). You'll also have more control over your number-one guy. Of course, by 'control' we mean that while he'll *always* be in the driver's seat, he might actually listen to your directions every now and then.

Your Work-out Programme

It's just like the ladies' programme: squeeze, hold, release. Repeat. And repeat. Build up your tolerance over the course of a few weeks, following the instructions above, until you can hold the squeeze for up to ten seconds, doing ten reps, three times a day. And add the rapid-fire squeezes, too. You can even try bearing down, though it probably won't come as naturally to you as it does to the ladies.

When you're bored or at a particularly dull party, try to make your penis bob up and down by flexing the muscles. You could even drape a napkin over it to add resistance and visual appeal — like the magician who makes a dove appear from behind his handkerchief. Just don't hang anything heavy on it: this is a delicate little twitch of a trick, not a weightlifting contest. And don't think for a second that building this muscle will build bulk. Because it won't. So get over it and just enjoy what the good Lord gave you.

When to Flex

Next time you're inside your partner (lucky dog), hold reeeallly still and try a little twitching action. See what she or he says. Or try squeezing your muscles right before, or right as, you come. Experiment while you're flogging the bishop to see what flexing does for you and your orgasm.

18

WET YOUR WHISTLE

The Importance of Lube

Let's get one thing straight: shop-bought personal lubricant is not just for leatherboys who want to go 'elbow deep'. Nor is lube a 'crutch' for people with faulty machinery. And reaching for the wet stuff doesn't mean you're 'not into it', 'frigid', or 'kinky'. First of all, not everyone's bits and pieces moisten up on demand. When it comes to guys, they have diddly-squat to offer in terms of natural lubricant — a couple of drops of pre-come aren't going to oil anyone's parts. And for women, natural lubrication doesn't necessarily go hand in hand with sexual arousal (nor does it always *indicate* sexual arousal — and it's certainly no guarantee that she's ready for penetration). Vaginal secretions in chicks are caused by hormones and hormones get tossed around more often than the new kid at school — everything from her menstrual cycle to pregnancy to menopause to sickness can affect how much natural lube she produces. In addition, smoking, caffeine, booze, weed, stress and cold medicine can all dry you up. So when you're a friend in need, man-made lubricant is a friend indeed.

Need more reasons to use lube? Because dick and vadge burn suck. Because her highly sensitive nooks and crannies can take more exploration when well lubed. Because it's a brand-new feeling — don't knock it till you've tried it. Because it lets you try positions that require an easy in. Because it lets you try orifices that don't have nature's lube working for them. Because it makes everything fit together just so, especially when the laws of physics seem to suggest that there's no way in hell everything's going to fit together just so. Because condoms feel better with a little lube (both outside and in — put a few drops on the head of the penis before rolling one on for a more touchy-feely lay). Because a lubricated condom is less likely to break. Because wet is sexy. Because we say so.

When to Lube?

Every time you go up the poop chute (even if it's just with a pinky). Every time you're putting your whole hand anywhere. Pretty much every time you give him a handjob (unless he's got an uncut specimen and doesn't need it, or he specifically requests a dry rubdown, or you're a Jedi Master). Occasionally during oral sex, if you're prone to dry mouth (or you just want to add some flava). When it comes to handwork for her, it's ladies' choice — though if she's never experienced a wet one, you should initiate her. She'll probably find that a little lube gives her clitoral head more stamina. (There's nothing worse than a clit that gets numb before it gets off.) As for vaginal penetration (with a toy or a penis), it depends on the vagina, the penis and the toy (and the day, the mood, the position, the barrier protection, the weather . . .). A pre-lubricated condom may not always be enough, especially if you're going loooong (or if the penetrating specimen is particularly long). Non-lubed barrier protection will dry things up pretty quickly (which is absolutely no excuse to forgo the barrier protection), so just add something slippery. Also, many dildos absorb a chick's natural juice supply way faster than a dick does.

What to Lube With?

Here's where it gets tricky, or sticky, if you will: you have more choices than the captain of the footie team at the school dance. First of all, the only DIY lube you should ever use on her is your own spit (assuming you're free of any mouth infections, like oral herpes) or her own private geyser (sometimes there's enough flowing down there to dip in with a finger and spread the wealth). You can get more creative with him, as long as he's not planning on sticking his willy in any of your orifices immediately after the lube job — see the sidebar for our suggestions on which household supplies to raid. But spit doesn't last — besides, it's so schooldays. Grown-ups buy lube. Man-made lubricants break down into three basic genres: oil-based, water-based and silicone-based. And within each of those groups, there are at least 57 varieties to choose from. (Do your best to ignore the fact that their brand names are only one rung up the cheese ladder from porno titles.) Ready? Set? Wet!

Oil-Based Lubes

Oils have more slippery stamina than the water-based variety (you rarely have to reapply) and you can find them pretty much anywhere (even the kitchen cupboard), but they're not the kind of lube you can use on just any occasion.

All oils destroy latex, so keep anything oily away from latex condoms, gloves, dental dams or diaphragms. Safer sex and oil just don't mix. And we're not only talking about lard; 'oil-based' includes petroleum products like Vaseline and hand lotion, too. Also, you shouldn't be using oil if there's a vagina involved: it's too damn hard to wash out of the body — it can hang out there for days, encouraging bacteria to cling on, which can lead to infections. (Some vaginas of steel never get bothered by oils, but if you're not sure you've got one of those, stay well away.)

So when *can* you use oils? On a dude's dong, if a handjob's all that's on the menu. For a full-body massage, if you can keep your hands from wandering to her privates. Going up the bum, either manually or with a polyurethane condom like Durex Avanti (oil won't degrade polyurethane). By the way, because the anal tissues are easily irritated, you should stick to pure, unscented products such as a lightweight vegetable oil. (But don't forget, if the person is allergic to peanuts, then their asshole will be allergic to peanut oil.) Stay away from petroleum-based products like Vaseline for backdoor love, since they'll just dry out the mucous membranes — but these products are fine for man-handjobs. Other oils worth greasing up with (for handjob use only) include Elbow Grease (available on the Net).

Water-Based Lubes

Water-based lubricants play well with others. Sometimes referred to as 'jellies', most of them are tasteless, odourless, non-staining and non-irritating (even to sensitive little vaginas). They can all be used safely with latex products and silicone toys and they all wash away in seconds with plain old water — which means they don't hang around in the veegee encouraging bad bacteria to grow. Their only downside is that they need to be reapplied fairly often — or just 'loosened' with water when they get tacky. (So keep a glass of water handy and if you have the option, get it in a pump dispenser for easy one-handed reapplication.) By the way, products called 'water-soluble' are not the same thing at all — they usually contain oil. So don't fall for that one.

How to choose a lube? It all depends where the lube is going. Some lubes are built for stamina (e.g., major butt action), others for taste, others to replicate vaginal juices, others for supersensitive vaginas. Don't buy anything containing nonoxynol-9 (see sidebar) and if the lube is going near a vagina, steer clear of products with glycerine (it's a form of sugar that can cause yeast infections in some chicks). Other than that, it's just a matter of test-driving the brands out there until you find your own personal best. Below, some of our water-based faves . . .

- Liquid Silk: this lube has the consistency of moisturiser. It lasts longer than any other water-based product, doesn't get sticky or tacky and is glycerine-free. Two thumbs up (wherever those thumbs are going). Maximus, by the same company, does pretty much the same thing except it's clear, rather than white. It's a matter of aesthetics.
- Pjur Aqua (or Pjur Eros Waterformulation): another flavourless, odourless, non-sticky lube. A real team player.
- Astroglide: one of the best-selling brands, thanks to its sweet taste and the fact that it mimics the body's natural lube. It does, however, contain glycerine.
- Slippery Stuff: thicker than Astroglide, this lube was invented for divers who had trouble getting in and out of their rubber suits. It's taste-free, glycerine-free and not too sticky. You'll probably have to Internet buy this one.
- ID Juicy Lube: if you've got a sweet tooth, this lube's for you. It comes in bubblegum, cherry, peach, passion fruit and watermelon. But, as with anything flavourful, this one's got glycerine in it. If you like it plain, stick to the original formula ID Lube.
- Probe (and Probe Classic): the thickest water-based lubricant out there, it's a fave among fisters. Might be tricky finding in the UK, but worth the search.

- **K-Y Jelly:** it's practically retro, it's been around for so long — K-Y is the original water-based lube. We don't recommend it because it gets gummy so fast and can't be rewet. But it *is* available pretty much anywhere (even in Texas, we've heard) and it is water-based. If you find yourself in a pinch (or in Texas), it'll do.

Getting Fancy: Silicone-Based Lubes

We have seen the future and it is slippery. Silicone-based lubes provide all the fun of oils but none of the nasty side-effects. Lubricated condoms have been employing it forever, but only recently has silicone liquid been offered by the bottle. It's safe on vaginas, safe with latex, sturdy enough for butt

play, lasts for hours (very convenient when you're wrist-deep and reapplication is not an easy option) and it can be washed away easily with soap and water. The only thing it's not compatible with is silicone toys (apparently it causes some bizarre chemical reaction). And the best thing ever is that it's completely waterproof. Bath time will never be the same again. It's a teensy bit more expensive than water-based lube, but you'll need so little of it (just a drop or two) that you'll probably end up saving dough. Silicone addicts claim that it feels warmer than other lubes and transmits sensation better. And unlike water-based products, silicone feels good all over the body.

The Germans have cornered the market on silicone lubes. So next time you're looking to make a little Nachtmusik, try out Venus or Eros, the two longest-lasting silicone products out there. They're both hypoallergenic and glycerine-free. Or try ID Millennium or Wet Platinum.

A Final Thought on Wet Sex

You don't have to lube the same way each time, so mix it up. Messy is sexy (not to mention easier), but sometimes you just want a good clean quickie fuck (like when you're doing it on Grandma's couch while she goes down the shops). The most important thing to remember is this: crotch burn is just not sexy. And that's our final word.

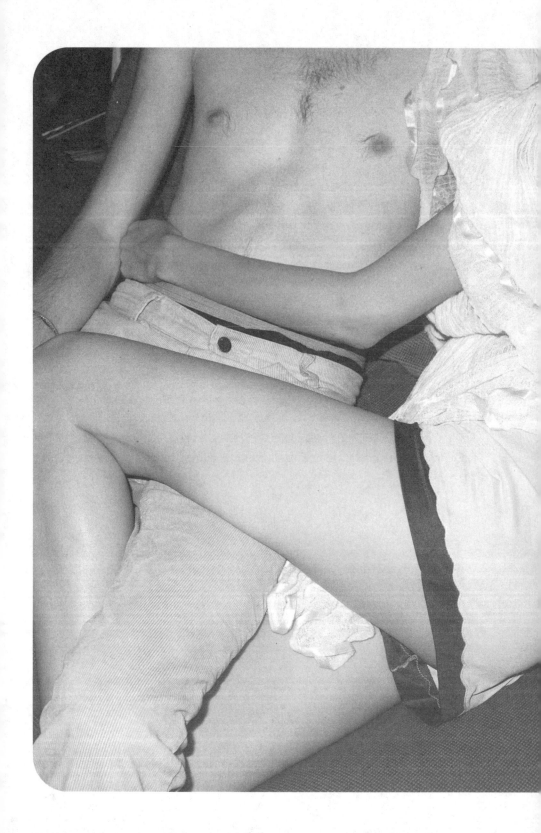

THE HIPBONE'S CONNECTED TO THE ...

The Below-the-Belt Anatomy Appendix

We've made liberal use of dirty words, silly slang and entertaining (at least to us) euphemisms throughout this book, in part because any word — especially 'penis' and 'vagina' — starts to look funny if you say it enough and in part because we didn't want to sound like a secondary school sex-ed textbook. To be responsible, we've dedicated the section below to the unadorned truth about what little boys and girls are made of, complete with medical lingo and a serious-as-cancer tone. (You'll find the euphemisms we employ most often at the end of each definition.) But please keep in mind that for every girl and every boy, there is a slightly different way that these parts fit together (anatomy) and work together (physiology) to make you special ... kinda like snowflakes. So think of the list below as a basic guide to the average body's bits and pieces. If yours don't work exactly as the manual says they should, it probably just means they broke the mould.

Ladies ...

- **Vulva:** The collective name for the external female genitals — not to be confused with just the vagina. The vulva includes the outer lips (labia majora), inner lips (labia minora), the head (glans) of the clitoris, the vaginal opening,

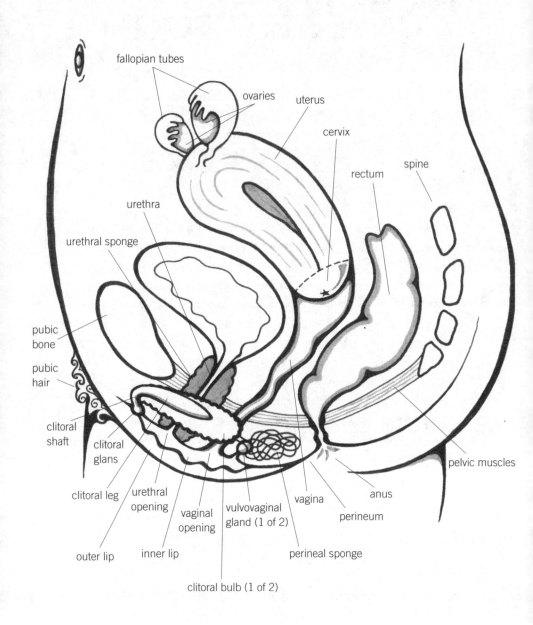

fallopian tubes

ovaries

uterus

cervix

spine

rectum

urethra

urethral sponge

pubic bone

pubic hair

clitoral shaft

clitoral glans

clitoral leg

urethral opening

vaginal opening

vulvovaginal gland (1 of 2)

vagina

anus

perineum

pelvic muscles

outer lip

inner lip

perineal sponge

clitoral bulb (1 of 2)

the urinary opening and the mons. For an illustration of the vulva, turn to page 40. (Aka the view, down there, down under.)

turn to page 40

- **Mons, or mons veneris, mons pubis:** The pad of fatty tissue that covers the pubic bone below the abdomen, above the labia and protects the pubic bone from impact during sexual intercourse. It's usually covered in pubic hair . . . or stubble. The mons veneris, Latin for 'Mountain of Venus' (after the Roman goddess of love) is sexually sensitive in some lucky women. (Aka the mound.)

- **Inner and outer labia:** Two sets of lips surrounding the clitoral glans, the urethra and the vaginal opening. The outer lips, or labia majora, are pads of fatty tissue usually covered in pubic hair that are comparable to the male scrotal sac; the inner lips, or labia minora, are usually hairless, with one often slightly bigger than another and correspond to the bottom side of the penis. The labia (especially the inner lips) are usually responsive to stimulation; some women's labia have more nerve endings than others and some women find inner labial stimulation more effective than direct clitoral stimulation. While the inner labia tend to be thinner and lighter in colour than the outer labia, sexual stimulation causes them to swell and turn darker. The inner labia may protrude farther than the outer labia. (Aka lips, labes, vertical smile.)

- **Clitoris:** Back in the day, people used to think the clitoris was just a little sensitive nubbin peeking through the hood where the tops of the labia meet. But now (thanks to books like *The Clitoral Truth* by Rebecca Chalker) we know that it's a complex organ of innervated erectile tissue (just like the penis), extending throughout the genital region, sometimes as much as 12 cm deep, that fills and swells with blood. That little nubbin is just the tip of the iceberg (officially called the head or the glans). Therefore, when you stimulate the urethra, vagina, or anus, you're indirectly stimulating the clitoris, too. It's the only organ in the human body (either female or male) whose sole purpose is to transmit sexual sensation. (Aka the clitoral network.)

male, female, other

Sometimes parts fit together a little more differently and people don't fit so neatly into this admittedly narrow-minded boy-girl dichotomy. They're called intersexes — people with ambiguous or atypical sex organs. Not to be confused with people who feel they are trapped in a body of the opposite sex — those people are called transsexuals. In some cases, surgeons have been called on to help align their external body with their internal gender identity.

- **Clitoral glans:** The glans (the sexual organ that corresponds to the head of the penis) is the head of the clitoris, the little nubbin mentioned above. The clitoral glans has 6–8,000 sensory nerve endings — more than any other structure in the human body, male or female — which is about four times as many as are on the (much larger) glans of the penis. It varies greatly (both from woman to woman and from day to day in each woman) in size, shape, colour and the extent to which it protrudes from the hood that's created by the folds of skin where the top of the labia meet (this is the region analogous to the foreskin). Anywhere from two to 20 mm in diameter, the clitoral glans can seem to disappear when it gets lost in all the surrounding swollen tissue during extreme arousal and/or when it retracts a bit during orgasm. While the clitoral network extends way back inside a woman, in this book, when we use the term 'clit', we're referring to the external head. (Aka the clit, head, little man in the boat, chickpea, bean, acorn, magic button.)
- **Clitoral shaft or body of the clitoris:** If you move your finger above the clitoral glans, over the hood and press down, you should feel some spongy tissue leading towards the pubic mound for about a centimetre or two. This is the clitoral shaft — the tough, rubbery and moveable cord extending from the glans beneath the skin. It can be sexually arousing for some women when pressed.
- **Crura or clitoral legs:** Beneath the skin's surface, the clitoral shaft forks sharply, forming two legs (crura) that extend down either side of the vagina, behind the labia, like a wishbone, for about seven cm.
- **Clitoral bulbs:** The clitoris has another two extensions that start where the shaft and crura meet and extend down underneath each inner lip — they are 'bulbs' of cavernous erectile tissue that fill with blood during arousal, just like the erectile tissue, or corpus cavernosum, of the penis. These are bigger and fuller than the crura.
- **Urethra:** Just beneath the clit, you'll find a small V or slit known as the urethral opening (or urinary opening); it's one end of the thin, four-cm-long tube known as the urethra, which conducts urine from the bladder out of the body. The urethra runs parallel to the top wall of the vagina and is surrounded by spongy erectile tissue, or corpus spongiosum (just like the urethra in men is). Like a roll of insulation, this 'urethral sponge' contains many tiny glands called paraurethral glands, which fill with an alkaline fluid (similar to the prostatic fluid of men) upon arousal. The oval five-

pence-coin-sized area of this tissue that can be felt through the ceiling of the vagina, commonly known as the G-spot, can sometimes be stimulated to the point of fluid expulsion through the urethra in some women (known as female ejaculation — see page 103 for more info). The urethral sponge and its glands are analogous to the prostate gland in men. (Aka the pee hole.)

- **Bladder:** The organ that collects and stores urine produced by the kidneys that is regularly emptied through the urethra.

- **Vagina:** The passage of folds (that can mould to whatever might be passing through) between the cervix and the world, also known as the birth canal. The vaginal walls are a mucous membrane (i.e., a thin layer of tissue that secretes mucus). If you've ever read the instructions for inserting a tampon, you'll know that this approximately seven- to 12-cm canal heads towards the small of your back at a 45-degree angle (rather than straight into your body). The back two-thirds of the vagina are smooth and not very sensitive; when aroused, this area can almost double in length and width (a process called tenting that makes vaginal fisting possible). The outer, nerve-heavy third of the vagina actually swells and thus tightens during arousal, thanks to the extensive clitoral tissue around it; the top part of this area will feel spongy — that's the urethral sponge on the other side of the vaginal wall (aka the G-spot). The vagina produces continuous secretions — whether during ovulation, pregnancy or sexual arousal — to provide lubrication (different from the lubrication provided by the vulvovaginal glands mentioned below), help keep the vagina clean and maintain its acidity to prevent infections. (Aka the vadge, veegee, vg, cooch, coochie, cooter, yoni, wilma.)

- **Vulvovaginal glands, vestibular glands or Bartholin's glands:** Two internal bean-sized glands just below the vaginal opening. They provide a bit of lubrication during sexual excitement — just a few drops of viscous fluid — released via all-but-invisible ducts on the inner lips. They're generally too small to notice, but sometimes you can feel them if they get infected and swell.

- **Hymen:** A thin membrane that surrounds the vaginal opening, partially blocking it but almost never covering the hole completely. Hymens come in all shapes and sizes: some women are born without one while others have to have them opened surgically. As a result of certain kinds of vaginal penetration, like masturbation and tampon use and other non-penetrative activities, like horseback riding and gymnastics, the hymen is usually stretched or torn before the first time a woman has partner sex. But there's a chance it hasn't stretched as far as it will go during intercourse, which is why it might still hurt or, in rare cases, bleed during the first few times. For most women it stretches easily; after being stretched or torn, little folds of hymen tissue remain visible just inside the vagina. (Aka the cherry, as in 'popping your cherry'.)

- **Cervix:** The gateway between the uterus (womb) and the vagina. It's a round fleshy dome with a small dimplelike opening in the centre called the os. The cervix changes position, colour and shape throughout a lifetime as well as during each menstrual cycle. It's usually the size of a cherry, but can be bigger, especially in women who have given birth. The tiny os opening is the gatekeeper: it won't let anything like a tampon, finger or penis pass. However, it allows his sexual fluids in during intercourse, fertility-promoting mucus out during ovulation (just in case any sperm come along), blood out during menstruation and babies out during labour (it can dilate to ten cm or more!). The space around the cervix on the vagina side is called the fornix and some women like this space explored with a finger. While the cervix has no nerve endings on its surface, it is sensitive to pressure — again, some women like the pressure of *full* penetration, others hate it.

- **Uterus:** This is where foetuses grow. It's sandwiched between the bladder on one side (which is beneath the abdominal wall) and the rectum on the other (which is near the tailbone). A non-pregnant uterus is about the size of a kiwi fruit or a small lemon. When you have menstrual cramps, this is where they're coming from. (Aka the baby maker and womb.)

- **Fallopian tubes:** Two identical egg-transport tubes, about 10 cm long, that extend out and back from either side of the upper end of the uterus, kind of like a ram's horns facing backwards (as *Our Bodies, Ourselves* describes them). The open, fringed ends float near the ovaries; during ovulation, when an egg is released from one of the ovaries, the millions of tiny hairs (called cilia) undulate to scoop up the egg and undulating muscle contractions push it along to the uterus. Somewhere along its journey, the egg hopes to find a sperm up for the challenge of fertilisation.

- **Ovaries:** These are two organs the size and shape of unshelled almonds located on either side and somewhat below the uterus (about 10 to 12 cm below your waist). The ovaries serve two functions: (1) to produce eggs and

(2) to produce female sex hormones (oestrogen and progesterone, among others). They are analogous to the testes in dudes.

- **Pelvic floor muscles:** The pelvic floor muscles — including the PC or pubo-coccygeus muscle and the bulbocavernosus muscle — are a group of muscles that help hold the pelvic organs in place and provide support for other internal organs all the way up to your diaphragm. They pass around the urethra, vagina and anus and contract during arousal and orgasm. So stronger pelvic muscles (conditioned by doing kegel exercises) mean stronger Os. See page 257 for more.

Bringing It All Together

During sexual arousal and (usually) rhythmic stimulation, blood rushes to the pelvis, filling the erectile tissue of the clitoris; glands fill with fluid; nerve cells become agitated (in a good way); the skin gets supersensitive, as do the nipples; the clitoral head protrudes as it becomes engorged; the shaft becomes more noticeable; the clitoral legs stiffen and stretch; the bulbs balloon so the vaginal opening tightens and the lips swell; the urethral sponge pushes against the roof of the vagina (and may produce 'female ejaculate'); the vagina tents and lubricates (in theory to help penile insertion and possible sperm transportation to an egg), as do the vulvovaginal glands; the muscles in the area begin to contract, creating tension in the area; everything becomes more sensitive due to the increased blood supply; and then eventually, *hopefully*, a series of quick, rhythmic muscular contractions known as an orgasm release that tension. Some researchers theorise that women are more likely to experience 'multiple orgasms' (one right after another without a prolonged recovery period) because the blood in the area does not drain away as quickly and suddenly after orgasm as it does in the penis.

... and Gentlemen

- **Penis:** Unlike many mammals, men's penises do not have a bone. Nor do they have any muscles — at least not in the shaft, where one would hope. (See pelvic muscles on page 278 for the *surrounding* muscles.) What the

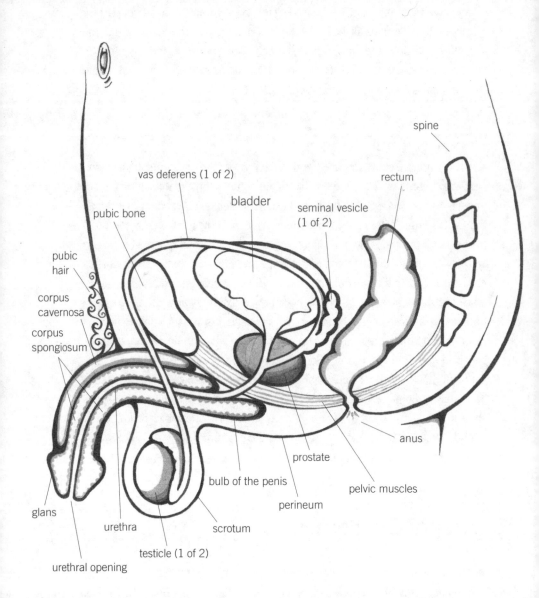

spine

vas deferens (1 of 2)

bladder

pubic bone

seminal vesicle
(1 of 2)

rectum

pubic
hair

corpus
cavernosa

corpus
spongiosum

glans

urethra

bulb of the penis

testicle (1 of 2)

scrotum

prostate

perineum

pelvic muscles

anus

urethral opening

penis does have is two long tubes running along its length, called corpus cavernosa, which are made of spongy erectile tissue and blood vessels. These cylinders are analogous to the clitoral bulbs in women. The base of the penis actually extends into the body, almost back to the anus. The two corpus cavernosa fork at the base of the penis, under the prostate and continue back, where they attach to the pelvic bone. (If you press on the perineum during an erection, you might be able to feel them.) The internal portion of the penis is known as the root, or bulb. (Aka cock, peter, schlong, willy, twig — as in 'twig and berries' — peepee, Mr Happy, Mr Pokey, John Thomas, Peter, skin flute, dong, johnson, one-eyed wonder worm, chorizo, knob, unit, rig, hot dog, gherkin, stewart, lingam, Mr Man, kielbasa, sausage, chub.)

- Glans: The head of the penis. With the highest concentration of nerve endings on the penis, the glans is the most sensitive area (especially in uncircumcised men) and is analogous to the head of the clitoris. (Aka the head, tip, helmet, hat.)

- Corona or coronal ridge: This is the ring of flesh at the base of the glans, where it meets the shaft of the penis. (Aka the crown.)

- Frenulum or frenum: A very sensitive thin strip of skin on the underside of the penis that connects the shaft to the head. In uncircumcised men, the frenulum tethers the foreskin and keeps it from retracting too far; in circumcised men, part or all of the frenulum may be missing (which is why uncircumcised guys claim more penile sensitivity).

- Foreskin or prepuce: In uncircumcised men, this layer of skin with some nerve endings covers the glans when the penis is flaccid, like a hood; it retracts during an erection. Small glands under the foreskin secrete an oily substance, which, when mixed with dead skin cells, forms a cottage cheese-like white paste called smegma. Circumcised men do not produce smegma. (Aka a polo neck or hood; uncircumcised penises are sometimes called polo necks or polodicks.)

- Urinary opening, urethral opening or meatus: The opening at the tip of the penis that is an exit for both urine and semen. (Aka the pee hole.)

- Urethra: This thin tube runs from the bladder, through the prostate gland, along the bottom of the penile shaft under the two corpus cavernosa, ending at the urethral opening at the glans. It transports urine from the bladder when you pee and prostatic fluid from the prostate and semen from the testicles when you ejaculate. The urethra is surrounded by a cylinder of spongy erectile tissue called the corpus spongiosum, which you can feel as the ridge on the underside of the penis. This ridge, known as the raphe, runs from the frenulum down the shaft, along the middle of the scrotum to the anus.

- **Testicles or testes:** Varying in size from grapes to eggs, with one often hanging lower than the other, the testicles are two glands that produce both testosterone and sperm. The sperm exit the testicles into the epididymis, a soft mass (that's actually a coiled-up tube) at the back and top of the testicles that connect to the vas deferens, see page 278. (Aka balls, the twins, the boys, berries — as in 'twig and berries'.)
- **Scrotum or scrotal sac:** The loose, hairy sac of skin that contains the testicles. The scrotum protects the testicles and keeps them from getting too hot or too cold (as extreme temperatures affect sperm production). During arousal, physical activity, or a cold spell, a muscle in the sac called the cremaster contracts to raise the sac closer to your body; during a warm shower, it relaxes to lower the sac. (Aka the ball sac.)
- **Vas deferens:** Two small tubes connecting the epididymis to the urethra for sperm expulsion. As sperm travel along these tubes towards the urethra, they collect semen ingredients from the seminal vesicles. The vas deferens are cut during a vasectomy.
- **Seminal vesicles:** Glands between the base of the bladder and the prostate that produce nutrients for the semen. These nutrients help transport the sperm and protect them after they have left the penis.
- **Semen or ejaculate:** The testicles produce sperm. During arousal, the sperm move out of the testicles through the epididymis, then through the vas deferens into the urethra, where they mix with several fluids (including prostatic fluid and nutrients from the seminal vesicles) to produce semen. This cocktail is expelled from the body via the urethra when a man ejaculates. Before ejaculation, the Cowper's glands (located near the bulb of the penis) secrete an alkaline fluid that neutralises any urine that may be left in the man's urethra and helps the sperm survive in the acidic vaginal environment. (Aka come, love juice, man juice, little guys [usually just refers to the sperm], spunk, seed, white gold.)
- **Prostate gland:** Similar in function to the seminal vesicles, this gland produces fluid that helps transport sperm and protects them after they have left

the penis. It's located behind the pubic bone just below the bladder, close to the root of the penis and is analogous to the female G-spot. (Aka the male G-spot or walnut.)

- **Pelvic muscles:** This muscle group forms a figure eight around the genitals and contracts involuntarily during orgasm. You can contract them *voluntarily* to halt the flow of urine. Toning them can help with sexual control and urinary incontinence. See page 257 for more.

Bringing It All Together

In response to sexual stimulation (mental, visual and/or physical), the brain sends signals via the nervous system that trigger blood flow into the penis along the corpus cavernosa. The spongy erectile tissue of these cylinders absorbs the blood, making the penis stiff (an erection); the engorged cylinders press against the membrane surrounding them and this pressure temporarily shuts down the walls of the veins that usually carry blood away, so the blood can't escape (at least, not as quickly as usual). An erect penis can hold eight times as much blood as a flaccid one, though it doesn't grow in *direct* proportion to its flaccid size. Not all erections point up — some point out, or even down (especially later in life, when the ligament controlling the angle has been stretched).

Prolonged (or perhaps not so prolonged) sexual tension causes the muscles near the prostate gland to contract, sending fluids from the prostate gland and seminal vesicles into the urethra. Seconds later, the valve between the bladder and urethra is closed. The fluid is then propelled down the urethra, picking up the sperm along the way from the testes and this collection of fluids, semen, is expelled out of the penis — what's known as ejaculation. (This is why it's such a pain to wake up with both morning wood and an intense need to pee: the male body is designed to do just one at a time.) 'Retrograde ejaculation' means that the semen never makes it out of the urethral opening and instead is absorbed back into the bladder — it sometimes happens after prostate or bladder surgery, in spinal injury cases, or during injaculation (orgasm without ejaculation, see page 104). It doesn't hurt and isn't harmful on an occasional basis: while some Tantric sex practitioners like Woody Harrelson sing its praises, we wouldn't recommend attempting it regularly, since some doctors think the practice might be connected to prostate or fertility problems.

... Everyone ...

- **Genitals:** The external sex and reproductive organs: the vulva in women and the penis/scrotum combo in men. Some people may be referring to the external and internal reproductive organs when they use the term 'genitals'. (Aka the groin, crotch, down there, family jewels.)
- **Pubic hair:** 'Wild' hair found on and around the genitals, including the perineum and around the anus, too. During puberty, the androgens (sex hormones) floating around your body turn all the follicles in your pubic area to flat, curly-hair follicles. Good for collecting your natural 'sex musk' to attract mates. May be subject to trimming, shaving and waxing, depending on the culture and one's personal aesthetics or sense of hygiene. (Aka pubes, pubies, short and curlies, bush, rug.)
- **Pubic bone:** When we say pubic bone, we are actually talking about the pubic symphysis, the joint where the pubic bones meet. The pubic bones are the lower frontal parts of the pelvic bones, or hip gird. Both sexes have fatty tissue protecting this area of the pubic bones; in women, this is the mons; in men, it's the area just north of where his unit starts (in cold weather, the penis may actually withdraw into this tissue). While you can't actually feel the joint, you can feel the general bony area beneath this fatty tissue. The pelvic floor muscles, among others, are connected to the pelvic bones. The bladder is directly behind the pubic symphysis.
- **Perineum:** The short stretch of skin starting below the vulva in women and below the testicles in men and extending, in both cases, to the anus. Underneath this skin is a dense network of blood vessels, sometimes called the perineal body, which fills with blood during sexual arousal. It's rich in nerve endings. Beneath this lie the pelvic floor muscles, which contract during arousal and orgasm. (Aka the taint or chin rest.)
- **Anus:** The external opening, or exit end, of the digestive tract. It consists of two sphincter (ringlike) muscles that form the inch-long, tubelike anal canal. First, there's the external sphincter, which is controlled by the central nervous system (i.e., you control it, most of the time). A couple of centimetres or so deeper lies the internal sphincter, which is under the jurisdiction of the autonomic nervous system (i.e., it usually responds involuntarily). On the plus side, the anus has a high concentration of nerve endings, is

interconnected with the pelvic muscles and has elastic folds of tissue that can expand to accommodate probing probes. On the downside, this is where you get 'rhoids. (Aka the asshole, arsehole, bumhole, ass, starfish, chocolate kiss, puckered kiss, doughnut hole, tootsie tip, black hole, tooky.)

- **Rectum:** The tube that transports food from the large intestine to the anus, that is, out of the body. It's ten to 15 cm long and has two curves along its length that give it the shape of a lazy S. The first bend in the road, closest to the exit, is formed by the pubo-rectal sling, which contracts when you have to go, to help keep you from pooing your pants. The second, less pronounced curve comes a few inches down the road. The rectal canal is designed purely as a passageway; it's the colon where faeces are stored. It lies just beyond your rectum, about 20 to 25 cm in from your anus. (Aka the ass, poop chute, the deck, Hershey highway, Cadbury's carriageway, dirt road.)

Class dismissed.

BIBLIOGRAPHY

We can't guarantee the accuracy of any information you might find in the books and websites listed below.

Books

Addington, Deborah. *A Hand in the Bush: The Fine Art of Vaginal Fisting.* Greenery Press, 1998.

Anderson, Dan. *Sex Tips for Gay Guys.* St Martin's Press, 2001.

Anderson, Dan and Maggie Berman. *Sex Tips for Straight Women from a Gay Man.* HarperCollins, 2002.

Angier, Natalie. *Woman: An Intimate Geography.* Virago Press, 1999.

Barbach, Lonnie. *For Yourself: The Fulfilment of Female Sexuality.* Signet, 2000.

Bechtel, Stefan and Laurence Roy Stains. *Sex: A Man's Guide.* Rodale Books, 1997.

Boston Women's Health Collective. *Our Bodies, Ourselves.* Penguin, 1996.

Califia, Patrick. *Sensuous Magic: A Guide to S/M for Adventurous Couples.* Cleis Press, 2002.

Cattrall, Kim and Mark Levinson. *Satisfaction: The Art of the Female Orgasm*. HarperCollins, 2003.

Chalker, Rebecca. *The Clitoral Truth*. Seven Stories Press, 2000.

Comfort, Alex. *The New Joy of Sex*. Mitchell Beazley, 1991.

Cox, Tracey. *Hot Sex: How to Do It*. Bantam Books, 1999.

Douglass, PhD, Marcia and Lisa Douglass, PhD. *Are We Having Fun Yet?: The Intelligent Woman's Guide to Sex*. Little Brown, 1997.

Easton, Dossie and Catherine A. Liszt. *The Bottoming Book*. Greenery Press, 1997.

Eichel, Edward and Philip Nobile. *The Perfect Fit: How to Achieve Mutual Fulfilment and Monogamous Passion Through the New Intercourse*. New American Library, 1993.

Fisher, Helen E. *The Sex Contract: The Evolution of Human Behaviour*. Granada, 1983.

Goddard, Jamie and Kurt Brungard. *Lesbian Sex Secrets for Men: What Every Man Wants to Know About Making Love to a Woman and Never Asks*. Nexus, 2002.

Herrman, Bert. *Trust, the Hand Book: A Guide to the Sensual and Spiritual Art of Handballing*. Alamo Square, 1991.

Joannides, Paul. *Guide to Getting It On!* (3rd Edition). Vermilion, 2001.

Kline-Graber, RN, Georgia and Benjamin Graber, MD. *Woman's Orgasm: A Guide to Sexual Satisfaction*. Warner Books, 1998.

Massey, Doreen, ed. *Lovers' Guide Encyclopaedia: The Definitive Guide to Sex and You*. Thunder's Mouth Press, 1996.

Midori. *The Seductive Art of Japanese Bondage*. Greenery Press, 2002.

Morin, PhD, Jack. *Anal Pleasure & Health* (Revised 3rd Edition). Down There Press, 2000.

Paget, Lou. *How to Be a Great Lover: Girlfriend-to-Girlfriend Time-Tested Techniques That Will Blow His Mind*. Broadway Books, 1999.

Peterkin, Allan D. *The Bald-Headed Hermit & the Artichoke: An Erotic Thesaurus*. Arsenal Pulp Press, 1999.

Rogers, Ben, et al. *Going Down: The Instinct Guide to Oral Sex*. Alyson Publications, 2002.

Rowan, M.D., Edward L. *The Joy of Self-Pleasuring*. Prometheus Books, 2000.

Sonntag, Linda. *The Bedside Kama Sutra*. Hamlyn, 2002.

Spark, MD, Richard F. *Sexual Health for Men: The Complete Guide*. Perseus
    Publishing, 2000.
Taormino, Tristan. *Pucker Up*. HarperCollins, 2003.
Winks, Cathy. *The Good Vibrations Guide: The G-Spot*. Down There Press,
    1999.
Winks, Cathy and Anne Semans. *The New Good Vibrations Guide to Sex*.
    Cleis Press, 1997.

Websites

14-condoms.co.uk

AllSexGuide.com

AltSex.org

amfAR.org

ASHASTD.org

BedroomBondage.com/BondageU

blushingbuyer.co.uk

condomcare.co.uk

Fpa.co.uk

GoAskAlice.columbia.edu

GoodVibes.com

KFF.org

LeatherViews.com

lovehoney.co.uk

MayoHealth.org

MedLib.com

Nabco.org

Nerve.com

OrchidsLair.com

paramountpleasures.co.uk

passiononline.co.uk

phls.co.uk

PlannedParenthood.org

PuckerUp.com

RateMyCock.com

Salon.com

SeekWellness.com

SexHealth.org

SexualHealth.com

Sexuality.About.com

Sexuality.org

SexualRecords.com

StormyLeather.com

The-Clitoris.com

The-Penis.com

Tes.org

Viceland.com

WebMD.com

ACKNOWLEDGEMENTS

We'd like to give gushing thanks to Isabella Robertson, the erstwhile managing editor of Nerve Books, who got *The Big Bang* (which she so brilliantly titled) off the ground — and kept it soaring upward. Debbie Grossman, whose photo editing helped turn a sex manual into a work of art. Jenny Lim, for her tireless research on everything from foreplay to fisting. And our long-time design consultant, Joey Cavella, for helping make all things Nerve look cool.

Many thanks to the following doctors for their invaluable medical vetting: STD specialist Kenneth F. Trofatter, Jr, MD, PhD, Director of the Maternal-Fetal Medicine department of the Center for Women's Medicine at Greenville Hospital System in South Carolina. Urology expert John P. Mulhall, MD, Director of Sexual Medicine Programs at the Departments of Urology at Weill Medical College of Cornell University, New York Presbyterian Hospital and Memorial Sloan-Kettering Cancer Center in New York. And Bita Motesharrei, MD, a private practitioner in Virginia specialising in obstetrics and gynaecology. Thanks also to our medical proofreader, Rana Lee Adawi, MD, from Beth Israel Hospital here in New York City.

And last, but not least, the great team at Hodder & Stoughton — Katy Follain, Nicola Doherty and Jocasta Brownlee. Also: Hikma Abdulghani, Babes in Toyland, Brian Battjer, Ben Bloom, Rebecca Chalker, Sean Conrad, Kevin Cooley, Stuart Delves & Smithfield Bar, Liza Featherstone, Adam Glickman & Condomania, Good Vibrations, Nathan Jude & Center of Operations, Louis

Kanganis, Claudia Lake, Donna Lichaw, Jay Mandel, Michael Martin, Jenny Morse, Jack Murnighan, Emily Nussbaum, Krisana Palma, Alison Perelman, Chris Pisacane, Keith Price, Dr Carol Queen, Allyson Sharkey, Spring Street Networks, Grant Stoddard andra Stoll, Becky and Hannah Taylor, Marc Weinhouse and Jack Wright. Plus the Big Bang models — Loan Chabonal, Marcos Cougleton, Elissa Gennello, Jan Hilmer, Chris Kramer, Avril Lang, Cayleb Long, Jose Mariscal, Scott McBride, Benjamin Monnie, Joanna Mostor, Eli Rarey, Mika Saa, Theresa Schmidt, Michael Shedwell, Jenny Strahl, Lian Tal and Danielle Top. And of course, Nerve readers the world over, for being the funniest, smartest and best-looking audience a magazine could hope for.

— The Nerve Team

ABOUT THE AUTHORS

Em and Lo (Emma Taylor and Lorelei Sharkey), the Emily Posts of the modern bedroom, made their UK debut with a weekly column for the *Guardian Weekend* magazine debunking sex myths. After four years as Nerve.com's resident advice gurus and 'astrologists', they can now be found dishing about all things love-, sex-, and star-related on their own website, EmandLo.com. They also write a monthly sex advice column for *Men's Journal* magazine in the US. Both live in New York City, where they spend far too much time together. This is their first book. Their next book, *Sex Etiquette*, is out in 2005.

Nerve.com is the only intelligent magazine about sex and culture for women and men. Since 1997, Nerve has been publishing provocative essays, stimulating reporting and side-splitting commentary on a daily basis, as well as striking photographs of naked people that capture more than just their flesh. Described by *Entertainment Weekly* as '*Playboy*'s body with the *New Yorker*'s brain', Nerve has grown into a successful multimedia company, expanding into film, television, books, print and on-line personals. *The Big Bang* is Nerve's first book comprised of completely original, previously unpublished material.